PSALMS

Readings: A New Biblical Commentary

General Editor
John Jarick

PSALMS

Howard N. Wallace

SHEFFIELD PHOENIX PRESS

2009

Copyright © Sheffield Phoenix Press, 2009

Published by Sheffield Phoenix Press
Department of Biblical Studies, University of Sheffield
Sheffield S10 2TN

www.sheffieldphoenix.com

All rights reserved.
No part of this publication may be reproduced or transmitted
in any form or by any means, electronic or mechanical,
including photocopying, recording or any information storage
or retrieval system, without the publisher's permission in
writing.

A CIP catalogue record for this book
is available from the British Library

Typeset by Vikatan Publishing Solutions, Chennai, India

Printed by
Lightning Source

ISBN 978-1-906055-61-5 (hardback)
ISBN 978-1-906055-62-2 (paperback)

Contents

Preface	vii
Abbreviations	ix
Introduction	1
Book I	12
Psalm 1	12
Psalm 2	15
Psalm 3	20
Psalms 4–6	25
Psalm 7	26
Psalm 8	29
Psalms 9–10	33
Psalms 11–17	39
Psalm 18	40
Psalm 19	46
Psalms 20–21	53
Psalm 22	53
Psalm 23	59
Psalm 24	63
Psalm 25	66
Psalms 26–32	71
Psalm 33	72
Psalms 34–39	77
Psalm 40	80
Psalm 41	85
Book II	92
Psalms 42–45	92
Psalm 46	94
Psalms 47–49	98
Psalm 50	99
Psalm 51	103
Psalms 52–62	109

Psalm 63	113
Psalms 64–71	116
Psalm 72	118
Book III	123
Psalm 73	123
Psalm 74	128
Psalms 75–77	132
Psalm 78	133
Psalms 79–88	138
Psalm 89	143
Book IV	150
Psalm 90	150
Psalms 91–104	154
Psalms 105–106	158
Psalm 105	159
Psalm 106	161
Book V	166
Psalm 107	166
Psalms 108–109	169
Psalm 110	170
Psalms 111–117	173
Psalm 118	175
Psalm 119	180
Psalms 120–134	184
Psalms 135–145	187
Psalms 146–150	190
Bibliography	194
Index	197

Preface

Reading the Book of Psalms as a book is not a common practice. It has mostly been viewed as an anthology, and individual psalms selected and used for worship, devotion, preaching or study as desired. In recent decades the question of whether the Book of Psalms has an intended shape to it and the whole has a meaning over and above the sum of its parts has been discussed by many scholars. The Jewish and Christian psalm traditions, while often using psalms on an individual basis, have nevertheless associated the collection with King David in one way or another. A sense of the collection as a unity is suggested by that association. Moreover, religious orders and some others in the Christian tradition have often seen the benefit of reading through the Book of Psalms in numerical order over a given period of time, from a week up to six months depending on the discipline. This practice suggests that many have found devotional gain in the Psalter as a whole as well as in individual psalms. This reading of the Book of Psalms will take seriously both recent scholarly interest in the book as a whole and the traditional use and association of psalms with David. A survey of issues related to these matters is found in the Introduction.

This reading is based on the Hebrew text of Psalms (MT) but with constant attention to its translation in the NRSV. I have used translations of individual words or phrases from the NRSV within the text except where I think this does not give the full sense of the Hebrew. In those cases I have provided my own alternative to the NRSV with reference to other English versions where that is helpful. With regard to the name of God, 'Yahweh' is used throughout for the Tetragrammaton (NRSV: 'LORD'). 'God' is used to translate the Hebrew $^{e}l\bar{o}h\hat{\imath}m$, unless the Hebrew form is significant and the transliteration is retained. I have used the terms 'the Book of Psalms', 'the Psalms' and 'the Psalter' interchangeably, aware that the last term especially can have a more specific reference in some circumstances.

Some thanks are due to others in relation to this work. Firstly to the general editors who commissioned the work and have been patient in waiting for the manuscript. I have benefitted from the diligent work of successive research assistants, Dr Anne Elvey and Kylie Crabbe, and to the Melbourne College of Divinity for the grants that made this assistance possible. I am thankful to the Uniting Church Centre for Theology and Ministry for study leave in 2007 which gave me time for writing the bulk of the commentary, and to the staff of Mannix Library of the Catholic Theological College, East Melbourne, who provided a place where it could be done. Finally, my thanks go to my wife, Bronwyn, whose patient support over many years has helped make this commentary possible. She helps me keep such work as this commentary in perspective. To her I dedicate this book.

Abbreviations

BTB	*Biblical Theology Bulletin*
CBQ	*Catholic Theological Quarterly*
KTU	Text references taken from M. Dietrich et al. (eds.), *Die keilalphabetischen Texte aus Ugarit* (AOAT 24; Neukirchen-Vluyn: Neukirchener Verlag, 1976)
HSS	Harvard Semitic Studies
HTR	*Harvard Theological Review*
JBL	*Journal of Biblical Literature*
JSOT	*Journal for the Study of the Old Testament*
JSOTSup	*Journal for the Study of the Old Testament, Supplement Series*
LXX	Septuagint
Ms(s)	manuscript(s)
MT	Masoretic Text
NAB	New American Bible
NIV	New International Version
NJB	New Jerusalem Bible
NJPS	New Jewish Publication Society *TaNaK*.
NRSV	New Revised Standard Version
REB	Revised English Bible
Syr.	Syriac version
VT	*Vetus Testamentum*
Vulg.	Vulgate
ZAW	*Zeitschift für die alttestamentliche Wissenschaft*

Introduction

David and Psalms in Tradition

The Psalms belong to David. That has been so for a long time in both Christian and Jewish tradition. Luther remarked that the Psalms pointed to Christ in the words of 'the illustrious prophet David'.[1] Earlier, the great Christian preacher Chrysostom (347–407 CE) spoke of David as active whenever the Psalms were sung.[2] Jerome expressed a similar opinion.[3] Among early Jewish writings, Josephus (*Ant.* VII, 305 etc.), the Babylonian Talmud (e.g. *B. Pesahim* 117a), and the Midrash on Psalms, *Midrash Tehillim*, all, in one way or another, attest to a close association of David and the Psalms.

The tradition has roots in biblical and ancient non-biblical writings. The New Testament directly attributes the words of psalms to David, e.g. Mk 12.35-37 (quoting Ps. 110.1), Acts 2.25-28 (Ps. 16.8-11), 4.25-26 (Ps. 2.1-2) and Heb. 4.7 (Ps. 95.7). The last two are interesting because neither psalm is associated with David in the Hebrew text (MT). Similarly, in the work *The Words of Gad the Seer* (1st century CE), Psalms 145 and 144 are quoted with revised superscriptions relating them more firmly to David.[4] Ecclesiasticus 47.8-10 (2nd century BCE) pushes the tradition further back celebrating David not only as an arranger of liturgy but as composer, singer, and a person of great faith. Beyond that the tradition is less clear. The

---

1. M. Luther, *Luther's Works. Vol 10. First Lectures on the Psalms. I Psalms 1–75* (H.C. Oswald [ed.]; St Louis: Concordia Publishing House, 1974), 8.

2. Quoted in J.M. Neale and R.F. Littledale, *A Commentary on the Psalms from Primitive and Mediaeval Writers* (London: Joseph Masters & Co., 1884), vol 1.1.

3. Quoted in A.F. Kirkpatrick, *The Book of Psalms* (Cambridge: The University Press, 1906), c. Quote from a letter from Bethlehem to Marcella.

4. M. Bar-Ilan, 'The date of *The Words of Gad the Seer*', *JBL* 109 (1990), 475–92.

connection of David with music and poetry in 1 Sam. 16.14-23; 2 Sam. 1.19-27; 22.2-51 and 23.1-7 (cf. Amos 6.5) may also have had some influence, although we should not confuse David's roles as musician, poet, and psalmist too readily.[5] Only the Books of Chronicles associate David with Levitical singers and temple liturgy so his association with psalms could have developed around the time of the Chronicler. The use of psalms in various ways within the Books of Chronicles, and particularly in 1 Chronicles 16, confirms this.[6]

The association with David is marked in a number of ways within the Book of Psalms itself. A considerable number of psalms have as part of their superscription the phrase *l^edāwîd* which can be translated in several ways: 'of David' (NRSV; NJB; NJPS); 'for David' (REB); 'concerning David' etc. Thirteen psalms are connected with events in David's life by means of an extended superscription (Pss. 3; 7; 18; 34; 51; 52; 54; 56; 57; 59; 60; 63; and 142). Finally, a third group refer to David within the body of the psalm (Pss. 18; 78; 89; 132; 144; cf. 122.5). Different textual traditions of the Book of Psalms demonstrate variation in direct association with David. The MT has 73 psalms with at least *l^edāwîd* in the superscription. The number is higher in the LXX (84 psalms). Some later Greek recensions change *tō david* ('to, for David) to *tou david* ('of David') suggesting authorship more firmly.[7] In the Dead Sea Scrolls Psalms manuscripts additional canonical psalms are attributed to David as well as some non-biblical works. The largest psalm scroll, 11QPs^a, states in a prose segment:

> And David, son of Jesse, was wise, and a light like the light of the sun, and literate, and discerning and perfect in all his ways before God and humankind. And the Lord gave him a discerning

---

5. A.M. Cooper, 'The Life and Times of King David according to the Book of Psalms', in R.E. Friedman (ed.), *The Poet and the Historian: Essays in Literary and Historical Biblical Criticism* (HSS 26; Chico CA: Scholars, 1983), 117–31 (127–30).

6. H.N. Wallace, 'What Chronicles has to say about Psalms', in M.P. Graham and S.L. McKenzie (eds.), *The Chronicler as Author: Studies in Text and Texture* (JSOTSup 263; Sheffield: SAP, 1999), 267–91 (284–91). Note the quotation of Pss. 105.1–15; 96.1–13; and 106.1, 47–48 in 1 Chron. 16.8–36 and Ps. 132.8–10 in 2 Chron. 6.41–42.

7. A. Pietersma, 'David in the Greek Psalms', *VT* XXX/2 (1980), 213–226.

spirit. And he wrote 3600 psalms; ... And all the songs that he composed were 446, ... And the total was 4050. All these he composed through prophecy which was given to him from before the Most High.

The association of the Psalms with David is rooted deep within the Psalms tradition. It expanded over time, and became widespread. The perception of the association varied from one situation to another involving, in various circumstances, David as author, David as ideal king, David as model pray-er as well as other aspects. The association has in turn, been a powerful tool in the reading and interpretation of the Psalms. It is the aim of this work to take this association seriously in the context of a literary reading of the Psalms. But first, we must examine further the nature of the association.

Study of the Psalms as a Whole

The study of the Psalms over the last century has been dominated by issues of genre and cultic performance. Psalms have been studied mainly as individual texts or in groupings based on those criteria. Much has been gained but many issues have defied consensus including matters of the dating of many psalms and the contexts within which they were used. The lack of specific detail in many cases has meant that these questions have often been left open. Individual psalms have been seen as expressions of personal piety, elements of temple liturgies, part of royal ceremonies or wisdom school practices etc., depending largely on genre determinations and other assumptions made about them. Suggestions as to the identity of the psalmist have also varied from anonymous individuals to various priestly guilds to the king himself. In many cases literary studies of particular psalms have proved more fruitful than historical ones. The superscriptions attached to the Psalms have largely been ignored during this time.

In recent decades, however, increasing attention has been given to the study of the Psalter as a whole, both in terms of the history of the collection and the significance of its shape. Specifically, there has been interest in whether there is any intention, particularly any theological intention, behind the collection as a whole. A number of points suggest this possibility. They include the five book structure of the Psalter with their doxologies and different organisational techniques (based on

4   Introduction

either author or Hebrew genre designations).[8] Psalms 1 and 2 have been linked redactionally to provide an introduction to the collection,[9] while Psalms 146–50 form a concluding group. Contrasting editorial frameworks, a royal one (Psalms 2; 72; 89) and a wisdom one (Psalms 1; 42–43; 73; 90), have been identified.[10] There is movement within the collection from a predominance of lament psalms at the beginning to ones of praise at the end, and from more individual psalms to more collective ones.[11] In addition, word and thematic connections exist between certain psalms,[12] earlier material has been reused in writing new psalms (e.g. Ps. 108 = Pss. 57 + 60),[13] and redactional supplements have turned individual psalms into communal and national ones.[14] The lack of cultic or worship concerns in either the frame to the Psalter or within the majority of psalms suggests that many have been loosed from their cultic contexts now to be read as Scripture.[15]

8.   The five books are: I Psalms 1–41; II Psalms 42–72; III Psalms 73–89; IV Psalms 90–106; and V Psalms 107–150. The concluding doxologies are: Pss. 41.13; 72.18-19; 89.52; 106.48 and Ps. 150.
9.   G.H. Wilson, 'The Shape of the Book of Psalms', *Interpretation* 46/2 (1992), 129–42 (132–33); B.S. Childs, *Introduction to the Old Testament as Scripture* (Philadelphia: Fortress, 1979), 516; P.D. Miller, 'The Beginning of the Psalter', in J.C. McCann (ed.), *The Shape and Shaping of the Psalter* (JSOTSup 159; Sheffield: JSOT, 1993), 83–92 (88–89).
10.   Wilson, 'The Shape of the Book of Psalms', 133–34.
11.   Wilson, 'The Shape of the Book of Psalms', 138–39.
12.   E.g. J.P. Brennan, 'Psalms 1–8: Some Hidden Harmonies', *BTB* 10/1 (1980), 25–29 (28).
13.   Childs, *Introduction*, 514.
14.   M. Marttila, *Collective Reinterpretation in the Psalms* (Tübingen: Mohr Siebeck, 2006), 78. For further discussion on indications of intention in the Psalter see: P.C. Craigie, *Psalms 1–50 with 2004 Supplement by Marvin E. Tate* (Word; NP: Thomas Nelson, 2004), 445–72, G.H. Wilson, 'The Structure of the Psalter', in P.S. Johnston and D.G. Firth (eds.), *Interpreting the Psalms: Issues and Approaches* (Leicester: Apollos, 2005), 229–246 (229–234).
15.   J.L. Mays, 'Psalm 118 in the Light of Canonical Analysis', in G.M. Tucker et al. (eds.), *Canon, Theology, and Old Testament Interpretation: Essays in Honour of Brevard S. Childs* (Philadelphia: Fortress, 1988), 299–311 (307); E. Zenger, 'The Composition and Theology of the Fifth Book of Psalms. Psalms 107–145', *JSOT* 80 (1998), 77–102; and 'Der Psalter als Heiligtum' in. B. Ego et al. (eds.), *Gemeinde*

A major contributor to the discussion of the shaping of the Psalter has been Gerald Wilson. Rather than a gradual development of the Psalter, Wilson sees a two stage development. Books I–III were stabilized first and the final Psalter, including Books IV–V, was given shape in the 1st century CE. This is supported by the evidence of the Dead Sea Psalms scrolls.[16] Both sections have been edited in an effort to address the disaster of the Exile. Psalms 2, 72 and 89 have been placed at the seams of the first three books in order to speak of the hope of the Davidic monarchy and its demise. Book III ends with Yahweh's rejection of David (Psalm 89). Books IV and V were edited and added later by sages in order to redirect the hopes of the reader from the Davidic monarchy, and the frailty of human kings, to the kingship of Yahweh. Wisdom psalms, or ones influenced by that tradition, were placed at the beginning of the collection (Psalm 1) and at the start of Books IV and V (Psalms 90, 107) and the end of Book V (Psalm 145 then the *hallel* Psalms 146–50). Prominence was given to the Yahweh *mālak* ('Yahweh is king') psalms (Psalms 93, 95–99).[17] Moreover, a shift in perspective at the start of Book IV taking the reader back to the time of Moses, signals a major interpretive point, namely that the solution to the Exile lies in a reaffirmation of Yahweh's kingship and *torah* obedience. Others have argued that the solution to the problem of Exile is not

---

ohne Tempel: Community without Temple (Tübingen: Mohr Siebeck, 1999), 115–32.

16. G.H. Wilson, *The Editing of the Hebrew Psalter* (Chico, CA: Scholars, 1985), 121 following J.A. Sanders. Also 'A first century C.E. date for the closing of the Hebrew Psalter?' in J.J. Adler (ed.), *Sefer Haim M.I. Gevaryahu: Memorial Volume* (Jerusalem: World Jewish Bible Center, 1990), 136–43. Cf. also P.W. Flint, *The Dead Sea Psalms Scrolls and the Book of Psalms* (Leiden: Brill, 1997), 143–49.

17. G.H. Wilson, 'King, Messiah, and the Reign of God: Revisiting the Royal Psalms and the Shape of the Psalter' in P.W. Flint and P.D. Miller (eds.), *The Book of Psalms: Composition and Reception* (Leiden: Brill, 2005), 391–406 (391–93); also 'The Qumran psalms manuscripts and consecutive arrangement of psalms in the Hebrew Psalter', *CBQ* 45 (1983), 377–88; 'Evidence of editorial divisions in the Hebrew Psalter', *VT* XXXIV/3 (1984), 337–52; 'Understanding the Purposeful Arrangement of the Psalms in the Psalter: Pitfalls and Promise' in McCann (ed.), *The Shape and Shaping of the Psalter*, 42–51; and 'The Structure of the Psalter' in Johnston and Firth (eds.), *Interpreting the Psalms*, 229–46.

simply confined to Books IV and V but is already addressed in Books I–III.[18]

Mark Smith developed this argument in another direction. One problem he saw with Wilson's view was: 'How is the historical orientation of Books I–III to be reconciled with the general eschatological orientation of the Psalter?' To put it another way, how do Books IV and V relate to the 'historical' David? A further question arises from the work of Brevard Childs as to why the superscriptions relating to episodes in David's life cluster around Psalms 50–60. Smith argues that the superscriptions reflect a post-exilic context where David is the founder of the cult (cf. 1 and 2 Chronicles). The psalms attributed to Korah and Asaph were gathered around Psalms 50–60 because those Levites were under David's authority. Books I and II, therefore, refer to the historical David and his life. Book III supplements the earlier books while there is a shift in temporal perspective in Books IV and V referring to the period after the return from Exile.[19]

Norman Whybray undertook an early sustained critique of the above approach.[20] His main criticisms related to the precise use of the final Psalter, the methods of analysis used, and whether there is any significant progression in thought or mood in any movement detected within the Psalter.[21] A consequence of his critique is that we may be talking about an intention expressed in less than a watertight fashion. We certainly have to take into account matters noted in the discussion such as the fact that there are royal psalms in Books IV and V even after the demise of the Davidic monarchy in Psalm 89 (e.g. Pss. 101; 110; 132; and 144.1-11). There are also psalms of praise of God's sovereignty in Books I–III (e.g. Pss. 8; 11; 16; 23; 24; 27.1-6, and 29 etc.). Moreover, the problem introduced by Psalm 89 is revisited in relation to Exile in Psalm 106, even after the stress on the sovereignty of God in Book IV. The intention evident within the final

---

18. J.C. McCann, 'Books I–III and the Editorial Purpose of the Hebrew Psalter' in McCann (ed.), *The Shape and Shaping of the Psalter*, 93–107; N.L. deClaissé-Walford, *Reading from the Beginning: The Shaping of the Hebrew Psalter* (Macon, GA: Mercer University, 1997).

19. M.S. Smith, 'The Theology of the Redaction of the Psalter: Some Observations', *ZAW* 104 (1992), 408–412 (409–10).

20. N. Whybray, *Reading the Psalms as a Book* (Sheffield: SAP, 1996).

21. Whybray, *Reading*, 31–35.

shaping of the Psalter is complex and multi-layered to say the least.

Several other issues play important roles in the discussion of the significance of the shaping of the Psalter. One is *torah*. Three psalms focus on this, Psalms 1, 19 and 119 and there are many echoes of *torah* elsewhere in the Psalter (e.g. Pss. 18; 25; 33; 78; 89; 93; 94; 99; 103; 105; 111; 112; 147; 148 etc.). The place of Psalm 1 as introduction and the weight of Psalm 119 give prominence to the matter of *torah* and suggest that it is a key to piety within the Psalms. This is so regardless of whether we understand *torah* in terms of the traditional Law of Moses or as 'teaching, instruction' relating to all forms of God's revelation.[22] The pairing of Psalms 1 and 2 as an introduction to the Psalter brings *torah* and the reign of Yahweh into close connection. The latter is related to human kingship in Books I–III, but since the final editing of the Psalter took place after Exile, psalms which speak of human kingship take on an eschatological ring. This in turn puts *torah* piety, as promoted by the Psalter, into an eschatological frame.[23]

A second issue is the way David is presented through the psalm superscriptions. The portrayal of David in relation to psalmody and temple liturgy in the Books of Chronicles and the way he is presented as psalmist in 2 Samuel 22 and 23, open the way to perceive David not only as author of psalms but as an ideal pray-er of them. The life of David, thus, becomes a hermeneutical key to the interpretation of the psalms. The fact that his life is not presented chronologically in the superscriptions reinforces this conclusion.[24] Of course, the life of David portrayed is that of the great king. While this might be seen as an obstacle to

---

22. See J.L. Mays, 'The place of the Torah-psalms in the Psalter', *JBL* 106/1 (1987), 3–12; J. Leveson, 'The Sources of Torah: Psalm 119 and the Modes of revelations in Second Temple Judaism' in P.D. Miller et al. (eds.), *Ancient Israelite Religion: Essays in Honor of Frank Moore Cross* (Philadelphia: Fortress, 1987), 559–74.

23. Mays, 'The place of the Torah-psalms', 10; Brennan, 'Psalms 1–8', 28–29.

24. See J.L. Mays, 'The David of the Psalms', *Interpretation* 40 (1986), 143–155; Childs, *Introduction*, 521; Cooper, 'The Life and Times of King David', 125; and H.P. Nasuti, 'The Interpretive Significance of Sequence and Selection in the Book of Psalms' in Flint and Miller (eds.), *The Book of Psalms*, 311–39 (326) who traces such a view to Gregory of Nyssa (c.335–c.395 CE).

8   *Introduction*

other pray-ers,[25] the fact that he is portrayed in his full humanity, negates any sense of isolation. This is evident in terms of his sinfulness (e.g. Psalm 51), his sense often of separation from God (e.g. Psalms 10; 22), and in other forms of distress as evident in the many lament psalms. As Childs remarks:

> David is pictured simply as a man, indeed chosen by God for the sake of Israel, but who displays all the strengths and weaknesses of all human beings.... The psalms are transmitted as the sacred psalms of David, but they testify to all the common troubles and joys of ordinary human life in which all persons participate.[26]

The picture of David created in the Psalter is as complex as is found elsewhere in post-exilic literature.[27] To pray the psalms thus becomes an experience of praying them with David whatever the circumstance. David becomes a beacon of hope for all Israel.[28] In the post-exilic period when the earlier securities of the faith, especially the Temple, were no longer considered invulnerable, it gives new freedom. As Cooper remarks: 'Attributing the liturgy to David gives psalmody a legitimacy that is independent of, in fact prior to, the Temple.'[29]

Connected to the person of David is the issue of 'messiah' in the Psalter. The first clear evidence we get of Jewish hope in a Davidic *messiah* (named 'Son of David') comes in the *Psalms of Solomon* 17 (c. 60 BCE). Prior to that the hopes emanating from the Davidic tradition and covenant are seen as fulfilled in other ways (e.g. Ecclus. 45.23-26; 1 Macc. 2.57).[30] Any *messianic* hope we might find in the Psalter developed uniquely in relation to

---

25. See for such an objection E.M. Menn, 'No Ordinary Lament: Relecture and the Identity of the Distressed in Psalm 22', *HTR* 93/4 (2000), 301–41 (301–10).

26. Childs, *Introduction*, 521. Cf. also G.T. Sheppard, 'Theology and the Book of Psalms', *Interpretation* 46/2 (1992), 143–155 (147–48).

27. J. Luyten, 'David and the Psalms' in L. Leijssen (ed.), *Les psaumes: prières de l'humanitè d'Israël, de l'Église. Hommage à Jos Luyten* (Leuven: Abdij Keizersberg, 1990), 57–76 (59).

28. Luyten, 'David and the Psalms', 76; Mays, 'The David of the Psalms', 155.

29. Cooper, 'The Life and Times of King David', 129.

30. K.E. Pomykala, *The Davidic Dynasty Tradition in Early Judaism: Its History and Significance for Messianism* (Atlanta: Scholars, 1995), 265–71 for summary.

that text. In this regard we note that the superscriptions to the psalms which refer to episodes in David's life effectively point back to him as an ideal character from the past. A sense of looking forward, as implied in a *messianic* hope, is gained only through the sense of movement, especially in relation to the history of Israel, implied in the Psalter. It is aided by the movement of Israel's history beyond the life of David following Book II. Nevertheless, this Davidic *messianism* is not yet the full blown version that will emerge in *Pss. Sol.* 17 or in some of the Dead Sea Scrolls. There is hope for a renewed leadership of Israel modeled on David and associated with his dynasty (e.g. Pss. 132; 144), but it is what has been called '"messianic" in royalist sense only'.[31] This is a subtle form of *messianism* in which a king, who knows human toil and weakness, rules victoriously. He is an exemplar of faithfulness and trust in Yahweh for the people with his piety grounded in *torah* observance. His own model is also David.[32] The high point of *messianic* speculation with regard to the Psalter comes only with the LXX version.[33]

Reading the Book of Psalms

This reading of the Book of Psalms will take seriously both the recent scholarly interest in the book as a whole mentioned above and the traditional use and association of psalms with David. I will read the Book of Psalms as if they are David's. In some cases this will imply authorship, in others a more complex and developed association is demanded. I am not implying that many, if any at all, of the psalms were authored by David or in his time. The authorship and original context of various psalms is a matter for historical study. In many places the conclusions of such study will be evident in the reading. What I want to do in the reading is take the association of the psalms with David seriously and read the collection as though it was David's or associated closely with him.

---

31. S.E. Gillingham, 'The Messiah in the Psalms: A question of reception history and the Psalter' in J. Day (ed.), *King and Messiah in Israel and the ancient Near East: Proceedings of the Oxford Old Testament Seminar* (Sheffield: SAP, 1998), 209–237 (227–28).

32. Cf. J.A. Grant, 'The Psalms and the King' in Johnston and Firth (eds.), *Interpreting the Psalms*, 101–18 (117).

33. J. Schaper, *Eschatology in the Greek Psalter* (Tübingen: J.B.C. Moor, 1995), 151.

As we take the traditional association of the psalms with David seriously, we realize that we are dealing with David in two basic guises—one in which he is the subject or object of the discourse of the Psalter, and another in which he is the author of the psalms.[34] Our reading of the Psalms must take these two guises into account. It also needs to take into account the other aspects which play important roles in the shaping of the Psalter. They include not only the life of David himself but also the story of Israel, *torah*, kingship and the reign of God, eschatology and *messianism*, to name a few. Which aspect(s) one sees as more important and which psalms are selected to illustrate this influences how one sees and describes the shape of the Psalter and its significance.[35]

This reading of the Psalter will involve, therefore, a look back to the life of David and, following the references in Book III to events associated with the Exile, a look forward with hope for a different future and a new royal reign reflecting the reign of Yahweh. In David's life and in terms of the model he becomes for a new royal reign there is a model for all faithful people. It is in light of this that the disasters of Exile can be faced. This is already embodied in the introduction of Psalms 1 and 2 together. They will shape the reading of all the psalms to follow. The past, in terms of both David's life and the history of Israel, holds the key to future well-being and faithfulness which will find its fulfilment in the unhindered praise of God by all that has breath (Ps. 150.6). Marvin Tate sums the situation up well:

> The 'blessed' person travels through the Psalter in pain and lament, with David as companion, until David's messianic voice proclaims the wisdom and praise of Yahweh in the great crescendo at the end of the Psalter.[36]

The length limitation in the *Readings* series places some constraints on reading the Book of Psalms. Not all psalms can be treated with equal weight, at least not if something useful is to be said. I have, therefore, selected 35 psalms for a more detailed

---

34. Cf. also J.M. Auwers, 'Le David des psaumes et les psaumes de David' in L. Desrousseaux and J. Vermeylen (eds.), *Figures de David á travers la Bible* (Paris: Les Éditions du Cerf, 1999), 187–224.

35. Nasuti, 'The Interpretive Significance of Sequence', 311–18.

36. Craigie, *Psalms 1–50 with 2004 Supplement*, 461. Comment in supplement by Tate.

reading. These have been selected on the basis of how they contribute to the reading of the Book of Psalms as a whole, e.g. those at the beginning and ends of books within the Book of Psalms or which have another significant function in the collection, or in some instances because they are an important example of a particular type of psalm. I have, however, wanted to see each psalm in its place in the collection so I have provided brief comments on those psalms or groups of psalms which fit between those selected for more detailed comment. The selection of specific psalms for detailed comment occasionally cuts across the 'older', smaller collections within the whole. This is noted where necessary but hopefully does not obscure the journey with David through the Psalter as a whole.

Book I

Psalm 1

Without delay the psalmist introduces us to the subject of the collection, *hā'îš*, 'the man'. We are told first that he is *'ašrê*, 'blessed' or 'happy' but what this means is only disclosed slowly over the course of the psalm, and then mostly by defining what it is *not* or by the use of metaphor. *'ašrê* is a significant word in the Psalter as a whole, always with a human, never God, as its referent. It occurs most frequently in Books I (9 times) and V (11 times) and in each of the closing psalms in Books I–IV.

In the Psalter, the blessing or happiness implied by *'ašrê* always relates to an existing situation, never something hoped for or awaited. Moreover, it requires something from the person. In Psalm 1, the man's blessing is associated with what he does not do, namely, follow (lit. 'walk in') the advice of the wicked, associate (lit. 'stand') with sinners or sit with scoffers. Not only do these three expressions cover all possible forms of illicit endeavour, from the active to the intellectual, they also convey a sense of movement, from 'walking' through 'standing' to 'sitting'. The final act implies permanent residency and stability.

Only after having heard what the blessed man does not do, do we begin to hear what he in fact does do. Verse 2 begins with a conjunction which implies a strong contrast. The blessed man does not participate in the activities, conspiracies or company of the wicked, but *rather* delights in the *torah* and constantly recites it, as the Hebrew word *hāgâ* implies. The importance of attitude, or that which gives direction to deeds, is stressed in the verse, not just activity itself. The hallmark of this man's life is a desire for *torah*, giving it constant attention and rehearsing its content. This *torah* is the basis for the piety of the prayers and hymns that follow in the Psalter, yet it is also enhanced by that piety.

The place of the *torah* in the life of the blessed man is developed through metaphor. He is 'like a tree planted by streams of water which yields its fruit in season and whose leaf does not wither'. In everything it/he does, it/he prospers. The ambiguity of the last clause in v. 3 is deliberate. While the verse speaks of the tree, it can also be referring back to the man who is compared to the tree, and the final verb 'have success, prosper' can speak of human success, for good or bad (e.g. Ezek. 16.13; Jer. 12.1) or fruitful agricultural production (e.g. Ezek. 17.9-10). The metaphor conjures up all sorts of images and ideas that add to our understanding of this blessed man. He has been 'planted' or 'transplanted' (*šātûl*) beside streams of water. The verb does not indicate planting in general, but a deliberate action in order to help preserve the plant and help it withstand harsh conditions (see Jer. 17.8; Ezek. 17.8, 10; 19.10; Ps. 92.13). The man is also settled in a place that constantly nourishes him, ensures his growth and stability, and allows him to prosper. As one planted, he is sustained and cared for by another, Yahweh, whose *torah* is the man's constant focus. While the tree, or the man, might make everything it/he does prosper, it is clear that the source of the prosperity lies elsewhere, in the streams that feed it, and the hand that planted it. The metaphor, therefore, speaks of a reality not evident to others, especially the wicked.

The metaphor in Ps. 1.3 recalls Jer. 17.8, which also describes those who trust Yahweh. More importantly the image of a tree planted by life giving streams echoes the idea of the divine enclosure with its life-giving waters and supernatural trees. There are similarities with the description of Eden (Gen. 2.4b–3.24) but more particularly with the temple precincts and images of trees planted within them (Pss. 52.8; 92.12-14; and especially Ezek. 47.12). However, the stress in this passage is on the *torah* observance of the man. The *torah* functions in this psalm just as the temple does elsewhere, as the 'place' of divine presence and the source of the man's security and life.

The reference to the *torah* in Ps. 1.2 reminds us of the law relating to the king in Deut. 17.18-20. In that passage the king is required to write a copy of the *torah* (i.e. Deuteronomy) in the presence of the priests. He is to read it all his life so that he will learn to fear Yahweh and keep all the words of the *torah* 'to do them'. He will not consider himself above his people, nor depart from the commands, so that he and his descendants may live long. The similarities to Psalm 1 include the careful, constant commitment of the king to the law, so that he might not go astray but prosper. While Deuteronomy 17 is concerned about the limitation of royal power and authority, it also seeks to ensure that what lies at the heart of the king's reign is *torah* and not simply power. Psalm 1 speaks of a life focused on *torah*, which shuns the ways of the wicked. The reference to *torah* in Ps. 1.2 has an even closer affinity to Josh. 1.7-8 where Joshua, after succeeding Moses as leader of Israel, is urged to be strong and to do all the *torah* in order that he may be wise in all he does. Verse 8, which has indications of a later interpolation in the story, is particularly close to Ps. 1.2, with its call to recite the book of the *torah* day and night so that Joshua will do all according to what is written in it. If he does all this he will be successful, using the same word as we find in Ps. 1.3. These passages suggest that Psalm 1 be read in a royal context, or at least one involving a position of high leadership, although the case is not definite. All we can say is that while our reading of Psalm 1 might allow a royal interpretation of the blessed man, it does not demand it.

In contrast to the man 'like a tree', the wicked are likened to chaff (v. 4). Another strong expression of contrast introduces this verse. The description of the man in vv. 2-3 is thus distinguished sharply from the statements about the way of the wicked (v. 1) and the metaphor of the chaff (v. 5). The syntax of the description echoes what is the case in life. The wicked, like chaff, are devoid of life sustaining water and are blown by the wind (cf. Hos. 13.3). They are under the influence of others, unlike the blessed one who is not so influenced. It is the wicked who in the end (v. 5) will not stand, either in justice or in the company of the righteous. There is no way for them to rise from their scoffer's seat in v. 1. What seemed to be secure and stable proves to be a snare from which there is no way out. Just as the blessed man did not join the company of the wicked in v. 1, so now the wicked cannot join the company of the righteous. As with the blessed man, we do not yet know who these wicked are. We know only of their 'way' and we are learning of their end.

The psalm ends in v. 6 with the statement that 'Yahweh knows the way of the righteous, but the way of the wicked perishes'. It draws the argument of the psalm, developed through metaphor and other poetic devices, to a conclusion. It gives a theological assessment of the two ways outlined in the psalm. The blessed man of vv. 1-3 is not mentioned individually again. He now has company as we include him among the righteous in v. 6. However, that does not mean, as an anonymous individual, he is simply typical of the righteous. We will learn his name and identity in due course. For the moment he remains unnamed. Verse 6 will allow him to become a model for that group, but we are not there yet. The ambiguity in this final verse builds on that already noted in v. 2 and allows the possibility of a royal interpretation of the one who meditates on the *torah*.

The 'way of the righteous' is what has been described so far in the activities of the blessed man. It incorporates delight in and constant recitation of the law and the avoidance of detrimental associations. What it means for Yahweh to know the 'way of the righteous' can be gleaned in part by going back to the image of the tree in v. 3. Further, the verb 'to know' implies a commitment to a special relationship. This is all part of the present experience of the blessed man. By contrast, the 'way of the wicked' perishes, recalling the lifeless, blown chaff of v. 4. The 'way of the wicked' is not the same expression as the 'way of sinners' in v. 1, but the two are equivalent. In v. 5 the terms 'sinners' and 'wicked' appear in parallel. While the nouns in v. 1, 'wicked', 'sinners' and 'scoffers', add different nuances to the way avoided by the man, together they embrace all who participate in illegal activity. Just as the verbs 'know' and 'perish' appear at opposite ends of v. 6, so too the outlook for each of these ways stands in stark contrast to the other. Of course, any observant reader/hearer will recognize that what is described here does not coincide with experience. Sinners do not simply perish. In fact, v. 1, with its description of what the blessed man does not do, presumes that the wicked are ever present to tempt him. Verse 6, therefore, demands an eschatological interpretation, and suggests the same for the 'judgment' and the 'company of the righteous' in v. 5. These terms suggest a future hope, but one which is grounded in present experience, at least in part. The perishing of the wicked may not yet be a reality. On the other hand, the happy state of the blessed man is already part of his experience.

At the end of the psalm we are no clearer as to the identity of the blessed man than in v. 1, but we do perceive his destiny. He has not spoken, nor has he been spoken to. He has remained one about whom only others speak.

Psalm 2

The transition from Psalm 1 to Psalm 2 is abrupt. Without any preparatory word, we leave the world of personal piety and *torah* and move to that of royal power and international relations. But Psalms 1 and 2 can be seen as a two-part introduction to the Psalter. There are a number of connections between them. Most apparent is the blessing formula (*'ašrê*), which frames the two psalms at Pss. 1.1 and 2.12. Several vocabulary links also exist: 'sit' in 1.1 and 2.4; 'meditate' in 1.2 and 'plot' in 2.1 are the same Hebrew root, *hgh*; and there is a close connection between 'way' and 'perish' in 1.6 and 2.12. Finally, similar ideas pervade the two psalms. There is a contrast in each psalm. In Psalm 1 it is between the blessed man and the wicked, while in Psalm 2 Yahweh's anointed king stands over against the rulers of the nations. Each psalm begins with the latter party taking counsel together and seeking either to ensnare or plot against the one favoured by Yahweh. In the end, however, the wicked and the nations perish in their way or face that possibility. In contrast, the blessed man in Psalm 1 meditates on the *torah*, while the king recites Yahweh's statute in Psalm 2. By means of these connections the subjects of Psalms 1 and 2, namely individual *torah* piety and national security, are closely linked. Moreover, the unnamed individual in Psalm 1 and Yahweh's king in Psalm 2 are brought together.

Following Psalm 1 the psalmist continues to speak at the start of Psalm 2. Verses 1-3 outline the plot and intrigue that goes on in the world of international relations. The psalm may reflect verbal defiance before battle (cf. 1 Sam. 17.41-49; 2 Kgs 18.19-35; 19.10-13; 2 Chron. 13.4-12) or vassal accusations against an overlord. But we are not told of any specific context or indeed whether any actual conflict lies behind the psalm. The psalm remains open to any or all such possibilities. What we are told, however, is that any such defiance is in vain, and we know that even before we know against whom this defiance is expressed. Information about the objects of the intrigue, Yahweh and his anointed, is kept until the end of v. 2, thus focusing our attention on them. Foreign kings and peoples feel imprisoned by them and seek freedom from them (v. 3). The rather mocking question of 'why do the nations conspire', and the fact that the quote in v. 3 consists of only vague protestations, serve to strengthen the statement in v. 1, that any intrigue is futile. With the absence of details of the rebellion, the reader/hearer is left to conclude that the plot will fail principally because of the ones against whom it is hatched. Yahweh and his anointed are unassailable, like the tree in Psalm 1. We know nothing else as yet about the nature of their kingship and rule, or of any of the challenges they will face. A hint as to the former is given at the end of Psalm 2 where the kings and rulers of the earth are called to wisdom and the final blessing is open to all, but these things will be explored in the rest of the Psalter.

The scene changes in vv. 4-6. We leave the realm of the kings of the earth and their plotting and enter the heavenly realm. The psalmist describes the scene. The central character is called 'he who is enthroned (sits) in the heavens'. While we know from v. 2 that it speaks of Yahweh, the stress on his position as king in heaven, in contrast to the kings of the earth, underlines his unassailability and the futility of their plotting. His laughter and derision arise from his position and, ultimately, are as threatening to his opponents as any physical confrontation. Elsewhere, laughter is Yahweh's response to his enemies (Pss. 37.12-13; 59.8), and is associated with the irresistible force of the Assyrians in an earlier time (Hab. 1.5-11).

The laughter turns to spoken word in v. 5. Here we get close to the heart of the matter. The one enthroned in heaven is not threatened by any mutterings of the kings of the earth, and his word is sufficient to exercise his authority. He speaks in anger and fury, to be sure, but it is his word that terrifies potential opponents. There is no actual or even threatened display of force. This terrifying word simply takes the shape of a declaration of kingship (v. 6): 'I have set my king on Zion, my holy hill'. The doubling of the pronoun 'I' at the start of the verse in the Hebrew gives it emphasis. The first person pronoun appears two more times in this brief statement: 'my king' and 'my holy hill'. The phrase '*my* king', found only here in the speech of Yahweh, clearly grants the divine king's authority to his human counterpart. Human royal authority is grounded in divine authority. The fact that the king is set on Yahweh's 'holy hill', or more properly his 'holy mountain', recalling the mythic abode of the divine king, further symbolizes this. The divine king has 'set' his earthly counterpart in the place of divine authority.

We reach the centre of the psalm at the beginning of the next section, vv. 7-9. For the first time in the psalms someone other than the psalmist speaks, namely the human king, Yahweh's anointed. However, the form of this king's speech is notable. He does not speak out of his own, recently granted authority. His entire speech is a quotation of the divine speech, possibly words from the coronation ceremony itself where the divine king declares of his earthly monarch: 'you are my son; today I have begotten you'. This divine speech is referred to as a *ḥôq yhwh*, a 'statute of Yahweh'. The word *ḥôq* appears infrequently in psalms but generally implies some fixed ordinance or boundary set by some authority, especially God (Pss. 81.5; 148.6). Elsewhere, it is associated or synonymous with *torah* (Ezra 7.10; Isa. 24.5). Just as the blessed man in Psalm 1 meditates on the *torah* day and night, the only thing we hear from the king in Psalm 2 is a quotation of the divine statute. Thus, a telling correspondence is struck as we move from divine to human speech, signifying the source of earthly authority and its exercise.

This is reinforced by the content of the speech. The human king quotes a divine promise to do with the conquest of the nations (vv. 8-9). However, there is an issue to do with the translation of the verbs in these verses. They can be translated as either future indicative or permissive. In other words, does v. 9 predict a future conquest in relation to an existing conflict, or does it give the earthly king permission to use his power if needed? The lack of contextual details in the psalm favours the latter. This is, in effect, the outworking of the divine response to any conspiracy and plotting on the part of the nations (v. 1). The kings of the nations ought to be fearful before the one begotten of Yahweh. He is powerful and he can use that power. Moreover, his power, and the source of their fear, lies not within himself or his earthly role. It lies with the one who calls him 'my son'.

In vv. 10-12 the psalmist returns as speaker, and the focus of discussion is again on the nations and the kings and rulers of the earth. A deliberate correspondence is created between v. 2ab and v. 10ab. The end of the psalm returns to the beginning. Only now, those who might conspire and plot are called to be wise and warned. They are now called to serve with fear (v. 11a), i.e. recognize and worship, the same lord against whom they conspire. They are now called to acknowledge his anointed, also against whom they plot (v. 12a). The translation of the beginning of v. 12 has always given problems. The Hebrew reads literally 'kiss the son'. This could be an instruction to do obeisance to Yahweh's monarch, declared to be Yahweh's 'son', but a difficulty is that the word 'son' is the Aramaic *bar* not the Hebrew *ben* of v. 7. Alternative readings involving various emendations to the Hebrew text have been proposed, e.g. the NRSV 'kiss his feet'. None is without difficulties. Moreover, other ancient versions of the psalm, while clearly having problems translating the MT, all reflect in some way the text of the MT. Given the parallels of v. 12 to v. 2, we might expect some reference to the human king in Zion. Further, it has been made clear in vv. 7-9 that the human king is endorsed by and carries the authority of his heavenly lord. It is appropriate then, that at the point where the kings of the earth are called to fear Yahweh they are also called to acknowledge his earthly representative. While the difficulties remain, it seems best to translate the beginning of v. 12 as 'kiss the son', presuming a call for obeisance similar to that seen in many ancient Near Eastern reliefs and statues which show people touching their heads to the foot of a new king.

The invitation set forth in vv. 10-12 should not be missed. While the rest of the psalm establishes the authority of the divine word in relation to the king in Zion, and hence the authority of the earthly king, and while he has the power to make the nations his heritage, the way is left open for those nations and their rulers to choose another way, a way of wisdom. Divine anger and retribution are not inevitable for conspirators and plotters. The nature of the kingship of Yahweh and his earthly monarch are not defined solely by this aggressive use of power. The full nature of this kingship will only be understood when we read other psalms but the final statement of the psalm, v. 12c, 'blessed are all taking refuge in him', does takes us a little further. This line stands alone at the end of Psalm 2, and through the same vocabulary forms an *inclusio* (where the beginning and the end are the same or similar) with Ps. 1.1. It may well have been placed in its current position for that reason. However, v. 12c also plays a number of roles in the context of Psalm 2. In Psalm 1, we noted the role ambiguity plays in interpretation. It also figures in Psalm 2. Who are those who take refuge? At one level, the immediate context of vv. 10-12b and the plural verb in v. 12c suggest that this blessed state is an offering to those who might otherwise consider conspiracy and plotting as their course of action. Further, the pronoun 'him' at the end of the line is unclear. Does it refer to Yahweh or his king? If the latter then blessedness is offered to those who adhere to the political structures sanctioned by Yahweh, including the kings and rulers of the earth. But we cannot forget the source of authority and power invested in those structures. The king in Zion draws authority only from Yahweh. He mediates divine kingship, and his word is derived from the divine declaration and promise. On the other hand, the description of the earthly king in Zion shows that he also finds his refuge in Yahweh, the one who grants him authority, power and sonship. In fact, he is not only vice-regent to Yahweh, but is a model for those who take refuge in Yahweh. The ideal king is also the ideal Israelite, a faithful servant of Yahweh. In this last context the blessedness of the man in Psalm 1 comes back into play in the *inclusio*. Human kingship is drawn back into the circle of those who neither partake of the conversations of conspiracy nor are cowered by them. Their refuge is in Yahweh in whose *torah* they delight day and night.

There is an openness to the future in Psalm 2, just like there is in Psalm 1. While each psalm speaks to the present, they also look to future events in terms of an unspecified judgment (Ps. 1.5) or the overcoming of conspiring rulers (Ps. 2.9). There is a timeless aspect to these psalms and they speak as much to the generations of the faithful to come or to kings of the future as they do to present ones. This forward look and the idealism of these psalms lend them to an eschatological interpretation. Such an interpretation is enhanced in Psalm 2 by reference to the anointed king as the mediator of divine authority. The roots of a messianic eschatological interpretation are thus in place. There were a number of attempts to interpret royal texts such as this messianically in early and medieval Judaism. The fact that the king is the only human, apart from the psalmist, to speak up to the end of Psalm 2 further reinforces this line of thought, especially in contexts where the demise of the Israelite monarchy is known as we will see in later psalms. The whole Psalter then is cast in this light, but as we have already noted, the messianism understood here is not one of military might only. It has been heavily qualified by the need for the king, the blessed one, to attend to the discipline of *torah* piety.

Psalm 3

In Psalms 1 and 2 we were introduced to the one who is blessed and the one who is the chosen king of Yahweh. In Psalm 3 the one who fills both those roles is named for the first time. The psalm bears the superscription 'A psalm of David (*mizmôr l^{e}dāwīd*) when he fled from Absalom his son'. While there are many possible translations for *l^{e}dāwīd* in psalm superscriptions ('of David', 'for David', 'dedicated to David') in this case *l^e* clearly means 'of' indicating that the words to follow are those of David himself. This is matched by a shift to the first person in the body of the psalm. Psalm 3 is set, therefore, in the context of David's flight from his son Absalom when the latter usurped the throne of Jerusalem (2 Samuel 15). The one whom the psalmist called blessed and chosen king, is suddenly exposed as one embroiled in family dissention and political rivalry. The voice of the one who meditates on the *torah* and takes refuge in Yahweh, is suddenly heard in the act of lament.

The psalm divides into three sections: vv. 1-3; 4-6; and 7-8. In vv. 1-3 David complains to Yahweh about the number of enemies that rise up (*qûm*) against him, that is, seek his life (cf. Pss. 54.3; 86.14). Three times the root *rbb*, 'to be numerous, many', is employed in vv. 1-2 in reference to these enemies. In the context of David's flight from Absalom the enemies set against him increase in number as the story proceeds, with first Absalom (2 Sam. 15.1-12) opposing David, and then Ahithophel (15.12), Mephiboshet (16.3), and Shimei (16.6) as well as others. They threaten David's place as king under Yahweh. So at this point the psalm lends itself to that context, but there are also points of variance between Psalm 3 and the 2 Samuel story. While in 2 Samuel David's enemies have challenged his place on the throne, for David the psalmist, the threat goes even deeper. In Ps. 3.1-2 the first two lines emphasize the personal threat to the psalmist, but in the last line we hear the enemies' words and understand the full nature of the attack. In contrast to the physical and political threat of 2 Samuel the real problem in the psalm is a theological one. The enemies taunt: 'There is no help for him in God' which strikes at the heart of the psalmist and his faith. We should note that the enemies speak about God (*'elōhîm*, v. 3b) at this point, whereas David prays to Yahweh (v. 2). We will see later that this distinction is significant. David's opponents in Psalm 3 are neither the international enemies of Psalm 2 nor the wicked who seek to ensnare in Psalm 1. The superscription suggests that the enemy can also be a son or other formerly loyal individual. This casts new light on the two earlier psalms. Enemies and those who entice faithlessness can include those who are closest. Enmity itself can be very subtle.

This first section of the psalm closes with a statement of confidence in Yahweh describing him as a 'shield' around David (cf. Pss. 7.10; 18.2, 30; 59.11 etc.), his 'glory' (*kābôd*) and the one who 'lifts up (his) head'. The term *kābôd* is the most complex. This is the only use of the phrase 'my glory' by a human speaking of Yahweh. On the other hand, the psalmist, others or Yahweh himself often speak of Yahweh's 'glory' (e.g. Pss. 19.1; 26.8; 29.1-2; 57.5, 11; 66.2; 97.6 etc.). The psalmist also uses *kābôd* to speak of wealth or honour (e.g. Pss. 49.17; 73.24). In this context, the psalmist both refers to Yahweh as his only honour, and the one who grants him honour. 'Lifting up the head' is also connected with victory over enemies, actual or anticipated (cf. Pss. 27.3, 6; 83.2; 110.7; Judg. 8.28).

The focus of the first section of the psalm is the enemies. In the central section, vv. 4-6, the focus shifts to David as psalmist. He speaks confidently that whenever he raises his voice to Yahweh in prayer, the latter answers him (v. 4) from 'his holy mountain' (NRSV: 'his holy hill'), a symbol of his sovereignty over creation. In Psalms 18 and 20, both royal psalms where the king struggles against enemies, Yahweh speaks from his temple in similar vein (cf. Pss. 18.6; 20.2, 6). David's statement is in direct opposition to that of the enemies who say there is no divine help for him. But he hangs on to his faith in Yahweh in hope and trust. Verse 5a, in which he states that when he has lain down and slept, Yahweh has awakened him, stands in parallel to v. 4. He is secure in life because Yahweh sustains him (v. 5b). While the main challenge to David is theological, the physical world with its daily cycle of events is not forgotten in the metaphors of the psalm. Even in his most vulnerable state (sleep) David has confidence in Yahweh and knows Yahweh's support each day. He boldly declares his lack of fear of the multitudes around him (v. 6), evoking thoughts of both the *many* enemies in vv. 1-2, and the statement that Yahweh is a shield *around* him (v. 3).

The central section of the psalm provides further points of comparison between Psalm 3 and the story of David's flight from Absalom. In the latter, David exhibits strong reliance on Yahweh when challenged by his opponents (cf. 2 Sam. 15.25; 16.11-12), and while in the psalm David seeks Yahweh's help from 'his holy mountain', in 2 Sam. 15.25 David asks for the ark to remain in Jerusalem as he flees the city. The city is the place where the symbol of Yahweh's presence resides and from where Yahweh will deal favorably with David.

The subject of the psalm changes again in the third section, vv. 7-8. David pleads with Yahweh to rise (*qûm*) against the enemies even as they rose against him in v. 1b. He asks Yahweh to deliver him using the verb from the same root as the noun 'help' in v. 2b. While the enemies stated that there was no help for David from God (*'elōhîm*), David names Yahweh as 'my God'. He proclaims in v. 8a that 'help' ('deliverance, salvation') belongs to Yahweh. As he echoes these earlier words of the psalm, David challenges his enemies, and, in particular, rebuts their theological statement.

The psalm ends with two statements of confidence which support David's plea for help. The first states that Yahweh smites the cheek of 'my enemies' and shatters the teeth of the wicked (v. 7b). These expressions can both be traced to legal contexts in the ancient Near East, although by the time they appear in this psalm they can be used figuratively to indicate the infliction of humiliation upon someone. However, a problem is encountered here with the use of the perfect form of the verbs in v. 7b. This usually indicates past action, but it is out of place in the lament given the imperative verb forms in v. 7a and the desire for a future blessing in v. 8. We could tie the psalm to some past action, but the perfect form can indicate some hoped for action by God in some psalms (e.g. Pss. 22.22; 31.5-6). Such use could lend itself to a softening of the distinction between past and present/future, and be a way of negotiating between confidence based on past action by God and hopes for present/future action. The ambiguity allows the imagery of the psalm to play on different levels. This is particularly the case if we read the psalm as that of David as he struggled with Absalom. In any event, the psalmist speaks with confidence of the physical threat of the enemies being overcome and of Yahweh effecting some difference in the world.

The second statement closes the theological argument, which is foundational for the resolution of the physical threat above. David states forcefully that deliverance belongs to Yahweh. This is in defiance of the enemies' statement of v. 3b. The intention of the enemies' assertion was to strip any sense of hope from the one who prays to Yahweh. David resists this. His confidence in v. 8 is based on the earlier expressions of confidence in the psalm. However, there is still an openness about it. The tension involved in trust is not easily dismissed. But that does not negate the power of the psalm. David's contention with the enemies over the usefulness of prayer, and ultimately over the efficacy of Yahweh, is itself in the form of a prayer. It serves to encourage trust and gives such trust expression.

The psalm concludes with a request for Yahweh's blessing upon his people. This is not the same word as used for blessing in Pss. 1:1 and 2:12 but is synonymous. We find this root word for blessing (*brk*) used a number of times to speak of God's blessing upon his people (Pss. 21.3, 6; 24.5; 45.2 and 129.8). The interesting aspect about Ps. 3.8, however, is that the blessing is called upon 'your people' and not upon David who has been the subject of the psalm. The psalm has significance beyond the context of David's flight from Absalom. It has significance for all Yahweh's people. The liturgical tone of this final verse allows the psalm to become part of the community's prayer (cf. 2 Sam. 6.18).

This broadening of the psalm's reference may also be evident in other aspects of the psalm. The superscript connects the psalm to David's flight from Absalom. While there are connections between the psalm and the story in 2 Samuel, there are also differences. In the psalm, Yahweh is called to act for David, but in 2 Samuel 18 David himself, having set up spies and informants, eventually overcomes Absalom. Moreover, in 2 Samuel David seeks mercy for his son Absalom. This mercy carries over to his dealings with others in 2 Samuel, namely Shimei (2 Sam. 19.18b-23) and Mephiboshet (vv. 24-30). However, in the psalm he recalls and seeks Yahweh's humiliation of his enemies (cf. 2 Sam. 18.5 etc. and Ps. 3.7). In addition, while in 2 Sam. 15.25 David looks toward Jerusalem as the place where the ark should stay, and hence is the place of Yahweh's presence, the term 'holy mountain' (Ps. 3.4) is not used of Jerusalem or the temple mount in or before David's time. Finally, the wider setting of the story in 2 Samuel, namely following David's seduction of Bathsheba and the murder of Uriah (2 Samuel 11), pictures David as a flawed and sinful character, something not even hinted at in the psalm.

These differences suggest that the close connection of Psalm 3 to the story in 2 Samuel is not assumed simply in historical terms. It invites further deliberation on the context within which a prayer such as Psalm 3 can be prayed. The fact that David's enemies in 2 Samuel include trusted companions and a son whom he loves suggests that the notion of 'enemy' cannot be limited to political opponents who stand at a distance. David's humiliating 'retreat' from Jerusalem exposes the painful cost of trust in Yahweh for the faithful servant. Moreover, the connection of David's flight to his sinful acts implies that the faithful servant of the psalm is nevertheless a blatant sinner. On the other hand, David's setting up of spies and informants suggests that trust and practical preparation may not be incompatible. These matters, in turn, draw the reader/hearer into a conversation around the context for such a prayer and encourage them to see connections with their own and other situations. The early Christian interpretation of David in this psalm as the forerunner of Christ in his sufferings and death is an example. The route taken by David in his flight from Absalom, through the Wadi Kidron (2 Sam. 15.23) and up the mount of Olives (2 Sam. 15.30), supports the later comparison to Christ in his agony.

Finally, some additional connections between Psalm 3 and Psalms 1–2 tie the beginning of the Psalter together. Reference to the wicked (Ps. 3.7, *rᵉšāʿîm*) recalls the threefold mention of them in Ps. 1.1, 5 and 6. In Psalm 1, the blessed one does not take the counsel of the wicked, and the latter cannot stand (*qûm*) in the judgment, but their way will perish. In Psalm 3 we see an example of the counsel of the wicked, namely that there is no deliverance in Yahweh, and understand something of the difficulty encountered and trust required to resist the temptation of such counsel. The reference to the 'holy mountain' in Ps. 3.5 recalls the use of the expression in 2.6. In Psalm 2 Yahweh speaks from heaven saying he has established his king in 'my holy mountain', which is identified with Zion. In Psalm 3 the psalmist has confidence that Yahweh will answer from 'his holy mountain'. Together, these psalms clearly locate Zion as the divine residence. The psalmist in Psalm 3 is the king of Psalm 2 who now takes refuge in Yahweh as Ps 2.12 urges. We see in Psalm 3 an example of what taking refuge can mean, in terms of both situation and trust required. The connection with the story of David's flight casts its own shadow on the meaning and context of refuge, and king David (as the psalmist) becomes the exemplar of those who take refuge.

Psalms 4–6

Psalm 4 could well continue the story of David's flight from Absalom, even though the superscription gives context. David calls on God to answer his prayer as he continues to be dogged by others who shame him and seek falsehood (v. 2). His 'honour' (*kābôd*) is put to shame (v. 2) but, since the Lord is called David's *kābôd* in Ps. 3.3, the shaming is not just an attack on David, but also against his God, thus continuing the theological assault of Psalm 3. However, David does not lose confidence in Yahweh (v. 4) and urges others to follow suit (vv. 4-5). While many seek Yahweh's protection, David knows this gladness and is a model for them (vv. 6-7). His confident rest in Yahweh (v. 8) echoes Yahweh's protection in such vulnerable situations as in Ps. 3.5.

In **Psalm 5**, David again moans and pleads to God for attention and hope (vv. 1-2) and trusts that in the morning Yahweh will hear his plea (v. 3, cf. Pss. 3.5; 4.4, 8). Yahweh does not delight in wickedness, and the boastful do not stand before him; they will perish (vv. 5-6; cf. Pss. 1:6 and 2:11). David asks Yahweh to make his way straight before him, consonant with the way of the upright in Psalm 1. As in Psalm 3 the attack born by David is verbal and he seeks an appropriate punishment for the mouths etc. of the wicked (v. 10). The psalm ends with the hope that all who love Yahweh's name, who take refuge in him, may rejoice, sing and find protection in Yahweh, confident of his blessing (cf. Pss. 1:1; 2:12)

The theme of lament at the attack of enemies continues in **Psalm 6** and David asks "How long?" (v. 3b). He pleads to Yahweh to be gracious (vv. 2-3a) because he languishes and is terrified. Yet he knows that his weeping in the night has been heard (vv. 8-9a) and that Yahweh has accepted his prayer (v. 9b). Now he wishes to see his shame and terror come upon his opponents.

Psalm 7

Another event in David's life stands behind this psalm. It is a song 'which he sang to Yahweh concerning Cush, a Benjaminite'. Unfortunately, there is no reference to a Benjaminite named Cush in 2 Samuel, leaving room only for conjecture over the connection. However, close to the story about Absalom in 2 Samuel there is reference to Shimei, a Benjaminite (2 Sam. 16.11; 19.16-17), who curses David as he flees Absalom. There is also reference in 2 Samuel 15-17 to Hushai, the Archite, a friend who acts as David's spy in Absalom's court. Thirdly, the reference could be to the Cushite messenger who brought news to David of Absolom's death (2 Sam. 18.21-32). This man is mostly called 'the Cushite' but in v. 21 is referred to as 'Cushi'. This last identification goes back at least to the LXX, where David sings Psalm 7 'upon hearing the words of Chousi'. This would make sense of the lament in the psalm, although David's enemy would not be 'Cushi' but likely Joab, a loyal friend who becomes an enemy in a matter of a few verses in 2 Samuel 18–19. Alternatively, we have to assume that the character referred to in the superscription belongs to a tradition that has not been recorded in the Bible, or the name is a euphemism for, or refers to, some other opponent of David such as Saul or Shimei. We should also note that Psalms 7 and 18 both break the normal pattern of formulae for superscriptions. They are also the only two where the event behind the superscition is not clearly identifiable.

Given this, it is still clear from the superscript that we are to read the Psalm as one from David himself. The association of Psalms 3 and 7 with stories from 2 Samuel 15–19 suggests further that the whole of the collection from Psalm 3 to Psalm 7 is to be read in that context. A number of elements in the psalm also relate it to Psalm 2 and support a possible royal context. In both, 'the peoples' ($l^{e\,\prime}ummîm$) are aligned against Yahweh and his king (Ps. 2.1; 7.6); the endeavour is futile (2.4; 7.15-16) and the enemies are defeated (2.9; 7.12-13); Yahweh has power over all the earth (2.7; 7.7-8); Yahweh protects and supports the king (2.8; 7.6); there is an offer of mercy to the enemies (2.11-12; 7.12); and in both Yahweh is a refuge for his king and people (2.12; 7.1). Whatever the event behind the psalm, be it personal or political or both, David draws on the promised protection of Yahweh when faced with the deadly pursuit of his enemies.

David begins by declaring that Yahweh is his refuge (v. 1). To date he has only stated in a general way that those who take refuge in Yahweh are blessed or rejoice (Pss. 2.12; 5.11). Now he overtly includes himself in that group and as such becomes a model for them. He takes this refuge lest his enemy overtake him. He employs the metaphor of the stalking and attack of a ravenous lion (v. 2) to convey both the suddenness of his terror and his own inability to escape.

David pleads innocence in vv. 3-5, implying righteous action on his part and injustice on the part of his pursuers. God should know this. If he is not innocent then David is willing for Yahweh to let him be pursued and trampled in the dust. The hunting metaphor continues. But the psalm itself is built on the premises that Yahweh has not acted so and that David does not deserve such a terrible fate. He relies upon Yahweh as the one who dispenses justice for all. Both this theme and the hunting metaphor are developed as the psalm progresses (see especially vv. 12-13, 15).

Verse 4 presents a number of textual problems, especially v. 4b. The NRSV translates the verb $wā^{\,\prime a}hall^e ṣâ$ as '(I had) plundered' in order to make sense of the line, but why would David not have cause to 'plunder' an enemy? The verb is better translated as 'rescue' and with the amendment (not unreasonable) of 'my enemy' to 'his enemy', the line can read 'or rescued his enemy without cause.' Alternatively 'without cause' could relate to both actions in v. 4: 'if I have paid back my friend with harm or rescued his enemy without cause'. It is quite possible that an ancient treaty obligation underlies the verse and God is presented as not only judge but also as protector of the alliance. There may even be a veiled statement of the accusation that is brought against David in these verses.

David's honour (*kābôd*; NRSV: 'soul') is threatened in v. 5. A similar threat was evident in Ps. 4.2 but since in Ps. 3.3 Yahweh was seen as David's *kābôd* ('glory') it is unclear whether Yahweh too is shamed or 'poured' out in David's situation. David cries out for Yahweh to arise and awake and for the assembly to gather for judgment (vv. 6-7). The metaphor changes from one of hunting to that of juridical process. It may sound as though Yahweh is sleeping on the job, but in the ancient Near East divine sleep could be a sign of sovereignty, and the call for God to awaken a plea for justice to be exercised (cf. Pss. 35.23-24; 44.23-26; 59.4b-5; but also cf. Ps. 121.3-4). The call (v. 6) for Yahweh to arise recalls the cry to battle that went before the ark in the wilderness (Num. 10.35). This, combined with the fact that 'the peoples' can have the nuance of 'warriors' in some contexts, suggests that this council could be one of war as well as one of justice.

As well as judging the 'peoples' David also expects to be judged (v. 8), but he knows his own innocence, or righteousness. In the NRSV translation, David is also assured that God is a righteousness judge in this process (v. 11). He may even be employing a legal formula in his statement. But the Hebrew of vv. 11–13 is not entirely clear and is open to a number of interpretations. One such interpretation supported by some ancient (LXX in part) and medieval Jewish commentators runs something like: 'God judges the righteous, but God has indignation every day against the one who does not repent.' The one 'who does not repent' (or 'turn' as the Hebrew has it) is here the recipient of God's indignation. Moreover, the reluctance to turn and God's condemnation of that one is a regular occurrence. Various aspects of the theme of righteousness are carried through the psalm (vv. 8, 9, 10, 11, and 17). In this case David's prayer is built on a two-fold righteousness—his and God's, although in the end (v. 17) it is the righteousness of God that ultimately sustains him (cf. 1 Cor. 4.3-4). Any righteousness he possesses is in relation to the charge at hand and subject to any necessary repentance. At least David knows that, unlike the ravenous lion, there is some hope with Yahweh. It is also evident that the language of the psalm has changed slightly from very personal language about David's situation in vv. 1-6, to language in which David pleads for vindication from God who judges all with righteousness (vv. 7-16). David's personal plea for deliverance is gradually seen in the context of all who are righteous or repent.

As the psalm proceeds in vv. 12-13 the hunting metaphor is picked up again. It is not clear, however, exactly who is the hunter who whets his sword, draws his bow, and prepares deadly weapons etc. The subject of the verbs in Hebrew is simply 'he'. Is it God in his judgment (as the NRSV adds), or is it the wicked who plots further evil acts? Maybe the ambiguity is deliberate. In either case, we see two sides to God's justice in the face of wickedness—vindicating the righteous and judging the wicked. And we see the irony of the plotting of the wicked. In another metaphorical twist, the sequence of the conception, development, and execution of their lies is likened to the processes of pregnancy and birth (v. 14; cf. Job 15.35). But one final play on the word 'turn' or repent spells out the fate of the wicked. The hunting metaphor returns one last time as the wicked fall in the trap which they have prepared for their prey, and their evil *returns* (Heb. *šûb*) upon their own heads (vv. 15-16). Yahweh returns on high (v. 7), but as the wicked do not turn ('repent'), so their evil will return on them. The possibility of repentance (v. 12a) is contrasted with but tied to Yahweh's own various 'turns' and 'returns'.

The psalm ends with a vow of praise, as is the case with most psalms of complaint. David vows to give thanks to Yahweh and to sing praise to the name of the Most High, ʿ*elyôn*. Earlier David called upon Yahweh to rise up onto the seat of judgment (v. 6). This is a claim for the sovereignty of his God. It is the surety of that that gives him confidence in his prayer. Now at the end, as if to underline it, David calls Yahweh ʿ*elyôn*, that ancient title of the Canaanite high god (cf. Gen. 14.22; Ps. 47.2). David's God is sovereign over all, one in whom David can indeed find refuge.

But one final point is to be noted about David. His vow, with the promise to sing and accompany that with music, as the Hebrew word *zmr* implies, puts him in the realm of the temple choristers. The connection to David, at least in the superscription, together with the voice of the psalmist himself vowing to sing his thanks to God, helps lay the foundation for the tradition of David as king and psalmist. As such he invites others into his praise.

Psalm 8

In Psalm 8 David takes up where he left off in Ps. 7.17 singing praises to the name of Yahweh. He proclaims the majesty of Yahweh's name (cf. Pss. 29.1-2; 89.15-16; Isaiah 6 etc.) in all the earth in the *inclusio* to Psalm 8 (vv. 1a, 9). This is the first psalm of praise or hymn David has sung. Every single verse is addressed to God. As such, Psalm 8 takes up not only the vow at the end of Psalm 7, but expresses fully the joy anticipated in the earlier lament psalms (Pss. 3.8; 4.7; 5.11; and 6.5b, 9). The absence of any reference to human guilt in Psalm 8 picks up the innocence protested by David in Psalm 7. The matter of human sin will not be forgotten in the larger scheme of things, but this is not the place for that discussion. There are other things to say about humankind, not just about David but about all people, for in addressing Yahweh as '*our* sovereign' David draws the community into his praise. Nor are these things just a hope for the future. He speaks about human praise even in the immediate context of lament over hard times (Psalms 4–7; 9–13).

The *inclusio* in vv. 1a, and 9 gives a sense of completeness to the psalm. All things about which David speaks or implies in this psalm, are enclosed within the sovereignty of Yahweh. It envelops all—in heaven and on earth—and that is the central point. The 'middle' of the psalm deals with how this is proclaimed. There is a movement within this 'middle' from the heavens to the earth and out to the far reaches of the earth. There is a general 'hourglass' shape to the psalm focused around the reference to humankind (vv. 4-5), whose representative, David, declares Yahweh as 'our sovereign' at the beginning and end of the psalm.

The body of the psalm begins with reference to the heavens (v. 1b) and we immediately encounter a major difficulty. Is Yahweh's glory 'set', 'put', 'chanted', 'sung', or 'worshipped' above the heavens? English translations and commentators differ because the Hebrew text, at best, involves a rare construction or, at worst, is corrupted. It is at least clear, however, that what happens to Yahweh's glory (so NRSV for *hôd*; better 'might, splendour') happens 'above the heavens'. The difficulty also relates to how v. 1b is related to v. 2. Do the babes and infants 'set' etc. Yahweh's glory above the heavens or do they found a 'bulwark' (so NRSV for *'ōz*; better 'strength') against the foes? We could understand this to say that even the inarticulate speech of babes and infants is strength against the Lord's enemies; even the utterances of the weakest of humans praise God and stand against 'the enemy and avenger' (or better 'revenge-seeker'). This is quite a revolutionary statement. Yahweh's enemy is usually seen as the great sea monster, representing chaos (Pss. 74.12-17; 89.8-11; Isa. 51.9-10; Job 26.10-13) and his weapon is sometimes his voice (Ps. 29.3-9). In Psalm 8, however, lowlier voices are

Yahweh's strength. This way of interpreting vv. 1b-2 is at least as old as the New Testament where Jesus quotes v. 2 in Mt. 21.16 (cf. also 1 Corinthians 1 and 2).

In v. 3, David ponders the wonders of God's handiwork in the heavens, possibly at night. His attention then moves (v. 4) to the insignificance of a human being in the grand scale of things. He even uses words ($^{e}nôš$ and ben-$^{,}ādām$) which can imply vulnerability and be indicative of individuals or humankind collectively. He speaks for himself and all humankind. But it is not the insignificance of humans that is of primary interest, it is rather the attention and concern Yahweh gives to them. The statements about humans need to be seen first and foremost in relation to God, which was the point of enclosing the psalm with vv. 1a and 9 (cf. Ps. 144:3). In v. 4 the reader/hearer is caught by the shift from the grandeur of the heavenly spheres to the smallness of the human frame, as well as the move from statement to question. Verse 5 explores the thought further. Within a chiastic arrangement (little lower than—*crowned with glory*—*given dominion over*—all things under the feet) David then moves back to a statement, but one which stands in stark contrast to the question in v. 4. Humans are a 'little lower' than God (or gods) but they are crowned with 'glory and honour'.

The words associated with humans in vv. 5-6 are important. In contrast to the generic language of v. 4, David now uses royal language: 'glory ($kābôd$) and honour ($hādār$)', 'given dominion' (causative of $māšal$, 'to rule'), 'put under their feet'. 'Glory and honour' are attributes usually associated with God (e.g. Pss. 19.1; 29.1-2, 9; 96.3-6; 104.1, 31 etc., although cf. Ps. 21.5 regarding the king). The language of granting 'dominion' is used elsewhere in relation to both God and the human monarch (cf. Pss. 22.28; 72.8; and 145.3). This echoes the royal language used of God in vv. 1 and 9 and ties in with the theme of creation, with its royal associations, in vv. 1-3 and 7-8 (cf. the Genesis 1 creation account). Giving humans dominion over the works of God's hands (v. 6) recalls the 'work of (God's) fingers' in v. 3 and lifts humankind to great heights. While humans may seem insignificant in the grand scheme of things, they have been crowned with almost the status of their creator and granted dominion over all other creatures. The symbols of God's dominion in creation may seem to belittle humankind, but the divine gift of dominion raises those insignificant creatures to royal status.

There is a democratization of kingship in this passage similar to Genesis 1, although we ought not to assume this is a polemic against hereditary kingship. Kings still have status and power (see e.g. Psalm 72) but they share certain qualities and responsibilities with all humankind. Kings as well as 'ordinary' mortals, share the awareness of their own insignificance within creation as well as the wonder of Yahweh's care for them. And all people, not just kings, share responsibility for the order and care of creation.

This royal language invites reflection on Psalm 8 in comparison to the laments that have preceded it. We encountered the word 'glory' (*kābôd*) in those psalms. In Ps. 3.3, Yahweh was David's *kābôd*, but in Pss. 4.2 and 7.5 his *kābôd* (NRSV: 'soul') was threatened. David, like other human beings, suffered and was in both mortal and spiritual danger. Now in Psalm 8 he proclaims that Yahweh grants all humankind 'glory' (*kābôd*). Their 'glory' comes not from position in the world, but from God. It is human standing before God that is important. This was proclaimed in Psalm 7, but is reiterated here in stronger, more general terms. Even the weakest and most defenceless of humans, babes and infants, do not only praise Yahweh above the heavens, but can be strength against Yahweh's enemies in that their utterance of the name of Yahweh, even if unintelligible, elicits Yahweh's power. The same is true for the king, who has become weak and vulnerable in his suffering, but now praises Yahweh's majestic name. Yahweh as creator is seen as true refuge for the weak. As psalmist, David stands again in a representative role. The general point above may find further support through the use of the small particle *māh*, 'how', in Ps. 8.1b, 9. The same particle is used in the sense of 'what' at the start of v. 4. It also recalls the exclamation in Ps. 3.1 'O Lord, how (*māh*) many are my foes!' and the question in Ps. 4.2 'How long (*ʿad-māh*), you people, shall my honour suffer shame?' The answer to David's plight, and the general human condition, is found in the praise of God.

It should be noted in passing that the phrase 'enemy and avenger' (Ps. 8.2) appears elsewhere in the psalms only in Ps. 44.16, which deals with the suffering of Israel. The place of suffering in human experience is not dealt with directly in Psalm 8, but is taken up in Psalm 73 and in the treatment of the quote of Ps. 8.4 in Job 7.17.

There is a movement in the psalm from the expanse of the heavens to the earth and then out again. There is also a good deal of cross-referencing within this movement. Through the very structure of the psalm David underlines his point. There is no simple hierarchy in creation, moving from greater significance and power to less, but there is rather an intricate and interrelated whole. In addition to the use of royal language for both God and humans, and the reference to the work of God's hand/fingers in the two halves of the psalm, the '*all* things' put under human feet in v. 6 echoes '*all* the earth' within which God's name is majestic in vv. 1a and 9. The sovereignty of God, which encompasses all, is expressed in and praised by the most insignificant and vulnerable in creation. The ultimate focus of the psalm remains on God, as does the faith of David, the psalmist. To underline this, the only verb associated with human action in the psalm is 'looking' in v. 3.

Finally, a word should be said about the word 'dominion'. Modern humans think of dominion in different ways to their ancient counterparts. It is often thought of in terms of control, and in the way Psalm 8 and Genesis 1 have been used, especially in western society, in terms of domination and exploitation. But in the psalm, human dominion over other creatures is part of the glory and honour granted by God. It is neither an end in itself nor is it outside the domain of God's own sovereignty. In fact, it serves to proclaim God's 'majestic name in all the earth', in the words of the *inclusio*. To make this point, David extends human dominion in vv. 7-8 to things beyond human control: 'the beasts of the field, the birds of the air, and the fish of the sea, whatever passes along the paths of the seas'. The last reference could be an allusion to 'the great sea monsters' (cf. Gen. 1.21 and Leviathan of Ps. 104.26 etc.). David is making a statement, not so much about human dominion in activity and control, especially as expressed through kings in the ancient world, as about the 'mutual' relationship between humans and the created order and about the 'mutual' relationships within human society. Both sets of relationships have their reason for being focused in the sovereignty of God over all.

Psalms 9–10

Psalms 9 and 10 have long been considered one psalm. There are several reasons for this. Together they form an acrostic poem (where the first words of each section are arranged according to the order of the Hebrew alphabet), albeit one that is broken. There is no superscription to Psalm 10, an unusual situation for an independent psalm in Book I. They are treated as one psalm in the LXX. The term *selāh* is usually found within the body of a psalm, not at the end as with Psalm 9. Finally, there are a number of verbal and thematic connections between them. These include language describing 'the poor, oppressed' etc. (e.g. 9.10, 12, 18; 10.2, 12, 18), 'times of trouble' (9.10; 10.1), 'to seek' etc. (*dāraš*, 9.10, 12; 10.13, 15), 'avenge' (9.13; 10.13, 15), 'forget' (9.10, 12; 10.13, 15), 'nations ... perish' (9.6-7; 10.16), and 'Rise up, O Lord!' (9.19; 10.12). Since the acrostic is broken and the MT preserves them as separate psalms, it is possible two traditions operated at an early stage, one that saw them as two psalms, the other as a single work. We will read them as one in our present context.

Individual verses in this acrostic poem do not always fit together smoothly and may have come from originally independent sayings, especially in Psalm 9. Nevertheless, they witness to a general structure. Psalm 9 begins (vv. 1-12) with thanksgiving and praise for both what Yahweh has done and for who he is: enthroned, judging with righteousness, not forsaking the poor etc. It continues the tone of Psalm 8. However, it quickly turns to lament and pleads with Yahweh to act again in this way (vv. 13-18) and judge the nations (vv. 19-20). The order of thanksgiving then lament is unusual (although cf. Psalms 27; 40; and 89). Psalm 10 begins by asking why Yahweh is so far off when the wicked oppress the poor (vv. 1-11). It again calls onYahweh to rise, defeat the wicked and rescue the poor in 10.12-16. Finally, vv. 17-18 pick up the note at the end of Psalm 9 with a statement of assurance and trust in Yahweh to do justice for the poor.

This is another psalm of David, although no particular occasion is given. The superscription, 'according to *mûthlabbēn*', is possibly a musical setting, although the Targum for Psalms sees an allusion to 1 Sam. 17.4 and the story of David's battle with Goliath. The psalm could easily be read as from the king, as one of David's.

The fact that Psalm 9 begins with strong verbal memories of the end of Psalm 7 ('give thanks', 'sing praise' to God's 'name', and referring to God as '*elyôn*, 'Most High'; Pss. 7.17b; 9.2b) also infers David as the psalmist in Psalm 9. The reference to the divine 'name' in both places also draws these psalms into close association with Psalm 8, where the divine name is praised in the inclusio (vv. 1, 9). Thus, the praise in Psalm 8 becomes that vowed at the end of Psalm 7 and prefaces the thanksgiving and lament in Psalms 9 and following.

Ps. 9.3-4 contain other connections to Psalm 7. In v. 3 the enemies turn, stumble and fall, as they did into their own traps in Ps. 7.15, and Yahweh takes his throne and judges righteously in Ps. 9.4 as he did in Ps. 7.7-11. David then proclaims in three parallel lines that Yahweh has rebuked, destroyed ('made perish') and blotted out the nations/wicked (Ps. 9.5). The eternal nature of Yahweh's action is stressed even as the eternal result for the enemies is described, again in three parallel lines (v. 6). The verb 'to perish' (*'bd*, cf. Ps 1.6) is used three times in Ps. 9.3-6 to emphasize the point. The name of the enemies (i.e. their reputation) and their memory have perished, anticipating the notion of 'forgetting' which appears later in the psalm (vv. 12, 17, 18).

David speaks of Yahweh enthroned forever in vv. 7-10. He highlights Yahweh's righteous judgment and care for the oppressed. This is joined to the defeat of the enemies in the preceding verses. The one who 'sits in the heavens' (Ps. 2.4) not only laughs but carries on his serious kingly business. He is not only supremely powerful over his enemies but is a stronghold (twice mentioned) for the oppressed, who are more closely defined as those who 'know (Yahweh's) name', who trust in him and seek him. These are the ones who respond to the call to praise at the end of Ps. 7.17 and who participate in that praise in Psalm 8, and who in that psalm share in Yahweh's kingship. While Yahweh's kingship is the focus in this psalm, the human manifestation of that kingship is not lost to view.

The first section of the psalm concludes in vv. 11-12 where David's thanksgiving becomes an invitation to the congregation (pl. imperative) 'to give praise', using again the verb *zimmer* from Pss. 7.17 and 9.2. Yahweh, the one 'who dwells in Zion', is also the one who 'avenges blood', or literally 'seeks blood' (v. 12). The verb *dāraš* is the same as used for those who 'seek' Yahweh, and has both a cultic sense of seeking a god and a judicial sense of seeking retribution (cf. Gen. 9.5). Yahweh seeks revenge for crimes against those who seek him. Moreover, *zākar* ('to remember') and *šākaḥ* ('to forget') occur again highlighting the fact that Yahweh does not forget the poor (cf. 9.18; 10.12) even though others might forget Yahweh (9.17). Thus, through a series of word plays, the nature of Yahweh's kingship is set over against the violent action of the enemies/wicked.

As thanksgiving turns to lament, David seeks Yahweh's graciousness (vv. 13-14) in looking on the affliction caused by those who hate him. This could echo a scene from a royal installation but the language speaks generally of the 'poor' etc. While we may think of David as the psalmist, he speaks as one of the 'poor' in general, rather than from a position of privilege. As such he models for all one who beseeches Yahweh to raise him up from 'the gates of death' so that he might praise Yahweh in 'the gates of daughter Zion', the gates of life and the place of vindication.

The vivid images of hunting and trapping from Ps. 7.15-16 reappear in Ps. 9.15-16. The nations are again ensnared in their own traps. Three times David tells us this, interrupted only by a clause that interprets it all as Yahweh's judgment (v. 16a). The plea to Yahweh within the lament is built on the assurance of Yahweh's kingship (vv. 7-12, 13b-14). As one of those who are oppressed, David trusts that Yahweh will indeed take up his cause, as is fitting for a righteous king.

Themes of 'returning' (NRSV: 'depart'), 'forgetting', 'the poor', and 'perishing' come back in vv. 17-18. But again, sharp contrasts are made: the wicked 'return' to Sheol because they have 'forgotten' God (cf. v. 12; also 10.12). In contrast, Yahweh does not 'forget' 'the poor'. In fact, they will never be forgotten, nor will their hope ever perish. The parallel use of 'wicked' and 'nations' in these verses allows the plea to operate at both the level of the individual seeking aid, and at that of the people in national matters. National and ordinary contexts are brought together and David fills both roles of faithful individual and king. The psalm is, therefore, free to operate beyond its initial context.

Psalm 9 ends with a call to Yahweh to rise again (vv. 19-20), a call repeated in Ps. 10.12. It echoes the calls back in Pss. 3.7 and 7.6, and, as noted earlier, the battle cry that went before the ark in the wilderness (Num. 10.35). More importantly there are strong connections here with Psalm 8, especially through the word $'^e nôš$ ('mortal'). David uses the word twice in 9.19-20 to remind us that the nations which attempt to prevail against Yahweh are simply $'^e nôš$ ('mortal, human'). The same word was used to describe humans in comparison to Yahweh in Ps. 8.4a. And while in 9.19 the nations/$'^e nôš$ would seek to prevail ($'āzaz$, 'to be strong') against Yahweh, in 8.2 the related noun $'ōz$ ('strength/bulwark') described the secure defense of Yahweh against his foes. In Psalm 8 the glory of $'^e nôš$ is established by Yahweh, not by humans themselves, especially those who in Psalm 9 forget Yahweh and ultimately assume Yahweh has forgotten the evil they commit (Ps. 10.11, 12; although 'the righteous' could be the subject of v. 11).

David asks Yahweh in Ps. 10.1-2 why he is far off and hidden in these 'times of trouble'. His call presumes the statement in 9.9 where Yahweh is a stronghold for such times. The hiddenness of Yahweh, while a deep concern for David and the poor who suffer at the hand of the enemies, is seen by the latter as the very thing that enables them to do what they do (10.11). The irony is clear. David calls for Yahweh to be visible now to both the poor and the enemies, for the deliverance of the one and the judgment of the other. He then gives a lengthy description of these enemies of Yahweh in 10.3-11, concluding with a further reference to the hidden face of Yahweh, and thus creating an *inclusio*. The very description of the enemies undermines their position. If David knows what they are up to, so too then must Yahweh.

There are a number of textual and translation difficulties in these verses. Enough is clear, however, to know that the wicked, the nations, pursue their own interests and prosperity at the expense of the poor, and ignore Yahweh's judgments. While they deceive others, they also cultivate thoughts of their own security. The description of the wicked conceiving evil, being pregnant with mischief and giving birth to lies (Ps. 7.14) is surely played out in full here. The language of the hunt (cf. Psalm 7) returns again in v. 9. The poor and innocent are the victims in this language of violence, of murder, seizure, and lying in wait.

In vv. 12-18 David turns away from the description of the wicked and the implicit lament calling on Yahweh to rise again (cf. 9.30; also Pss. 3.8 and 7.7). He pleads with Yahweh to 'lift up his hand', possibly in an oath, or as a sign of intervention. Such a gesture is seen in Egypt in relation to the god of war and the king-god. David also pleads for Yahweh not to forget the oppressed. The wicked do not believe Yahweh calls them to account (*dāraš*, 'to seek') but we have already heard that Yahweh does 'seek' blood and avenge the poor, and does not forget them (9.12). David asserts boldly, contrary to the statements of the wicked in 10.11, 13, that Yahweh does indeed see (v. 14). He looks out situations of trouble and violence, in order to 'put his hand' to them. David pleads further for Yahweh to break the wicked and to 'seek' them out (v. 15). His confidence is in the eternal kingship of Yahweh (v. 16). It is the basis for everything, especially the perishing of the nations who oppress from the earth. Echoes of Psalms 1 and 2 are present. Yahweh will establish the hearts of the poor and do justice to the orphan and oppressed (vv. 17-18), again overturning the plotting of the wicked who were foolish enough to utter sayings against Yahweh in their hearts (vv. 11, 13). This strengthening of the hearts of the oppressed over against the confidence of the wicked hearkens back to Psalm 8 and its holding up of the weak.

The syntax of the last Hebrew clause of the psalm is uncertain. It is unclear who does the terrifying, Yahweh or the wicked, who is referred to as $'^e n\hat{o}š$, 'those from earth', the wicked or the poor, and who is subject and who object. On the basis of 9.19-20, it is possible that $'^e n\hat{o}š$ refers to the wicked. Psalm 9 ends with a desire that Yahweh judge the nations and that they (who will experience fear) may know they are $'^e n\hat{o}š$. The clause at the end of Psalm 10 could be a further statement of the hope that the terror caused by the wicked/nations will cease, and not just for the moment, but for ever.

While there is a unity within these two psalms, there is one difference. In Psalm 9 David offers thanksgiving and a plea as an individual, although in vv. 11-12 he calls for the community to participate in praise. He speaks frequently of 'the nations' but also equates them with 'my enemies' (vv. 3-4). In Psalm 10, on the other hand, he mainly laments and pleads on behalf of the poor and oppressed. With this a major concern for the poor is introduced into the Psalter. While there are elements that tie these psalms together, there is also movement between them.

We have noted that the superscription to Psalms 9–10, connections to Psalm 7, and some internal elements suggest that we read them as the words of David. Other connections strengthen this. The conjunction of the themes of eternal sovereignty of Yahweh (vv. 7-8) and divine support for the human monarch was also the theme of Psalm 2. In Ps. 10.14, Yahweh is described as a 'helper' of the orphan. That same term is applied to the king in Ps. 72.12 when speaking of his responsibility toward the poor. And we will also find that some of the terms introduced in Psalms 9–10 to speak of the poor and oppressed, notably $‘ānî$ ('poor, afflicted') and $'ebyôn$ ('poor'), are gathered again in the royal Psalm 72 (vv. 2, 4, 12-13).

Thus, Psalms 9–10 have been shaped to lead from the prayers of David for his own deliverance in a time of suffering, to his prayers on behalf of the oppressed and meek. His confidence in prayer is based in the eternal sovereignty of Yahweh (Pss. 9.7-8; 10.16), although his prayer also knows of the experience of

Yahweh's absence in times of trouble. But these aspects of David's prayer are not left there. While he fulfils his responsibilities in terms of his own trust in Yahweh and in his intercession for others, he also invites them to participate in his prayer. Between thanks and petition in Psalm 9, and having proclaimed the sovereignty of Yahweh, David declares Yahweh as a stronghold for the oppressed and for those 'who put their trust in' and 'seek' Yahweh (vv. 9-10). He then calls upon them to join in praise to Yahweh (vv. 11-12). At the end of Psalm 10, he prays confidently that Yahweh will hear also the desire of the poor, strengthen their heart, and hear their petition (v. 17); and this in the face of his seeming abandonment of them (vv. 1-11). David not only fulfils his royal responsibilities but invokes prayer and faith in others. His prayer for himself and others becomes a model for the faithful in their prayers. Moreover, the end of his prayer has an eschatological note to it. He prays that the meek will be heard by Yahweh and that terror may cease forever. The faithful are invited to pray as David, and to realize that all these prayers have an eschatological edge to them.

Psalms 11–17

David continues his lament in Psalms 11–14. In **Psalm 11** he takes refuge in Yahweh even in the face of the assaults of the wicked. His assurance is in the fact that Yahweh is in his holy temple, enthroned in heaven and sees all that transpires among humankind (vv. 4-5). The pain of the lament continues through **Psalm 13** as David pleads with Yahweh 'how long?' (13:1). He feels forgotten by Yahweh (cf. Pss. 9.5-6, 12, 17-18; 10.12-13), but in spite of this he remains confident of deliverance and maintains his vow of praise. In **Psalm 14** David believes the statements and actions of the wicked are futile, but feels alone in his faithfulness (Psalm 14.3), a theme that began in v. 1 of **Psalm 12**. Yahweh's deliverance, while eternal in nature, remains a future hope (Ps. 12.7), a theme also of the earlier laments. The eschatological nature of this hope is clear in Ps. 14.5, 7. In v. 5 David imagines that 'there' the wicked themselves will be in great terror as God will be found with the company of the righteous. This counters the statement in Ps. 10.18b.

David changes direction in **Psalm 15**. In this liturgical psalm he asks who can abide in Yahweh's tent, on his holy hill. A similar question will be asked in Ps. 24:3. The answer is given in terms of righteous behaviour, much of which contrasts with the activities of the wicked in earlier laments. An eschatological element again enters at the end of the psalm where those who approach the 'holy hill' will never be moved (Ps. 15.5c). The reference to the 'tent' and 'holy hill' recalls the immediate conclusion to Psalm 14 where David sought deliverance from Zion (v. 7) and where he described the righteous as the companions of God (v. 5). This 'holy hill' has been mentioned before, first as the place where Yahweh established his king (Ps. 2.6) and also as the place from which David sought help in his first lament (Ps. 3.4). What David describes in Psalm 15 applies above all to him, but the plural reference in v. 5c indicates it also applies to 'those who do these things', who follow in David's steps.

David seeks continued protection in **Psalm 16**. He feels secure and joyful in Yahweh's presence, one numbered among those referred to in Psalm 15. In **Psalm 17**, he again seeks Yahweh's deliverance, proclaiming his innocence, presumably along the lines of Psalm 15. The merciless oppression and apparent success of the wicked weigh heavily on him (cf. Psalm 10). In turn he attacks them with sarcasm in Ps. 17.14, speaking of blessing but implying punishment. The reference to sleep in v. 15, which recalls Psalms 3 and 4 shows David feels secure even at a time of extreme vulnerability.

Psalm 18

According to some Psalm 18 may be one of the most ancient of psalms, dating in its original composition to the eleventh or tenth century CE, and so coming from around the time of David. It could appear to be two psalms, an individual song of thanksgiving in vv. 1-30, and a royal thanksgiving in vv. 31-50. However, internal connections and the fact that a second, almost identical version of the entire psalm occurs in 2 Samuel 22, suggest that the psalm should be read as a single unit. As such it adds to our perception of David in the psalms.

Two important sections frame the psalm. In the first, vv. 1-19, David is concerned with some unspecified calamity and seeks Yahweh's help. The section is dominated by the description of Yahweh's appearance in vv. 7-15. In the second, vv. 31-45, David speaks about a past battle against unnamed enemies. The description of the battle and victory (vv. 37-42) is central to this section. Both sections begin with brief praise of Yahweh, and with particular reference to Yahweh as rock (vv. 2, 31), and end on a strong note of deliverance (vv. 17, 19 and 43). Between these two sections lies a more reflective passage (vv. 20-30), in which David speaks of his own righteousness and Yahweh's response. This passage ends with a reflection on the nature of Yahweh himself (vv. 25-30). The theme that Yahweh responds to his loyal and blameless people and delivers the 'humble' applies to both major sections of the psalm and ties them together. The psalm ends with brief praise of Yahweh referring to him again as rock and emphasizing his deliverance of the psalmist. This is explicitly associated with David and his descendants in v. 50. This is the first reference to David in the body of a psalm (cf. also Pss. 78.70; 89.3, 20, 35, 49; 132.1, 10-12, 17; 144.10; cf. Ps. 122.5).

The superscription to Psalm 18 expands the common $l^e d\bar{a}w\bar{\imath}d$ formula referring to David as 'servant of Yahweh' who sang this psalm 'when Yahweh delivered him from the hand of all his enemies, and from the hand of Saul'. The situation of David's deliverance remains rather general, and even though the reference to Saul strengthens the connection to David himself, no specific occasion is mentioned. The reference to Saul could even be a late expansion on the superscription.

Describing David as 'servant of Yahweh' is revealing in the context of the Psalter. The full phrase occurs again only in the superscription to Psalm 36. The self-designation of the psalmist as 'servant' in relation to Yahweh is frequent (e.g. Pss. 19.11, 13; 27.9; 31.16; 35.27 etc.), but reference to David specifically as Yahweh's servant also appears only in the two superscriptions and in those few psalms which mention David in the body of the psalm, although within those few it is frequent (Pss. 78.70; 89.3, 20, 39, 50; 132.10; 144.10; cf. also 2 Samuel 7 [several places] and 1 Sam. 25.39; 2 Sam. 3.18). Only three other 'servants of Yahweh' are named in the Psalter: Moses (Ps. 105.26); Abraham (Ps. 105.6, 42); and Israel (Ps. 136.22). Thus, David is the pre-eminent 'servant of Yahweh', standing in the line of Abraham and Moses, and now speaking as psalmist.

The reference in David's being delivered 'from the hand of Saul' is not clear. Saul becomes David's enemy from 1 Sam. 18.29 on and when other matters allow he pursues David even into the wilderness. David manages to escape on several occasions, but nothing in Ps. 18.1-19 connects the psalm with any episode in 1 Samuel 19–28. Moreover, vv. 31-45 of the psalm imply that David is already in a position of authority, possibly presuming his time of kingship in 2 Samuel. Thus, the context implied by the superscription remains vague. However, we should not presume the reference to Saul in the superscription has no connection at all with David's story in Samuel. The theme of David's loyalty and uprightness before Yahweh (cf. Ps. 18.21-30) is also present in Samuel (see 1 Sam. 19.1-7; 19.18-24; 20.16; 22.14; 24; 26; and 30.21-25). Thus, the superscription could well point to the events of 1 Samuel 19–28 in general, even if no one episode is indicated.

Other factors may have been at play when a version of the poem was appended to 2 Samuel in chapter 22. It is not clear which is the older version of the psalm, however, we note that even in the Samuel context David's loyalty and faithfulness shine through (e.g. 2 Sam. 21.1-14), the more so since Saul opposed Yahweh's choice of David. The superscription to the psalm is used to introduce the psalm in 2 Samuel 22 as one of a number of appendices to the story of David. In that place it serves to link David's escape from Saul to his deliverance from *all* his enemies and so becomes a thanksgiving for David's entire career in 1 and 2 Samuel.

David begins the psalm speaking about personal deliverance from unnamed enemies (vv. 1-19). He prefaces this with praise of Yahweh that is both intimate and extensive. He begins with the clause 'I love you' using a rare form of the verb, *riḥām*, 'to have compassion on someone' (cf. Ps. 103.13). Here, however, it is a statement of attitude toward another not one of action, and no doubt arising from personal experience. The statement is matched in v. 19b to form an *inclusio* for the first section in which it is said that Yahweh delights in David and so delivers him. David's description of Yahweh (vv. 1-2), which includes the longest list of predicates for Yahweh in the Psalter, is shaped by the military experience mentioned later in the psalm. Yahweh is strength, rock, fortress, deliverer, shield, horn of salvation, and stronghold, certainly worthy to be praised and called on, and one who can be trusted to respond (v. 3).

What David states in summary in v. 3 is explored in detail in vv. 4-19, although the Hebrew is occasionally corrupt (e.g. v. 11). The description of Yahweh as worthy of praise is now undergirded by David's description of divine action. His own situation is outlined briefly in vv. 4-5 in metaphorical language. He describes his confrontation with those who were too strong for him and hated him as a death-like experience (v. 17). Yet the one he loves hears his cry even from such a god-forsaken place and comes to him. Mention of the temple in v. 6 may seem an anomaly for David but in light of what follows, the temple referred to is not that built by Solomon (1 Kings 5–8) but Yahweh's heavenly abode. On the other hand, an allusion to the later Jerusalem temple cannot be missed, as the link between the heavenly and earthly temples is strong (cf. Ps. 20.2, 6).

David next describes the theophany, or appearance of Yahweh (vv. 7-15). The language suggests both the Sinai theophany (Exod. 19.16-25; cf. Judg. 5.4-5; Hab. 3.3-15) and the Canaanite theophany in the story of the god Baal. The effect is two-fold. The threat of David's 'mighty' enemies pales by comparison to the description of darkness, thunder, lightening etc. produced by Yahweh. Secondly, as the foundations of the world tremble and are laid bare, Yahweh's deliverance of the one who loves him is given cosmic significance (cf. Psalm 89 later). The assault on David is an assault on Yahweh's sovereignty, and his deliverance of David more than just an individual experience. The unusual appearance of a theophany in an individual thanksgiving psalm underscores this.

David finishes the first part of the psalm with a description of the actual deliverance. Yahweh reaches down to draw him out of the 'mighty waters' (*mayim rabbîm*), a term carrying connotations of the great cosmic waters of chaos (cf. Pss. 29.3; 77.20; 93.4; 144.7). What is otherwise striking is the rich array of synonyms for 'deliver' in vv. 16-19—'took' (*lāqaḥ*), 'drew out', 'delivered' (two Hebrew words), and 'brought out'. In each case the pronoun 'me' is the object as it is the object of the might, hate and confrontation of the enemy. The verb 'to take' may suggest even more. It is a common verb but is used in relation to righteous individuals who are taken up to heaven. This is so of the pre-flood heroes Enoch (Gen. 5.24) and Utnapishtim in the *Gilgamesh* epic. It is also the case when Elijah is taken up (2 Kgs 2.10). Thus, not only does David's deliverance have cosmic significance relating to Yahweh's sovereignty, but it also signals the exaltation of David himself. This is no run of the mill rescue.

In vv. 20-30 David becomes more reflective, considering why Yahweh has acted as he has. The section divides into two subsections, vv. 20-24, in which David reflects on his own righteousness, and vv. 25-30 in which he reflects more on Yahweh. Verses 20-24 are tightly structured. In vv. 21-23 David says he has kept Yahweh's ways, he has not put away (*sûr*)Yahweh's ordinances from before him even as the king in Deut. 17.20 was not to turn aside (*sûr*) from the commandments, and he has been blameless before Yahweh (cf. Deut. 18.13). In the latter two statements there is reciprocity as David and Yahweh (in terms of his law) stand before each other. A 'negative' statement balances each of these three positive ones: David has not wickedly departed from Yahweh, has not put away Yahweh's statutes, and has kept himself from guilt. The whole is surrounded by vv. 20 and 24 forming an inclusio through several repetitions, and explaining Yahweh's reward for such behaviour. The whole places David among the righteous described in Psalm 1, among those who may dwell on Yahweh's holy hill (Psalm 15), and among those who take refuge in Yahweh (Psalms 16 and 17).

In vv. 25-28 David is more concerned to speak of Yahweh's response to those who take refuge in him (v. 30; cf. v. 2). Yahweh's reciprocal action toward both the loyal, blameless and pure, and the 'crooked' is again the theme. In each of the first three cases the verb which describes Yahweh's action matches the human behaviour. In the last, however, the verbs change. With those who are 'false, or twisted', Yahweh 'wrestles' and 'acts astutely'. It is summed up in v. 27 as Yahweh delivers 'the poor' and brings down the haughty, repeating the theme of Psalms 9–10 and 14 (esp. v. 6). However, in describing Yahweh, David has also outlined the charge for Yahweh's king, as we will see later in Psalm 72 (esp. v. 4) and elsewhere. The echo of David's voice in the psalm is strengthened in v. 28 with his statement that it is Yahweh who 'light(s) my lamp'. *nēr*, 'lamp', is rare in psalms, but is particularly associated with David and his dynasty in 2 Sam. 21.17, 1 Kgs 11.36, and Ps. 132.17. Moreover, not only is Yahweh a shield for those who take refuge in him, but he strengthens his king, which seems to be the sense of v. 29, although the Hebrew text is difficult.

The way is now prepared for David to shift his attention in vv. 31-36 to his military victory. He begins with a rhetorical question 'Who is God except Yahweh, and who is a rock like our god?' (v. 31). This is followed by general praise of Yahweh in vv. 32-34, introduced by a series of Hebrew participles. This is not only a common way of expressing praise but emphasizes that this is the usual way Yahweh acts, especially toward his king. The statements about Yahweh do not just pertain to one occasion. David's praise and the description of Yahweh equipping him for battle continue as he speaks directly to Yahweh in vv. 35-36. David is entirely equipped for his task, in hands and feet as well as in protective equipment such as shield. He is swift and sure of foot. But all the time David stresses that it is Yahweh who has equipped him (v. 35). While the Hebrew of v. 35 has some problems, it is Yahweh's 'humility' or 'gentleness', rather than 'help' as reconstructed by some, which has done this. Such a notion ties in with vv. 25-27 and expressions elsewhere (e.g. Prov. 15.33; 18.12; 22.4; Zeph. 2.3).

David then turns to a first person description of an unspecified victory (vv. 37-42). A shift to describing the king as agent of victory is unusual in the Old Testament, where emphasis is always put on Yahweh's aid. The shift serves to give some emphasis to David himself. On the other hand, a fine balance between divine and Davidic agency in victory is kept. While David now does the pursuing and striking etc., he does so only because Yahweh has assisted. He can pursue and overtake (v. 37) because Yahweh has made his feet like a deer's (v. 33). The enemy falls under David's own steady feet (v. 38, cf. v. 36). He beats the enemy to dust (v. 42) with hands Yahweh has trained for war (v. 34), and Yahweh has girded him with strength (vv. 32 and 39). The theme of Yahweh's support is picked up again in vv. 43-45 as David summarizes his victory and the subjugation of the nations. He returns to addressing Yahweh directly, giving the latter credit for all. Divine aid undergirds all the king does as David knows full well, for he has trod this path before and been supported by Yahweh in the process.

As David nears the end of this psalm the interplay of its two halves comes to the fore. The start of v. 43 resembles the start of v. 17 'You/he delivered me from ...' although the Hebrew verb differs. He makes further connections in the final section of praise, vv. 46-49. The praise itself, which arises from the deliverance, echoes that at the start of the psalm, especially with the repetition of 'rock' and 'my salvation' (v. 46; cf. v. 2). Verse 48 provides an even stronger parallel to v. 17 at the end of the first major section with reference to deliverance from enemies. While the words used are not always the same, the references to support in v. 35 and to having a wide place for his steps in v. 36, recall similar statements in vv. 18-19. All this underlines that Yahweh is the one who in every way equips his king for victory, delivering him not only in times of personal calamity but in times of national threat. Moreover, the description of the personal deliverance, with its central theophany, casts both it and the national deliverance described in the latter half of the psalm, into the context of Yahweh's cosmic victories over chaos. Both are grounded in Yahweh's divine kingship and creative activity. As much as David is presented as an individual in the first half of the psalm, his deliverance represents that of all who take refuge in Yahweh.

The psalm ends with reference to David and his descendants in v. 50. Following v. 49, the verse gives further reason for praise, namely that Yahweh 'makes the victories of his king great, and acts faithfully toward his anointed, to David and his descendants forever'. It also provides a summation of all that has gone before. However, through the parallelism of 'king', 'anointed', 'David' and 'his descendants' and the final phrase 'forever', the context for the victory described is extended well beyond David. This victory, although given historical reference in the superscription, is available to all who follow in David's line.

The facts that v. 50 is not linked grammatically to the preceding, contains vocabulary not found elsewhere in the psalm, and that vv. 1-3 and 46-49 contain similar phrases and statements, suggest that v. 50 is a later addition to the psalm. Be that as it may, the inclusion of v. 50 creates with the superscription a 'new' *inclusio* for the psalm. It suggests that the psalm not only be read in its Davidic context but beyond that. This portrayal of David, both as ordinary person and king, functions as a paradigm for the faithful as well as a royal paradigm. David's life, faith and royal activity stand as a model for all kings to follow. David is an example of the king who, holding to the ways of Yahweh, cries out to Yahweh and is delivered.

Psalm 19

At the start of Psalm 19 David turns once again to praise (cf. Psalm 8), but praise of a particular slant. Not only does he praise the glory of God but in the latter half of the psalm (vv. 7-13) he praises the *torah* of Yahweh. This raises the question, as was also the case with Psalm 18, whether we are dealing here with two psalms. In addition to the shift in focus, there is a corresponding shift in the name of God from ʿ*ēl* to Yahweh, and a change in poetic style. On the other hand, a regularity in poetic structure throughout the psalm, certain word and thematic connections between the halves, and the idea of wholeness or completeness in each half, suggest a unity to the psalm with the shifts noted above deliberately and intricately bound to its main theme.

While shifts in style divide the psalm in two major sections, further subdivisions are evident. In vv. 1-4a David speaks of the glory of God proclaimed in the heavens, using two vivid metaphors (vv. 4b-6). Verses 7-9 shift the focus to a description of the *torah*, with vv. 10-13 focusing on the relation of humans to *torah*. Finally, a number of themes from the psalm are brought together in the petition in v. 14. The superscription to the psalm, identifying David as the psalmist, returns to the brief form familiar from Psalms 11; 13; 14; 15 etc.

There are connections with earlier psalms. David begins his praise in Psalm 19 through contemplation of the heavens (cf. Psalm 8), the place from which help came to David in the theophany in Psalm 18. However, Psalm 19 introduces new elements. Unlike Psalm 8, the praise of God's glory and handiwork is neither sung nor chanted, for, it seems, that while speech and knowledge are poured out and declared continuously 'their voice is not heard' (Ps. 19.3). How, then, are this speech and knowledge known, and what sort of knowledge are we considering? Is it knowledge about God, or God's own knowledge, which according to Prov. 3.20 was active in creation? These questions are addressed throughout the psalm.

In the opening section, vv. 1-4a, David states that this knowledge is proclaimed and reported in the grandeur of the heavens. The mention of $rāqî^{aʿ}$ ('firmament') in v. 1 recalls the same term in Genesis 1 and suggests that creation itself is the handiwork mentioned. Elsewhere, God's 'handiwork' can encompass such things as deeds of salvation (cf. e.g. Pss. 28.5; 92.5) or even precepts (cf. Ps. 111.7-8), a point which could support the unity of Psalm 19.

Creation in both its spatial (heavens and firmament) and temporal aspects (day and night) declares the glory of God. The purpose of this proclamation is unclear in this first section of the psalm. The facts that the heavens do the declaring, and that, on one possible translation of v. 3b, 'their voice is not heard', suggest that this praise is primarily an inner cosmic matter and not necessarily intended for human hearing. That is, the cosmos has its own praise to give God, independent of human praise. Such praise, not open to human perception, is known elsewhere in the ancient Near East. In one text from Ugarit, a Syrian coastal city destroyed about 1200 BCE, we read of the god Baal sending a message to his sister Anat which includes the following:

> For I have a message I must tell you,
> a word that I must repeat to you;
> a word of trees and a whisper of stones,
> a meeting of heaven with earth,
> the depths with the stars.
> I understand lightening, which the heavens do not know,
> a word which humans do not know,
> and which the multitude of the earth does not understand.
>
> (KTU 1.3 iii 17–24)

Thus, the 'voice' and words that go out throughout the earth (Ps. 19.4a) are not for human edification. They are part of creation itself and, one might venture, sustain creation. In this sense a parallel will be drawn with the role of *torah* in the second half of the psalm.

But it is also possible to translate the last clause of v. 3 as 'without their voice being heard.' In this case, what is central is the need to 'hear' this 'voice' and these words that go out through the earth. David observes the beauty of the sky, and perceives in it the glory of God. Such reflections were part of the wisdom tradition as, for example, in Prov. 6.6-9 or chapters 25–28 where many sayings build upon observations in the natural world. There is a delightful poetic interplay between seeing and hearing in this opening section of Psalm 19.

A difficulty is the translation of the word *qawwām* (v. 4a), rendered by the NRSV as 'voice'. The Hebrew word elsewhere means 'a string, thread, line' (e.g. 1 Kgs 17.23) sometimes in the sense of a measuring line. The NRSV is following an emendation of *qawwām* to *qôlām*, 'their voice', a translation initially seen in the LXX. However we read or emend the text, it is clear from the parallel clause that the words of this 'silent' speech reach the uttermost parts of the earth.

In vv. 4b-6 David underscores the point made in vv. 1-4a. His extended treatment of the sun in these verses is unusual in the Old Testament. He uses two metaphors in v. 5 to make his point: that of the sun as a bridegroom coming forth from his wedding canopy and then as a strong warrior running his course. Each proceeds with joy until completion of his destined journey.

Ancient Near Eastern mythology concerning the sun possibly lies behind this section, although David renders the material thoroughly within his own theological world. The sun was considered a god throughout the ancient Near East, and in many cases one of great stature. In Mesopotamia, his consort is often called 'the bride' and he himself is frequently given the epithet of 'hero' or 'warrior'. In Ps. 19.4b-6, however, the sun functions as a representative of God's handiwork. Moreover, God makes a tent for it, possibly envisaging its nightly abode. It does not have a palace or temple of its own, but a tent, thus signifying it as part *of* creation and subordinate to the God of whom David speaks. While he strips the sun of any sense of deity, he draws on the ancient qualities of the sun god to extend the theme of praise. The sun's rays shine forth each new day, undimmed and unhindered, bringing light and life to all creation and defeating the forces of darkness. Its rays are not contained; it lights up every corner of the world as it relentlessly pursues its path from one end of the cosmos to the other. Its 'course' is complete and 'nothing is hid from its heat' (v. 6). The metaphors make the point, as both the bridegroom and the warrior are intent on reaching their goal. Such is also the case with the silent word of praise that spreads through all creation.

The theme of pervasiveness ties this section to vv. 1-4a, and the note of joy in the metaphors undergirds the positive force of praise in the cosmos. But we also note that the sun god is connected to law and justice in the ancient Near East. This lends further strength to seeing unity in Psalm 19, for the notions of both life-endowment and judgment are involved with *torah*, the subject of the next section. Verse 6, thereby ties the psalm together, even as it provides through the word 'heavens' an *inclusio* for the first section (vv. 1-6)

In vv. 7-10 David abruptly changes the subject of the psalm to *torah*. Other shifts also occur. While humankind is somewhat distanced from the revelation of God in the first half of the psalm, where there are no words etc., now all is open. *torah* is described chiefly in terms of its relation to and benefits for humans. The first half of Psalm 19 stands in contrast to the human focused message of the earlier psalm of praise, Psalm 8, but now the psalm swings back to that earlier focus. We move also from speaking about *ʾēl*, 'God', to talking about Yahweh. Moreover, the image of God shifts from the passive figure in vv. 1-6, whose revelation needs to be discerned, to an active one teaching and transforming humankind through *torah*.

These verses have been carefully constructed. Six words are used in vv. 7-9 for *torah*, translated 'law' (*torah* itself), 'decrees', 'precepts', 'commandment', 'fear', and 'ordinances'. The listing and order of these words is unique in Psalm 19. In the Hebrew there is a repeated pattern with these nouns: two singular nouns are followed by a plural one. In each half verse which is governed by one of these synonyms, an adjective describes *torah*: 'perfect', 'sure', 'right', 'clear', 'pure', and 'true'. Finally, in vv. 7-8 the effect on humankind is described: reviving life, making the simple wise, rejoicing the heart, and enlightening the eyes. Mention of the 'fear' of Yahweh may sound odd here. The phrase usually refers to an attitude of the believer toward God, something akin to worship. Here, however, it is possibly used to refer to a quality of *torah* itself, namely the faith codified therein (cf. 2 Kgs 17.25-28; Ps. 34.12; Isa. 29.13).

The influence of *torah* on the life of humankind is broad. It affects not only individual and corporate behaviour, but has intellectual, aesthetic and personal benefits. Like the sun earlier in the psalm, it does not leave an area of life untouched. The joy it brings echoes that of the bridegroom and the victorious warrior. This reference to *torah* is not just about a lifeless body of regulations, but essentially about the will of Yahweh.

The pattern established in vv. 7-8 shifts in v. 9 with further statements about the intrinsic qualities of *torah* itself. *torah* endures forever and is altogether righteous. In each statement in vv. 7-9, the inclusion of the words 'of Yahweh' clearly qualifies the synonym for *torah*. There is no doubt who initiates this knowledge among humans and transforms life, just as there is no doubt whose glory and handiwork are proclaimed silently throughout the cosmos. The section concludes in v. 10 with a statement on the desirability of Yahweh's *torah*. It is more desirable than even the finest gold, or honey. Both gold and honey are found in nature, that is, not made by human hands, underlining Yahweh as the source, and are a yellow/golden colour. In both aspects there is an allusion back to the reference to the sun earlier in the psalm.

This section of the psalm not only points back to the first half of Psalm 19, but has several links through various words and verbal roots back to Psalm 18. The connection is particularly strong with the more reflective passage of that psalm in which David speaks of his own righteousness and Yahweh's response (Ps. 18.20-30). These verbal connections include: 'righteous' (Pss. 18.20, 24; 19.9), 'return' (18.20, 24; 19.7), 'keep' (18.21, 23; 19.11), 'judgment' (18.22; 19.9), 'blameless' (18.23, 25[2x]; 19.7), 'pure, complete' (18.20, 24, 26; 19.8), and 'eyes' (18.24; 19.8). Both psalms ground human behaviour in Yahweh's *torah*. The section also has connections with other wisdom texts and was possibly influential in the later identification of *torah* with wisdom (see Prov. 4.10-23; Sirach 24; and Bar. 3.9-4.4).

The focus shifts again in vv. 11-13. This time, in direct address to Yahweh, David speaks of the human response to *torah*. Reference to the psalmist as 'your servant' picks up the reference to David as servant in the superscription to Psalm 18. Consistent with Psalm 1, David is guided by Yahweh's *torah*. He is 'warned' by it (so NRSV in Ps. 19.11) and protected from the influence and power of the 'insolent'. While the word is not used in Psalm 1, it is certainly reminiscent of the groups from whom the psalmist keeps himself in that psalm as well as of the enemies mentioned in other psalms. This 'warning' role was also the role of the prophets (cf. Ezek. 3.15-21; 33.1-9). However, while the Hebrew *nizhār* means 'he is warned', the same root *zhr* can mean 'to shine, lighten' in late Biblical Hebrew (cf. Dan. 12.3). It might mean that David is 'enlightened' by *torah*, thereby setting up another deliberate play on the earlier image of the sun.

David finds there is 'much reward' or a 'great end' in keeping *torah* (v. 11; cf. Ps. 119.33, 112). *torah* is the means by which Yahweh protects his servant, who by observance can be like *torah* itself, complete (NRSV: 'blameless') and innocent (v. 13). In the hearing of *torah* self-understanding is gained (cf. 2 Kgs 22.11-13; Neh. 8.9-12). Thus the theme of judgment re-enters the psalm, recalling yet another aspect of the reference to the sun in vv. 4b-6. The pervasiveness of the word of Yahweh is also implied. Just as the knowledge of God pervades the world and nothing is hid from its searching rays (v. 6), so David, the observant king, would let *torah* pervade his life in being 'warned/enlightened', blessed, reproached, and protected. *torah*, like the sun and creation itself, carries forward the revelation of God in a totally pervasive way.

In the very last verse, v. 14, David returns to the theme of words. But, while words have been the focus of the psalm from the beginning, there has also been a narrowing in the form of the words considered, from the silent 'words' of the heavens to those of *torah*, now to the psalmist's own words. David prays that his words might be acceptable to Yahweh, that is, consistent with the word that pervades the cosmos and revives life through *torah*. This reminds one of the question put in the middle of Psalm 8: 'what are human beings that you are mindful of them?' Behind that question and here in Psalm 19 there is the implied possibility that the insignificance of humans, or the unacceptability of their words, could lead to a godless, life-less existence. However, it was suggested in Psalm 8 that the Lord, whose name is majestic throughout the earth, does have concern for weak humans, and in Psalm 19 we learn, in a similar vein, that frail human speech and thought can be consistent with the divine word filling creation and revealed in *torah*. God himself grants the possibility of life. Moreover, in Ps. 19.14 David urges that the ardent prayer of the faithful servant should be to seek that greater consistency and harmony.

The language of 'acceptability' recalls that of the temple sacrifice (cf. Isa. 60.7; Mal. 2.13). It also recalls the 'language of sacrifice' focused around *torah* earlier in the psalm (Ps. 19.8, 'pure'). But the language of 'acceptability' is also applied, especially in wisdom contexts, to individual behaviour including speech (see Prov. 10.32; 12.2; 14.9). This implies two things. Speech and meditation on *torah* (using the same Hebrew root *hāgāh* as in Ps. 1.2) become ways of acceptance with Yahweh and of conforming to the will of Yahweh. Secondly, the psalmist has been influenced strongly by the protocols and language of the royal court. This strongly reinforces the notion of David as the psalmist. The detailed connections with the royal Psalm 18, already noted, strengthen this notion. Reference to Yahweh as 'rock' (Ps. 19.14), while frequent in the psalms, only begins with Ps. 18.2. The title 'redeemer' is not frequent in psalms, appearing only in combination with 'rock' here and in Ps. 78.35, another royal psalm. At the beginning of Psalm 18 the epithet 'rock' is connected to 'deliverer' (v. 2), synonymous with 'redeemer' (cf. Ps. 144.2). The connections of Psalm 19 to Psalms 1 and 2 around *torah* meditation and with the royal Psalm 18 in particular, underline David as a model pray-er who observes *torah*. His prayer not only instructs other *torah* faithful servants, but suggests the acceptability of the words of all who pray this psalm after him.

Psalms 20–21

We return to specifically royal psalms with Psalms 20 and 21. In Psalm 18 David spoke of his own trust in Yahweh, his deliverer especially in time of threat (from Saul), and the one worthy of praise. He spoke bluntly about his inability to save himself and ended the psalm with thanksgiving for Yahweh's having answered his prayer. **Psalm 20** begins again with a plea for Yahweh to aid the king in time of threat. Although no specific enemy is mentioned, David's troubles with Saul in Psalm 18 come to mind. The psalmist, now separate to David, speaks to him focusing on the temple, the place from which Yahweh's help comes and where the king expresses his 'heart's desire' through sacrifice (v. 4). The cultic language and idea of 'acceptability' found at the end of Psalms 19 is, therefore, echoed in this prayer. At the heart of Psalm 20 is the assurance of divine assistance for those who trust not in human strength but in the name of Yahweh (vv. 6-8; cf. Ps. 3.8; Deut. 20.1-4). But in the use of the pronoun 'our' (v. 7) the psalmist has broadened the prayer beyond the affairs of David to those of all his people. The plea in v. 1 for Yahweh to answer the king is paralleled by the prayer for Yahweh to 'answer us' (v. 9). As in Psalm 8, royal powers and privileges have been democratized.

Psalm 21 takes up the joy of David at his deliverance. Proximity to Psalm 20 suggests that this joy is the result of the earlier prayer. Yahweh again responds to the desire of David's heart (v. 2), a desire expressed in total trust (v. 7). The end of the psalm speaks of how the king will overcome his enemies, although again it is clear that this is really Yahweh's work (v. 5). As in the plea at the end of Psalm 20, the prayer for the king anticipates future threats (Ps. 21.8-12). Neither trusting prayer nor divine deliverance are one-off events but become part of an ongoing relationship. The end of Psalm 21 thus prepares us to encounter the pathos of Psalm 22. It also reminds us in v. 13 of the power and presence of Yahweh which is worthy of praise, qualities celebrated and described in Psalm 19 as pervading the cosmos.

Psalm 22

After a prayer for the victory of the king (Psalm 20) followed by rejoicing and thanksgiving for an answer to prayer (Psalm 21), the sudden cry of desolation in Psalm 22 comes as a shock. In a way it ought not because the structure of Psalm 22, with lament followed by a hymn of praise, repeats the pattern of the preceding two psalms. In this psalm, however, we hear of the troubles of the king not from his supporters but from his own lips.

The superscription attributes the psalm to David but offers little by way of context. Later in the psalm, however, we will read phrases which will turn us back to the royal Psalm 18. The connection with David will be strengthened there. The reference to 'the deer of the dawn' in the superscription is uncertain and could indicate either a musical setting or a sacrificial context. In Christian tradition the psalm has been associated with the suffering of Jesus. It became an interpretative tool for understanding the passion of Jesus (cf. Matt. 27.32-46; Mark 15.21-34) and has been traditionally associated with the Good Friday liturgy. In Jewish tradition, on the other hand, some have understood the superscription as David looking ahead to the time of the Persian Empire and the suffering of the Jewish people in dispersion. In particular, it has been associated with the story of Esther and the threat against her people under Haman and King Ahasuerus. The 'deer of the dawn' is seen as a reference to Queen Esther and the suffering of the psalmist interpreted corporately in relation to the whole Jewish community.

The psalm is divided into two major sections, the lament in vv. 1-21a and the hymn of praise in vv. 21b-31. Each of these major sections is developed by means of a pattern of two. The lament is divided into two halves, vv. 1-11 and vv. 12-21a, with David pleading for God not to be far away at the end of each (vv. 11 and 19-21a). Verses 1-11 contain two complaints (vv. 1-2 and 6-8) after each of which David declares past trust in God. The second half of the lament has two descriptions of those who surround David (portrayed as ravenous beasts, vv. 12-13 and 16) each followed by a statement that he is close to death (vv. 14-15 and 17-18). The twofold prospect of death counters the twofold reference to birth and beginnings. All seems at an end.

The hymn of praise at the end of the psalm also has two distinct sections. In the first, vv. 21b-26, David sings God's praise in the congregation. In the second, vv. 27-31, his praise of God is widened to take in all the nations and the ends of the earth as well as the dying and those yet to be born.

The psalm begins with the most desperate of cries wherein David asks why God has abandoned him and is so far from him (v. 1). David still claims a strong relationship with God whom he addresses as '*my* God, *my* God'. Such words suggest in the ancient Near East an intimate and exclusive attachment, but the distance between them is now so great that it seems God can neither help nor hear David's words. God's honour is at stake when there is no answer to David's cry uttered day and night (v. 2). Time alone will not resolve David's problem; it is one of both space and time.

Twice in the lament section David recalls how things were different in the past. In vv. 3-5 he recalls the faith of the ancestors and later he will recall his own earlier experience (vv. 9-10). The Hebrew of v. 3 is not clear. It could be understood as the NRSV translates it: 'You are holy, enthroned on the praises of Israel.' Alternatively we can read it as some ancient Greek translations did, reading 'holy' as 'holy ones' or 'holiness' and understanding 'praises of Israel' as a divine epithet. We would translate the phrase then as 'enthroned among the holy ones/in holiness, the praise of Israel'. While the latter is a stronger statement about God's sovereignty, the former, in stressing God enthroned on Israel's praises, gets to the heart of the lament. God's sovereignty is at stake in David's dilemma. If God does not answer, will David continue to praise and will God be any longer enthroned? Three times in vv. 4-5 David refers to the trust placed in God by the ancestors and three times he recalls that God delivered them. This might function as a motivation for God's response. But David's predicament and statement of the trust of the ancestors echoes his own statements as king in Psalms 20–21 in the words 'help' (Pss. 20.6; 21.1, 5; 22.1), 'answer' (20.1, 6; 22.2) and 'trust' (21.7; 22.4-5). The king himself feels abandoned by God.

In vv. 6-8 David returns to his lament describing himself in the most abject terms. This description stands in sharp contrast to the view of humankind given in Psalm 8. His feeling of abandonment by God is matched by a sense of scorn and isolation within the community, the same community which has provided him with examples of trust and deliverance in the past. The language David uses is traditional for laments (cf. Ps 44.13-16 in regard to national enemies, and 109.25; also Isa. 37.22-23). Here, however, no words of salvation follow, only the questioning of the mockers (v. 8), which bears close resemblance to earlier words from David's foes (Ps. 3.2). The words also recall Ps. 18.19. The expressions in 18.19 and 22.8 are virtually identical despite their different contexts (also cf. 1 Sam. 22.20). They occur no where else in the Hebrew Scriptures, although similar expressions refer to the divine care of the ancestors (Ps. 44.3), the divine bestowal of prosperity (Deut. 30.9), and the election of Solomon (1 Kgs 10.9 = 2 Chron. 9.8). A deliberate connection is made to

Psalm 18 giving the words of the mockers a heightened level of meaning. Their taunt is a direct challenge to David's earlier words. The matter of trust and deliverance is the subject of this present lament. The mockers' use of his words makes the present situation all the more difficult. On the other hand, it is also a strong reminder that past trust has been vindicated in deliverance and the present struggle is worth pursuing.

David reflects again on the past in vv. 9-10, although this time it is his own past. In a chiastic structure (birth-nurture-nurture-birth) God is described in terms of both a midwife at his birth and as nurse afterward. Since birth God has been 'my God' to David. This reminds us of the adoption of the king as 'son' in Psalm 2. David's own past trust in God, and quite possibly by allusion his adoption, are also motivation for God to respond to him. In the statement in v. 10 and in the plea in v. 11 the language of vv. 1-2 ('my God', 'far') is repeated tying the first section of the psalm together.

In the second half of the lament (vv. 12-21a) the complaint is more sustained as David describes his predicament in vivid terms. In a series of vivid animal and other metaphors and similes David alternates between the description of his enemies ('bulls', 'ravening and roaring lion', 'dogs'; vv. 12-13 and 16) and his own condition ('poured out like water', 'heart is like wax', a 'potsherd'; vv. 14-15 and 17-18). The use of such language is already familiar in the Psalter, especially that of a lion in v. 13 (cf. Pss. 7.2; 10.9 and 17.12; also 35.17 and 91.13 to come).

This animal language has a number of effects. First, it clearly conveys that David is absolutely helpless in his predicament. His enemies are like powerful beasts and he does not have the strength to resist them. Secondly, in using animal imagery David is not simply abusing his enemies. In the ancient Near East such imagery described powerful individuals (cf. Deut. 32.14; Amos 4.1; and Gen 49.24 where God is called the 'bull of Jacob' [NRSV: 'Mighty One of Jacob']). Its use in the psalm underlines the power of David's enemies. Thirdly, animal imagery was used in Mesopotamia sometimes to describe the demonic powers thought responsible for sickness and suffering. The effect of all this is to emphasize David's inability to resist the powers, both human and cosmic, that are lined up against him. His need for assistance from God is clear. The language of death in vv. 15, 17-18 is hyperbole, describing David's predicament in extreme terms, a situation also exhibited in some Mesopotamian literature.

The last line of v. 16 has long been recognized as difficult. In the Hebrew it reads 'like a lion my hands and my feet'. This makes little sense although the lion image fits the language of the psalm. One solution, which was adopted as early as the LXX, has been to alter the Hebrew of 'like a lion' to form a verb meaning 'to bore, pierce or dig' and to read 'they pierced'. Many early Christian commentators interpreted this in relation to Christ's crucifixion. Other proposals suggest altering the Hebrew to a verb 'to be shrunken, shriveled' or 'to be consumed' making the hands and feet the subject (so the NRSV).

The lament concludes with a longer plea for deliverance, vv. 19-21a. The repetition of the word 'far' ties this section back to the end of the first part of the lament (v. 11) as well as to its beginning (v. 1). The mention of the dog and lion reiterates the main images of this latter half of the lament. There is constant movement back and forth in David's thought and expression.

The psalm shifts from lament to praise and thanksgiving in v. 21. However, there are two problems in reading this verse. The last word in the verse in Hebrew reads 'you have answered me'. The NRSV has interpreted this as 'you have rescued me' reading v. 21b ('From the horns of the wild oxen you have rescued me.') as the beginning of the praise section, thereby separating the two halves and the parallel elements of v. 21. It also suggests, or maybe presumes, that the praise at the end of lament psalms comes after some external, unrecorded pronouncement by a priest or other official that God has heard David's lament. If, however, we keep the parallel elements of v. 21 together it makes a fitting conclusion to the lament section. But then there is the problem of how to understand 'you have answered me'. This word could be seen as the beginning of the thanksgiving, thus separating lament and thanks by time and circumstance. Alternatively, it could be seen as a transitional statement holding lament and praise together. Divine revelation and David's confidence come not after some comforting words by a third party, but from within the very turmoil of his situation. The suffering is no longer evidence of God being 'far away'. Rather, God is hidden, even in revelation, and God's answer to suffering is perceived in and through the crisis, metaphorically 'from the horns of the wild oxen'. The future sense of the praise which follows, which for the most part remains a vow, gives the praise an eschatological quality, something already experienced but which awaits fulfillment. Moreover, the answer which David acknowledges is not something that follows his complaint and precedes his praise. Praise itself is a gift from God and the means of David's deliverance. He has found in his own praise the answer for which he longed back in v. 2.

The praise that is vowed in vv. 22-31 falls into two sections: praise in the congregation (vv. 22-26) and praise that stretches to the ends of the earth (vv. 27-31). In language as extravagant as that of the lament, David praises God to his present generation. This praise will even spread to those beyond the 'offspring of Israel' (v. 27) and future generations. David's trust in the midst of lament was in part based on the trust of past generations and his own trust since birth. The trust of those who have now gone down to the dust will be vindicated by the trust of those yet to come (vv. 29-31; cf. Psalms 69; 102).

The nations are viewed more favourably in this psalm than elsewhere. In general, the nations are seen as enemies who have been or are to be defeated. Where they worship Israel's God they are usually called to do so (e.g. Pss. 67.4; 72.11, 17; 86.9). In this case, however, they remember and turn of their own accord. The implication here, since the nations have no memory of Israel's God to recall, is that they will change their allegiance. The language is reminiscent of the royal psalms.

The translation of v. 29 has given problems. The Hebrew reads 'all the fat ones of the earth have eaten and bowed down'. Minor emendations give the reading in the NRSV: 'To him, indeed, shall all who sleep in the earth bow down.' This gives better parallelism within the verse speaking of those about to die. On the other hand we could read the Hebrew as it is and see the verse speaking of 'all the fat ones of the earth', meaning those alive. Thus the verse speaks of both those alive and those about to die who worship Yahweh. But even the descendants of those who die will worship thus stressing the sovereignty of Yahweh over all generations (v. 31).

In the course of this psalm, David's distress becomes a source of praise and joy for the whole community. His sense of distance from God and associated suffering becomes the catalyst for the ends of the earth knowing the divine presence. While there is no evident liturgical action associated with the psalm, although the references to eating in v. 26 might have been drawn from a ritual thanksgiving meal, the community context becomes evident in vv. 3-5, and especially in the second half of the psalm (vv. 23-24 and 27-31). In this regard, the suffering of David is unlike that experienced by Job or Jeremiah in lonely isolation.

The vagueness of the description of David's sufferings allows the psalm to be associated with other cases of affliction. Thus, over and above the connection to David, the psalm has been associated with many other biblical figures (Moses and the Israelites; Hezekiah and Isaiah in the *Midrash*) and in Christianity and Judaism in general with Jesus and Esther respectively. In each case the community takes up the prayer of David as the latter half of the psalm suggests.

Psalm 23

Psalm 23 is one of David's most well-known psalms. Its brevity belies its power and beauty. Two metaphors dominate the psalm and through them and the associated images, Psalm 23 has promoted trust in God in countless generations since David's time.

The first metaphor is that of the shepherd (vv. 1-4). The second is that of the banquet table (v. 5). However, the poem is more complicated than that for v. 3 already ends with a reason for the confidence of vv. 1-3 and in v. 4, while the shepherd metaphor continues, there is a change to direct address to the Lord which continues into the banquet metaphor in v. 5. In v. 6 we return to speaking about the Lord in the third person.

The richness of the psalm is developed through the many layers of meaning in the two basic metaphors. Both can be associated with kings and gods in Israel and the ancient Near East. The epithet of shepherd for God is found in Gen. 49.24; Isa. 40.11; Ezek. 34.11-16 (cf. Pss. 80.1; 95.7; and 100.3). It is found elsewhere in the ancient Near East, for example in relation to the Mesopotamian sun-god Shamash, or Pharaoh in Egypt. The idea of banqueting in the presence of enemies can also allude to a royal victory celebration after the defeat of a foe. So the metaphors of the psalm have royal overtones and are consistent with David as psalmist. However, there is a twist in that the human king now speaks from the point of view of the 'sheep' or the 'guest' at the banquet, giving the shepherd or host roles to his heavenly Lord and trusting completely in the latter's protection and provision. The multiplicity of images could lead to a questioning of the psalm's unity. On the other hand, the very flow of images could be seen to hold the psalm together.

The superscription does not connect the psalm with a particular event in David's life, although the content suggests a period when David was driven into the wilderness and in some danger.

The narrative of 2 Samuel 15–21 might serve as a backdrop with its episodes of provision while David is in flight from Absalom (2 Sam. 16.1-4; 17.27-29) and David's victory over Absalom and other opponents in the end. The section is then followed by 2 Samuel 22 which reproduces Psalm 18 as noted earlier. The connection is not detailed but suggestive. It provides another perspective on Psalm 23 itself. While Yahweh's provision for David is clear the call for David to trust becomes more complex and difficult. The 'enemies' in whose presence he banquets are no longer distant opponents but family and former allies, and the 'darkest valley' can be experienced in contexts of deep intimacy. The cost of trust in Yahweh can be very great, including deep personal pain. In this context Psalm 23 becomes a complement to Psalm 3.

Psalm 23 can also be associated with the traditions of exodus, wilderness wanderings and entry into Canaan. The imagery of Yahweh as shepherd, of wandering and provision, together with some common vocabulary (cf. Ps. 23.2-3 ['pastures', 'leads'] with Exod. 15.13 ['abode', 'guides']) and phraseology (cf. Ps. 23.5 with 78.19) suggest this, possibly even in conjunction with Israel's later experience of exile. In both cases the individual psalmist stands for the people. Finally, Midrash *Tehillim* also connects Psalm 23 with the patriarch Jacob who, on his death bed, blessed Joseph remarking that 'God has been my shepherd all my life to this day' (Gen. 48.15).

David begins the psalm with the image of the provision made for the sheep by the shepherd (vv. 1-3). It is clear that the psalm is about Yahweh's provision from the start. The use of the divine name only in vv. 1 and 6 provides an *inclusio* for the psalm literally enveloping David's statements within references to Yahweh.

The psalm begins with the great affirmation 'Yahweh is my shepherd, I shall not want', or 'I lack nothing' (cf. Ps. 27.1). It is a bold statement of faith and trust attributing to Yahweh royal language and imagery used elsewhere of kings and gods in Israel and the ancient Near East as noted above. 'Shepherd' could possibly allude to a divine throne name like other names given to Yahweh (e.g. Gen. 16.13; 33.20; Exod. 15.3; Judg. 5.5; Ps. 24.10 etc.). While this initial affirmation seems straightforward, it is open to a number of interpretations. While 'Yahweh is my shepherd' is usually read as a principal clause in an affirmative manner, it could also be read circumstantially shifting emphasis to the nature and responsibilities (vv. 2-3) of the one designated shepherd. Such a reading could touch on some of the anxieties of the sheep. The phrase 'I shall not want' might also imply not being removed from the shepherd's presence. Verse 3a (NRSV: 'he restores my soul') would, therefore, become a classic statement of the lost sheep found, and the phrase 'paths of righteousness' (lit. Heb.; so the RSV etc.) possibly implying a pious or moral life, would need to be read as 'right paths' or 'correct way' (so NRSV etc.; cf. Ps. 27.11).

The initial statement in v. 3a can even be interpreted more strongly than the common 'he restores my soul', giving 'he returns/revives my life', possibly indicating a near to death experience for David (cf. v. 4). Not only is David revived, he is guided (vv. 2b, 3b) and all for the sake of Yahweh's name (cf. Ps. 31.3). Closeness to Yahweh means provision and life for David. The opposite means isolation and helplessness in the face of danger and even death. Thus, Psalm 23 provides an important counter to the initial statements of Psalm 22 and essentially expresses the inner side of the outer public statements at the end of that psalm.

The matter of divine presence with David stands at the centre of v. 4. He enters what reads literally in the Hebrew 'in the valley of the shadow of death' ($b^e g\bar{e}$' $salm\bar{a}wet$), although this unusual phrase is better rendered metaphorically as 'the darkest valley' or more vividly 'the valley of deep gloom/shadow' (cf. Jer. 2.6). Even in such a place he can proclaim, 'I fear no evil', echoing (in the Hebrew) the earlier 'I shall not want'. The reason for such confidence is the presence of Yahweh with him.

David maintains the shepherd image speaking of the guidance of Yahweh's 'rod' and 'staff' which 'comfort' him. The shift in this verse to direct address ('you') moves the relationship to a more intimate level. Maybe a stronger expression could be used here than the translation 'comfort', for while the range of verbs with which the Hebrew word is elsewhere associated suggests elements of compassion, redemption and protection, more than an inner peace in the face of trouble is indicated. Military victory or judicial vindication could be implied suggesting a closer association with the context of David in 2 Samuel 15–21. This would also fit a metaphorical understanding of 'rod' and 'staff' as something like 'justice' and 'mercy'.

David employs the second main image, the host and banquet, in v. 5. It is not totally disconnected to the preceding image as the theme of protection persists (cf. also Ps. 78.19). Moreover, both speak of food and drink (pasture/water; table/cup). Reference to banqueting in the presence of enemies recalls the darkest valley and the presence of evil in v. 4. There could be a reference to a thanksgiving sacrifice in this verse (cf. Ps. 27.6) or to a meal at which the psalmist is vindicated before his enemies, but reference to anointing with oil connected to wine in v. 5 ('my cup overflows'; cf. 'your intoxicating cup' in LXX) suggests rather the joy of celebration (cf. Ps. 104.15; Amos 6.6; Eccl. 9.7-9). Thus, Psalm 23 moves from protection of David in the face of dire threat to security and joy even in the presence of enemies.

The final verse begins with the Hebrew emphatic particle $'ak$, which often introduces a point in sharp contrast to what precedes it or a truth newly perceived. The enemies of the previous verse are supplanted in v. 6 by Yahweh's 'goodness' and 'mercy' ($hesed$; possibly 'covenant loyalty') which will now 'pursue' ($rādap$; so LXX; cf. NRSV: 'follow') David (cf. Ps. 43.3). $rādap$ has a number of associations which can all be relevant for its use in Psalm 23. It frequently carries the sense of hostile pursuit (e.g. Gen. 14.14; 44.4; Ps. 7.1, 5 etc.). When used in association with goodness, righteousness or peace, it is usually the individual who pursues those qualities (e.g. Pss. 38.20; 34.14; Prov. 21.21; Isa. 51.1 etc.). Finally, it has a close association with the language of covenant curses when a covenant has been broken (see Deut. 28.45). The usual sense of the verb in each of these cases is overturned in Ps. 23:6. It is no longer fear and evil that pursue David (v. 4); nor does he need to pursue goodness; and in Yahweh's presence the covenant curses are far removed. All has been overturned as Yahweh's 'goodness' and 'mercy' now pursue him.

In v. 6 David tells of the unceasing nature of this protection and joy, at least for his 'length of days' or 'his whole life long'. It is not often that one contemplates dwelling in the house of Yahweh, i.e. the temple, for the whole of life (cf. Ps. 27.4) so interpreting the phrase in terms of the land (cf. Hos. 9.3-4) or kinship structures is possible, but the exaggerated sense of other statements in the psalm ought not to be forgotten too quickly.

The reference to Yahweh in the third person in vv. 1 and 6 ties these verses together. If the initial clause in v. 1 is understood circumstantially then a further connection is made with v. 6 where each verse begins with a reason for the consequence then described. The feeling of security evoked by the imagery in the psalm is confirmed by the structure of the psalm.

The metaphors and the language of the psalm affirm the connection to David in the superscription. The reference to the temple in v. 6, which in Jerusalem theology is inseparable from kingship, supports the connection. But there is a twist as noted above. The one who is king and seen as shepherd or host speaks as the 'sheep' and 'guest' of Yahweh. The image of the banquet itself in v. 5 might assist this turn around. On the basis of some parallels in the ancient Near East, the image could be one of the human king in the role of vassal to the divine king who hosts the former in lavish style. While the language may be appropriate to a vassal before his suzerain, it strikes an accord with all who would put their trust in Yahweh. The king seeks the same care from Yahweh as do his people. He faces dark places and enemies that threaten just as they do. But he also expresses trust in his 'shepherd-king' despite great anxiety, and he can celebrate the deliverance of Yahweh. As representative of his people, he knows the gamut of feelings associated with faithfulness in the face of danger, and he invites his people to join in his prayer and make his words their own. But this is not the only shift in interpretation to which the psalm is open. All but one verb is in the imperfect form leaving the interpretation ambiguous: is it a proclamation of what David experiences in the present or what might be? The psalm remains open to both communal and eschatological perspectives.

Psalm 24

Psalm 24 has three distinct sections: vv. 1-2, a hymn of praise to the creator; vv. 3-6 which answers questions about who may ascend the mountain of Yahweh; and vv. 7-10 which seems to be an entrance liturgy for Yahweh. The sharp differences between the three sections in genre, style and content give an impression of disunity to the psalm and suggest it has been stitched together from earlier, separate compositions. However, some stylistic features and theological links between the sections reveal a unity beyond matters of genre.

The superscription to the psalm is the basic attribution to David. The LXX version, however, adds 'for the first day of the week' indicating usage in early Jewish worship, based on the reference to creation. The suggested liturgical structure of the psalm, especially in vv. 7-10, could suggest a number of cultic contexts for the psalm—divine enthronement, a New Year festival, some dedication ceremony or possibly even a cultic enactment of an entry of Yahweh into the netherworld. The connection with David also suggests an association with the entry of the ark of God into Jerusalem, recorded in 2 Sam. 6.16-19. However, there is no direct reference to the ark in Psalm 24 or clear attestation to the carrying of the ark in liturgical procession in the Jerusalem cult.

David begins the psalm proclaiming Yahweh as creator and sovereign of the world and all its peoples (vv. 1-2). The reference to the seas and rivers (v. 2) could be an allusion to an old creation myth featuring Yahweh battling against the sea monster (cf. Job 26.10-13; Pss. 74.12-17; 89.8-11). An expression of this myth is found in Ugaritic literature where Baal's conquest of Yam (titled 'Prince Sea/Judge River') results in his kingship, manifest in creation (KTU 1.2.iv.1–10, 32).

In vv. 3-6 the psalm takes a sharp turn in another direction. David asks the question, who can ascend the mountain of Yahweh? This question is followed by a response (vv. 4-5) and an affirmation (v. 6). A similar but more detailed structure and statement can be found in Psalm 15 (cf. also Isa. 33.14b-16). This is not, however, just as a concern for individual morals and righteous behaviour. In the ancient Near East, order in moral and religious matters was a reflection of creation's order, of a victory over chaos in all forms. Only four things are required of the one who would ascend, two in a positive mode and two in the negative—clean hands, a pure heart, not committing their life to what is false, and not swearing deceitfully. The first two deal with activity and thought/intention while the second set raises the general question of commitment and allegiance. Swearing deceitfully could imply making a false statement but it is likely the combination of that with false proclamations of allegiance (also implied by the verb 'to swear') that particularly irks David (cf. Jer. 5.2). The negative statements in Ps. 24.4b recall Ps. 1.1 and the description of what the blessed individual does not do. The whole of life is covered in this brief statement in Psalm 24. Instead of this person 'lifting up' their lives (NRSV: 'souls') to what is false, they will 'lift up' a blessing and righteousness from Yahweh (v. 5). The qualities they exhibit are also those of Yahweh.

Who might fit this description is left unstated, but it could easily apply to David as psalmist. Yahweh's 'holy mountain' was the place where Yahweh established his king (Ps. 2.6) and from where Yahweh answered David's plea in 3.4. What David described in Psalm 15 and does again more briefly in Psalm 24 applies above all to him. But not just to him, for in Ps. 24.6 the application is widened to all those who seek Yahweh, or who seek the face of 'the God of Jacob' as the emendation to MT (so LXX; cf. Ps. 75.9) attests. This shift from the individual to the community undergirds David's representative role again. At the same time it marks an appropriate conclusion to this section of the psalm.

Although vv. 3-6 seem to be on a different tack to vv. 1-2, an awareness of the mythic background to the psalm helps show how these sections fit together. In the Ugaritic myth of Baal and Yam mentioned above, after victory over Yam, the warrior king Baal processes to his mountain abode to take his throne. However, in Psalm 24 after victory over Sea/Rivers in vv. 1-2, we do not hear of the divine warrior's process. Instead, there is the question of who can ascend the divine mountain. While it has not been made clear in v. 3 that the question necessarily pertains to Yahweh's worshipers, the natural 'mythic' answer to the question would be Yahweh himself. That, however, is not the way vv. 4-6 unfolds. Instead, the question is answered in terms of who is the loyal worshiper who can accompany the divine king in the approach to his temple. This literary replacement of the divine king by the worshiper stresses that the qualities of the divine warrior who is victorious and creator need to be echoed in the worshiper. Adherence to the law as a way of life is this echoing and becomes a means of praise of the creator, thus expanding ways of celebrating divine kingship. The one who celebrates divine kingship is also the one in whose life Yahweh's kingship is manifest.

The tone of the psalm takes another sharp turn in the third section of the psalm (vv. 7-10). Theses verses are suggestive of a liturgy of processional entry into the temple or city. In terms of mythic patterns, the expected entry of the divine warrior and creator into his temple has been delayed in the psalm. Now, however, it comes with all the pageantry it calls for. The verses fall into two parts. After identical commands to the personified gates and doors (identified in the Aramaic Targums of Psalms as the gates 'of the house of the sanctuary' and the gates 'of the garden of Eden') to 'lift their heads' that the 'king of glory' may enter, a question comes back as to who is this 'king of glory' and the response follows. The pattern is present in each part. Moreover, the Hebrew of the questions indicates that a challenge is implied. Who dares call himself the 'king of glory' and demand entry? If a liturgy does lie behind these verses then it maintains the drama of the situation. The language emphasizes that identity must be established. In this context, the title 'king of glory' is appropriate. It is a generic title meaning a king worthy of glory and occurs nowhere else in the Hebrew Bible, although the title 'God of glory' will occur in Ps. 29.3 recalling this passage. The twofold response to the questions reveals first Yahweh as warrior, which spells out the creation aspect, and then as 'Yahweh of Hosts', possibly a throne name of Yahweh (cf. Isa. 6.5; Pss. 84.1, 3; 46.7, 11; 48.4-8; 89.5-14 etc.) with the 'Hosts' being the heavenly beings surrounding Yahweh. This could be another link with the ark of the covenant with its symbolic cherubim (Exod. 25.18-20) and hence with 2 Sam. 6.12-19. The personified gates and doors of the temple/city are thus called to lift up their heads and stand proud and confident as Yahweh of Hosts enters his domain, even as in vv. 3-6 the faithful 'lift up' the blessing that flows from innocent hands and pure heart in echo of the King of Glory.

The call for the gates to lift their heads may also echo a passage from the myth of Baal. Using similar language the text (KTU 1.2.i.20–29) describes the council of the gods cowering and lowering their heads to their knees when they see the messengers of Yam ('Prince Sea/Judge River') coming with a challenge. It is Baal who takes up this challenge calling the gods to raise their heads in victory as a rebuff to the forces of chaos. The address to the gates in Psalm 24 could be a call for recognition of and pride in the victory of Yahweh, the divine warrior and creator.

In Psalm 24 David stresses unambiguously who possesses the earth, Yahweh. He perhaps calls for that to be recognized liturgically. He also calls for that to be recognized and celebrated in the life of all in the company who seek Yahweh and would ascend the mountain of Yahweh. While David spoke in Psalm 23 of trust in the one who protects and sustains him in his darkest moments, in Psalm 24 he gives the theological foundation for that trust, calling the faithful to respond in obedience. Together these psalms speak of a mutual relationship of care and concern between the worshiper and Yahweh.

Psalm 25

In Psalm 25 David returns to words of lament. Individual psalms of trust and liturgies of entrance to Yahweh's house, even with pure hands and a clean heart, are not enough in the short term to dispel times of danger and possible shame.

This is the second acrostic psalm we have met. Generally each verse is introduced by the next letter of the Hebrew alphabet, however, there are some irregularities here. Since some of these irregularities are shared with the next acrostic psalm (Psalm 34) they could be deliberate, although the reason is not clear. The acrostic structure might first suggest a fragmented flow of thought but another structure relating to content is also evident in Psalm 25. It begins and ends with prayer in the form of direct speech to Yahweh (vv. 1-7; 16-22). Each of these prayers is divided into two. Verses 1-3 are concerned with enemies and potential shame while vv. 4-7 seek forgiveness and direction from Yahweh. In vv. 16-22 the prayers are reversed with vv. 16-18 speaking of forgiveness and vv. 19-22 concerned with deliverance. The centre section is a third person meditation also in two parts, first focusing on Yahweh's response to sinners (vv. 8-11) and then on the benefits of Yahweh's response for the sinner (vv. 12-15). The focus on enemies at the start and end of the psalm suggest that the psalmist is the king. Other points support this.

David begins by declaring he 'lifts his soul' (NRSV), or better 'his life', to Yahweh. The parallel line in v. 2a implies a statement of trust, but similar statements in Sumerian and Akkadian as well as in Pss. 86.4 and 143.8 suggest a context of flight seeking protection. At the same time the language of 'lifting' alludes to raising one's hands in prayer toward the temple (Pss. 28.2; 134.2) or at the evening sacrifice (Ps. 141.2). It makes a link with Psalm 24 with its several plays on the word 'lift'. This lament is thereby associated with other statements about trust and confidence in Yahweh.

Two sets of parallel lines develop the thought in vv. 2b-3. David seeks that he not be shamed, defined initially as the enemies exalting over him (v. 2b-c). In v. 3, however, the singular subject (David) is broadened to the plural of all those who wait for Yahweh. David's situation is related to the whole community of faithful and he asks now that shame be the fate of the enemies, now defined more specifically as those who act treacherously or falsely. These verses bring together ideas on shame expressed earlier in Pss. 4.2 and 6.10.

In the second half of the opening prayer David seeks to know and learn the ways and paths of Yahweh. This general thought is developed in the parallel lines. The ways and paths of Yahweh are defined in vv. 4-5a as Yahweh's truth in which David seeks to be led, using the verb related to the noun 'way' (*derek*). Truth in this psalm is not an abstract quality but a relational one. The reason David gives for this petition is that Yahweh is the God of his salvation (cf. Pss. 18.46; 24.5 and 27.1, 9) and the one for whom he has waited all the day. The theme of 'waiting' or hoping is introduced to the Psalter in this psalm (vv. 3, 5, and 21; cf. 27.14; 39.7 and 40.1), and in this, as in other matters, the life of David becomes a model for the community, as he waits constantly for Yahweh. But not only are Yahweh's ways and paths defined as 'truth' or 'faithfulness'. The teaching and learning of them are salvation.

The latter half of the second prayer, vv. 6-7, forms a small framed unit around the theme of memory. The verb 'remember' is mentioned three times (once in NRSV as 'be mindful'). David asks Yahweh to remember not his past, which is defined here by 'sins' and 'transgressions', but Yahweh's own compassion and 'love' (*ḥesed*). These things are eternal and while he does not want to ignore the weight of his own sin (cf. v. 11), David puts it in perspective by setting it alongside the things of Yahweh. Yahweh's own qualities and sovereignty are what is central for him. In reference to Yahweh's 'love' and 'goodness' in vv. 6-7 there is an echo of the divine things which pursue David all his days in Ps. 23.6. It is little wonder that he might be prepared to 'wait' for Yahweh all day long (25.5). Who Yahweh is makes such waiting possible. It is also little wonder that he would desire Yahweh's teaching since salvation and forgiveness are intricately bound with it.

In the first part of his meditation (vv. 8-11) David explores further Yahweh's nature, particularly in relation to Yahweh's people. Just as David has a desire to be taught (vv. 4-5), so Yahweh's own goodness and uprightness lead him to instruct sinners in the way, defined in vv. 9-10a as 'what is right' (cf. Ps. 23.3) and 'love' and 'faithfulness'. A mutual desire for instruction and learning, i.e. salvation, allows the life of the one who waits to reflect the qualities of Yahweh. The repetition of the words 'way' (*derek*), *ḥesed* and 'truth/faithfulness' in vv. 8b-10, picking up the earlier references, underlines the interrelationships here. But we ought not to miss the brief proviso at the end of v. 10. All this is for those who keep Yahweh's covenant and decrees. While Yahweh's *ḥesed* etc. is the basis for Yahweh's dealing with sinners, the responsibility for loyalty and obedience on the part of the faithful is not negated. Allusion to the exodus story strengthens this. The language of vv. 10-11 recalls that of Exod. 34:6-10. In that passage Yahweh addresses Moses after the people went astray waiting for him to come down from Mt Sinai. Several words (e.g. *ḥesed*, 'mercy', 'sin', 'transgression', 'pardon', 'faithfulness/truth') are clustered in both texts. Moreover, each is concerned with a renewal of covenant after some transgression.

The response of David, and all faithful ones, to the nature of Yahweh is stressed in v. 11. Having stressed Yahweh's mercy and 'love' and desiring to instruct the sinner in what is right, David proclaims his own need of forgiveness for his transgression is 'great'. But we cannot miss the way the verse is expressed. The 'greatness' of David's transgression is not the focus. Emphasis is placed on 'For your name's sake, Yahweh'. This further draws a connection with Ps. 23.3 where David was led in 'right paths for (Yahweh's) name's sake'. Psalm 25 is expounding on Psalm 23 at this point.

David opens the second meditation with a question. In some ways it is similar to the question in Ps. 24.3 but the effect and development are different. In Psalm 24 David went on to answer the question of who could ascend the mountain of Yahweh by listing the qualities of such a one, but here he answers the question of who fears Yahweh by detailing the consequences (i.e. blessings) for those who do fear. They will be instructed by Yahweh in the way they should choose, a synonymous phrase for 'what is right' (v. 9). They will 'abide' in 'goodness' (*ṭôb*) and possess the land, which while having a sense of 'prosperity' (NRSV) is more than just material well-being. It is a quality of Yahweh already connected in vv. 6-8 with justice, mercy and 'love'. The language of guidance in vv. 13-14 continues the allusion to the exodus begun in vv. 8-10. Finally, those who fear will be part of the circle of intimate friends (Hebrew *sôd*; NRSV: 'friendship') of Yahweh among whom private and supportive counsel is given. Knowing Yahweh's covenant is an important part of this counsel, so each section of the meditation ends with reference to covenant, one with a call to adherence (v. 10b), the other with an assurance of its availability and clarity (v. 14). And just as vv. 8-11 ended with David's response to the nature of Yahweh in v. 11, so the meditation on those who fear Yahweh ends with David's own attestation of his attention to Yahweh and his assurance in that (v. 15).

David returns to his prayer of lament in vv. 16-18. His plea emerges from the confidence of vv. 12-15. The focus is again on sin and distress and the 'troubles of (the) heart' (v. 17), although in seeking forgiveness David uses the word *nāsa'*, in contrast to the more technical term *sālaḥ* in v. 11. *nāsa'* in a less figurative sense means 'to lift' and was used as we noted in Ps. 24.4, 5, 7, and 9 and again in Ps. 25.1 above (cf. also Pss. 32.1, 5; 85.2; 99.8).

In the final section of the psalm David comes full circle. His plea continues but it moves back to the subject of the start of the psalm. A number of terms in these final verses echo the beginning of the psalm including 'enemies', 'my soul/life', 'shame' (especially in the phrase 'do not let me be put to shame, vv. 2b and 20b) and 'wait'. The basis of David's plea is that he has taken refuge in Yahweh and seeks for 'integrity' and 'uprightness' to keep him (v. 20). Finally, v. 22 stands out in the psalm for a number of reasons. First, the subject matter changes from David as psalmist to Israel. Secondly, the notion of 'troubles' returns picking up the word *ṣārôṭ* from v. 17. Thirdly, the line begins in Hebrew with the letter *pē* and stands outside the alphabetic sequence of first letters. The verse has possibly been added late to the psalm and could suggest the troubles of Israel in exile. In this last case, it is possible that the use of *pē* at this point is meant to pick up the first letter of the alphabet in v. 1, *'ālep*, and the middle one, *lāmed*, in v. 11 to form the word *'lp*, or *'ālep*, the first letter of the alphabet indicating the acrostic structure.

In Psalm 25 David lifts up his life to Yahweh even as he did not 'lift (his) life' to falsehood, but lifted a blessing from Yahweh in Ps. 24.5. Like the gates in 24.7 and 9 he lifts his head in pride and favour. We hear the words of the one who would ascend mountain of Yahweh. Following the words of trust and praise in the previous psalms, the themes of waiting, and seeking forgiveness in this psalm stress that the ascension of the mountain of Yahweh is not something easily undertaken. Nor is taking 'the way of the righteous' as set out in Psalm 1. David is aware, as in earlier laments, of struggles along the way, both external in terms of enemies, and internal 'troubles of the heart'. Deliverance from the things that would oppress the one who fears Yahweh, or from even choosing 'the way of the wicked', requires discipline and instruction. David needs to be taught by Yahweh. He is called to learn the ways of Yahweh which themselves reflect goodness, uprightness, integrity, mercy, and 'love'. But these are all the qualities of Yahweh. They are not only set out before

David to choose, but they also sustain him. Through them he is brought into the covenant community, the *sôd* of Yahweh.

The language of enemies suggests the context of kingship. The plea to be taught by Yahweh brings back thoughts of the law of the king in Deuteronomy (Deut. 17.18-20) and the possible allusion in Psalm 1, even though the word *torah* is not mentioned in Psalm 25. The sense of the psalm as one of David's is strengthened in this way. On the other hand, he clearly prays this psalm with the whole community of those who fear Yahweh. The danger from personal and internal troubles and sin is as severe as that from external national enemies. Thus, national and individual experiences in striving for faithfulness are related.

Psalms 26–32

If in part of Psalm 25 David meditates on Psalms 23–24, then in **Psalm 26** he continues in that vein. Several words from preceding psalms are repeated in Ps. 26.1-3 ('integrity', 'walk', 'trust', 'love', and 'faithfulness'). The phrase 'walk in integrity'. forms an *inclusio* in this psalm occurring again in v. 11. While Ps. 26.4-5 picks up themes from Psalm 1, the reference to washing 'hands in innocence' in 26.6 directly draws on the description of those who can ascend the mountain of Yahweh in Ps. 24.4. This is surely the prayer of one whose love for the house of Yahweh is great (cf. Ps. 23.6), who is confident in their prayer for redemption, and who is a model for the great congregation (v. 12).

David continues in **Psalm 27** where the troubles that beset him seem to have become more difficult. His pleas for deliverance are strengthened. Nevertheless, the trust about which he spoke earlier is reiterated and also strengthened. David seeks now to live in the house of Yahweh (v. 4; cf. 23.6), his head is 'lifted' in praise (v. 6; cf. Psalm 24), he desires again to be taught the ways of Yahweh (v. 11; cf. 25.4-5, 12), believes he will see the goodness of Yahweh (v. 13; cf. 23.6; 25.7-8) and maintains his hope in Yahweh (v. 14, 'wait for the Lord'; cf. 25.3, 21).

David's lament continues in **Psalms 28** with two variations. He focuses more on the ways and fate of his enemies (vv. 3-5) and finally breaks into full praise of Yahweh who 'has heard the sound of (his) pleadings' (vv. 6-7). He finishes by praying that his own saving experience as Yahweh's anointed may be extended to all Yahweh's people (vv. 8-9), that his shepherd (Ps. 23.1) may also be theirs (28.9). The praise at the end of Psalm 28 is extended in **Psalm 29**. In what might well be an old Canaanite hymn to

Baal which has been modified for worship of Yahweh, the heavenly host are called on to give glory to Yahweh. David praises the 'voice of Yahweh' in the language of the storm god ('voice' can = thunder), speaking of its great power. All this praise of the voice of Yahweh in the temple celebrates Yahweh's answering David's voice which was directed in supplication toward the sanctuary (Ps. 28.2). He concludes proclaiming Yahweh's kingship over creation in language similar to Ps. 24.1-2 and again prays for Yahweh to give strength and peace to his people (28.11).

Psalm 30 is a psalm of thanksgiving continuing the note of praise from Psalm 29. David's mourning has been turned to dancing (v. 10). He calls others to join him in his joy (v. 4). The superscription associates this psalm with the 'dedication of the temple'. The *Midrash* links the psalm with all three dedications (of Solomon's temple, 1 Kgs 8.63; after exile, Ezra 6.16-17; and in the second century BCE, 1 Macc. 4.52-59). After several psalms in which David longs to dwell in Yahweh's house (Pss. 23.6; 24.3; 26.8; 27.4) this dedication is not out of place. But the reason for thanks can quickly give way to further grief and distress as it does in **Psalm 31**. Nevertheless, David maintains his trust and in spite of the most severe scorn and threats of shame (vv. 9-18; cf. 25.2-3) he seeks the shelter of Yahweh's presence, urging others to wait with him (v. 24).

Psalm 32 is a mixed type of psalm in which David revels in Yahweh's forgiveness (vv. 1-5) and urges other faithful ones to offer prayer to Yahweh (v. 6). There is ambiguity in vv. 8-9. It is unclear whether these words are those of David daring to teach another the way they should go or we are hearing Yahweh's words to David in fulfilment of Ps. 24.4-5. It may not matter in the end because such instruction as David might give can only come from personal experience, a point constantly evoked as David regularly turns to address the community. He does so again at the end of this psalm calling them to shout for joy (v. 11).

Psalm 33

In Psalm 33 the community gives praise to Yahweh. The psalm is unusual for Book I of the Psalter in having no superscription (although the LXX and the Qumran manuscript 4QPs do add one). However, the connection to Psalm 32 is strong with three words from 32.11 repeated in 33.1: 'shout for joy', 'righteous', and 'upright', as well as the name Yahweh. The blessing with 'ašrê

(32.1-2 and 33.12; also cf. 34.8) and mention of 'the eye of Yahweh' (32.8; 33.18) also link the psalms. Thus, while the two psalms are different in aspects of content and genre, in Psalm 33 the community can be seen taking up the invitation to rejoice in Ps. 32.11. The two psalms are even seen as one in some ancient Hebrew manuscripts.

The twenty two verses of Psalm 33 equal the number of letters in the Hebrew alphabet, although the verses do not begin with successive letters as in acrostic psalms. There may be a hint at the acrostic structure implying completeness and reinforcing the message. In common with some acrostics there is a teaching element to the psalm. As such it may be seen to develop further the motif from Pss. 25.4-5, 12 and 27.11.

The psalm divides into four sections: a call to rejoice in vv. 1-5; vv. 6-12 on the word of Yahweh; vv. 13-19 on what Yahweh sees from heaven; and vv. 20-22 with the community's response. Repetition of words and phrases ties the psalm together. The hint at acrostic structure and the notion of Yahweh's creation by word (cf. Genesis 1) might suggest a post-exilic date for the psalm. On the other hand, it also has connections to earlier poems such as Exodus 15 and Judges 5.

Picking up the tenor of Ps. 32.11, David calls the community, referred to as the 'righteous' and 'upright', to praise Yahweh. He uses five separate imperatives: 'rejoice', 'praise' ('give thanks'), 'make melody', 'sing' and 'play skilfully' (vv. 1-3). Their praise is to be exuberant and a 'new song', although what that means is not yet clear. It is praise in word and music. The reason for praise is introduced immediately by *ki*, 'for', as in other hymns of praise. Five qualities of Yahweh match the five imperatives. Yahweh is 'upright', his work is done in 'faithfulness', he loves 'righteousness and justice', and his *ḥesed*, 'steadfast love', fills the earth (vv. 4-5). The name of Yahweh surrounds these qualities underlining the association. Although it is not yet clear, in these two verses David anticipates the foci of the praise to follow: the creative word of Yahweh (vv. 6-12, cf. v. 4) and human affairs emphasising those who hope in Yahweh's *ḥesed* (v. 18; cf. v. 5). The occurrence of 'upright' and 'righteousness' among Yahweh's qualities recalls the titles given to those called to rejoice in v. 1. Those who fear Yahweh and who are called to rejoice in him reflect the qualities of Yahweh. These words, used in relation to Yahweh's people, will occur together again only in Pss. 97.11 and 140.13.

In vv. 6 and 9 David picks up the theme of v. 4 and describes the role of Yahweh's word in creation. The reference brings to mind creation by divine word in Genesis 1 although it need not indicate a direct connection. The Egyptian god Ptah is said to have created through his word in the so-called Memphite Theology, and in Mesopotamia the words of deities were praised as powerful and effective. The idea could be much more ancient than the Genesis account. In addition, having spoken about creation through word, David goes on to allude to the old Canaanite and Mesopotamian creation myth of cosmic conflict with reference to the sea/deeps representative of chaos (v. 7; cf. Ps 24.1-2). He colourfully describes the defeat of the sea/deeps as putting them in storehouses (v. 7b) or damming/heaping them up (so MT in v. 7a). The Hebrew word used in v. 7a, *nēd*, means 'dam, heap' but is not common (cf. Exod 15.8, Ps. 78.13; and Josh. 3.13 and 16). The NRSV 'in a bottle' comes from the LXX which seems to have read the Hebrew word as *nĕ'ōd*, 'skin-bottle' (Josh. 9.4, 13; Judg. 4.19; Ps. 56.9 etc.). The reference to the old Canaanite and Mesopotamian creation myth might also allude to the exodus, the 'creation' of the people of Israel. The myth is employed in the story of the exodus and the use of vocabulary from the old poetic account in Exodus 15, specifically the use of *nēd*, 'dam, heap', and *tĕhômôt*, 'deeps' (Exod. 15.8; cf. Ps. 33.7) could bring that to mind.

David calls for 'all the earth' and 'all the inhabitants of the world' to fear Yahweh, or to 'stand in awe' of him. The same two verbs are used in Ps 22.23 (cf. also 25.12) in conjunction with the verb 'glorify' conveying a positive aspect of the sense of fear. A similar sense of both fear and praise was engendered in Psalm 29. In Ps. 33.8 the call 'to fear' and 'stand in awe' is oriented toward the future. David seeks to bring the people to praise. His call for a new future is, however, grounded in the past act of creation, with the verbs of v. 6 suggesting past activity. However, in v. 7 David describes Yahweh's gathering of the waters using participles, suggesting the possibility of an ongoing action. The power of Yahweh as creator, demonstrated by his word in the past, undergirds David's call, both here and in Psalm 29. Yahweh's act of creation is not confined to the past but is ongoing.

In this context vv. 10-12 might seem to introduce a new issue with Yahweh frustrating the plans of the people and the counsel of the nations (v. 10). By way of contrast the counsel and plans of Yahweh's heart are eternal. They 'stand' (*'āmad*) forever just as the earth 'stood firm' (*ʿāmad*) in v. 9. The subject may seem to have changed but both the counsel of the nations (v. 10) and that of Yahweh (v. 11) involve words thus picking up the theme begun in v. 6. The verbs used in v. 10 also imply opposition, suggesting that the human counsel described is consistent with the chaos symbolized by the sea/deeps. In both the act of creation and in human planning, that which contests Yahweh's word will not stand. Nothing opposes Yahweh's word in either the heavenly realm (v. 7) or the realm of human affairs (vv 10-11). The tenses implied in the verb forms is also significant (cf. vv. 6-8). In describing Yahweh's action toward human counsel, the verbs revert to past tense (v. 10). Thus even though the human counsel is a present issue, it has already been brought to nothing. In Yahweh's creation by word it has been defeated. Now, however, it is Yahweh's counsel, his word, which lasts. Verbs of continuous action are used (v. 11). These subtle shifts in tense in vv. 6-11 suggest that the power of Yahweh over all that opposes him has been demonstrated from the beginning. Finally, the sense of opposition in these verses contrasts with the correspondence between Yahweh and his people stressed earlier in vv. 1-5. Verses 9-12 echo Psalm 2 and the opposition of the nations to Yahweh and his anointed. In both cases blessing (*ʾašrê*) is upon the one who stands with Yahweh (Pss. 2.12; 33.12) or who resists the ways of the wicked (Ps. 1.1).

Verse 12 seems to contrast Israel and the nations (cf. Psalm 2). However, neither 'Israel' nor any of its synonyms is used anywhere in Psalm 33. The use of the word *gôy*, 'nation', in v. 12 in contrast to other words that could be used to speak of the nation/people of Israel, suggests that a broader perspective is emerging. The ambiguity of v. 12 is heightened with an allusion to the standard covenant formula with Israel ('I will be your God, and you will be my people', Deut. 26.17-19; cf. Exod. 6.7). Other language peculiar to the description of Israel as Yahweh's people is also present in the verse (*bāhar* 'to choose', and *nᵉḥālâ*, 'inheritance'). This combination of language will again appear in Book III (e.g. Pss. 74.1-2; 78.71-2) where it will be combined with the language of sheep/shepherd (e.g. Pss. 74.1; 79.13; 80.1). This combination of language has only just appeared in Book I (Ps. 28.9). Psalm 33, therefore, opens the possibility that other nations may well be included in those who fear Yahweh. We might recall that Psalm 2 left open the possibility for a change of heart within those who stood as Yahweh's foes (Ps. 2.10-11).

76   *Psalm 33*

A further shift takes place in vv. 13-18 as David focuses on the 'eye of Yahweh'. The language of kingship is also emphasized. As in the earlier parts of the psalm, five terms are used to speak of Yahweh's seeing: 'look down', 'see', 'watch', 'observe' (vv. 13-14) and in v. 18, 'eye' itself. Heaven and earth are separated at this point as Yahweh looks down (cf. Ps. 2.4). Three parallel statements introduce Yahweh's activity in vv. 13-15. The description of Yahweh increases over these verses to the fulsome description as the creator who fashions the hearts of humans. His activity increases from simply looking down and seeing humankind in v. 13 to observing all human deeds in v. 15, implying judgment by one intimately concerned with human affairs. The references to human hearts and deeds in v. 15 recalls those of Yahweh's heart and work in vv. 11 and 4 respectively, and sets up a basis for comparison. On the negative side, vv. 16-17, which echo the language of the old songs of Yahweh's wars (cf. Exod. 15.1-4; Judg. 5.18-22), express the futility of human power to save (cf. Pss. 76.4-7; 147.10-11; and Isa. 31.1). The positive conclusion in v. 18 to all this 'seeing' by Yahweh is that Yahweh's eye is on those who fear him and hope in his *ḥesed*, 'steadfast love'. This draws us back to the beginning of the psalm, especially v. 5, which concludes a positive comparison of the righteous and upright with Yahweh. Thus, the heavenly king, Yahweh, who delivers those who fear and hope in him, stands in contrast to earthly kings who cannot even depend on their own great armies to save them. Recurring motifs and words tie the major sections of the psalm together ('upright', vv. 1, 4; 'fear', vv. 8, 18; 'all the inhabitants of the earth', vv. 8, 14; 'people/peoples' and nation(s), vv. 10, 12; and 'steadfast love', vv. 5, 18, 22) and both major sections end with a statement of Yahweh's blessing/deliverance of his people. Verse 18 clearly states the confidence that stands behind v. 12. All this underlines the comparison, at the same time as it raises the question whether there is indeed continuity of purpose between Yahweh and his people.

The one who fears Yahweh is also one who hopes in Yahweh. Praise is not simply seen in an overt expression of joy and gladness of heart. It is that, but it is also trusting and waiting, with the implication of stillness and silence. The vocabulary of vv. 20-22 recalls the thoughts of vv 6-19 bringing the psalm to a conclusion: 'waiting' from v. 18, 'heart' from vv. 11 and 15, and *ḥesed*, 'steadfast love' from vv. 5 and 18. The motif of hope, treated in a positive way in vv. 19-22, stands in contrast to the vain hope for victory in v. 17. David now joins voices with the righteous to praise the Lord, pledging to wait for Yahweh with their *nepeš*, 'soul' or, more properly, 'life'. He has led the community to take up the invitation at the end of Psalm 32 and now it affirms his earlier statements. The whole community is 'glad' (32.11; 33.21) and affirms 'trust' (32.10; 33.21) in Yahweh's *hesed* (32.10; 33.18, 22).

David uses the language of creation and of Yahweh as creator to engender faith and hope in the community and to get them singing a 'new song'. This is the first time we hear this call to a new song. In what sense it is new remains a mystery for the moment. But to ask whether the psalm has anything *new* to say might miss the point. Creation is clearly an ongoing process in the psalm, or at least continues to bestow its benefits. To sing praise in the context of creation is to continue the whole process of responding to the ongoing work of the creator. What we say or do in our praise may not be new in the sense of being different or novel. It is new, however, in the sense of celebrating something which has happened, continues to do so and will go on into the future. It is new in the sense of being our present response to the creative acts of Yahweh in our own time and place. That response includes not just 'clean hands and a pure heart' (Ps. 24.3-6) but also a constant hope and waiting in Yahweh. It is hope that must be maintained in the face of opposition and false hopes. Yahweh does not promise to remove David or the community from the threat of death or the hardship of famine, but rather to deliver them and keep them alive (v. 19). It is a matter of in whom one ultimately places trust. There could be an eschatological aspect to this new song, a foreshadowing of an ultimate hope in which the whole earth participates. But if it is that, it is not just a hope to be realized at some distant time. It is a hope that opens out toward the future from present experience. This psalm establishes a portrait of David as psalmist which goes beyond his position as king with its basis in power and military might to suggest one whose only hope is Yahweh.

Psalms 34–39

Psalm 34 is another acrostic psalm. In it David heavily employs words related to the face and the organs of speech and hearing ('mouth', 'face', 'taste', 'eyes/sight', 'ears/hearing', 'tongue', 'lips'). He draws the community into his thanksgiving to Yahweh (vv. 3, 8). His own experience is an example (vv. 4-6) for others of how Yahweh rescues those who fear him (vv. 9, 11; cf. Pss. 25.12, 14; 31.19; 33.8, 18 etc.). David strives to teach them through his own words (vv. 11-14), having been taught himself by Yahweh (Pss. 25.4, 5, 12; 27.11). Psalm 34 finishes with reassurance of Yahweh's rescue and care for the righteous (cf. Pss. 32.11; 33.1). Repetition of the clause 'the eye(s) of Yahweh is(are) on ...' from Ps. 33.18 introduces the theme and it is extended by connecting it with the language of the 'ears' and 'face' of Yahweh in 34.15-18.

The superscription of this psalm relates it to the brief episode of 1 Sam. 21.10-15 in which David, fleeing Saul, sought protection with King Achish of Gath, only to fear for his life there. By feigning madness he was able to escape. The Samuel narrative has a number of verbal connections with Psalm 34. The Hebrew translated reasonably in the NRSV superscription of Psalm 34 'he feigned madness' and in 1 Sam. 21.13 'he changed his behaviour' means literally 'he changed his taste'. This rare expression links with the psalm's call to 'taste and see that Yahweh is good' (v. 8). The same Hebrew root *hll* is used in Ps. 34.2 in a form meaning 'boast' and in 1 Sam. 21.13 in another form meaning 'pretend madness'. However, David's fear in 1 Samuel is also picked up in the psalm by way of contrast with its theme of the 'fear of Yahweh'. The psalm becomes an example for the community of how one 'fear' can be replaced by a more beneficial one. The point is underlined further by the Psalm superscription replacing the Philistine king Achish of Gath by Abimelech of Gerar, a figure whom Abraham and Isaac also feared (Genesis 20; 26).

After the thanksgiving of Psalm 34 we hear in **Psalm 35** the voice of Yahweh's servant in the midst of affliction. The assurance of Yahweh's care and rescue of the righteous in their affliction turns quickly to an expression of the depth of that affliction and David's impatience at Yahweh's inactivity. Through long sections of complaint, plea and imprecation David details the activities of his enemies (vv. 1-8, 11-16, 19-21, 26-27). His impatience with Yahweh's inactivity becomes stronger as he pleads for Yahweh not to be silent and to wake up (vv. 17, 22-25; cf. Psalm 44). The question of 'How long?' echoes Psalm 13. He desires his pursuers to be like the chaff the wicked were compared to in Ps. 1.4. At the end of each of the three major sections of Psalm 35 in vv. 9-10, 18, and 28, there is a somewhat restrained promise of praise. The movement back and forth between the elements of lament and the constant shifts in language and metaphor (legal, military, agricultural, hunting, thuggery and abuse) may seem confusing but they contribute to a sense of the rising shame, confusion and dishonour David feels (v. 26) and his increasing frustration with Yahweh. Yet in whom else may David hope except Yahweh who is incomparable, defends the weak (v. 10) and vindicates his servants (v. 27; cf. 34.22). David's 'vindication' (ṣedeq, v. 27) is tied to Yahweh's 'righteousness' (ṣedeq, v. 28). It is Yahweh who is said to delight in his 'welfare' (šālôm, v. 27) who can overcome enemies who do not speak 'peace' (šālôm, v. 20). The passage in 1 Sam. 24.9-19, where David speaks to Saul pointing out his own mercy toward Saul in the face of the latter's pursuit of David, could suggest a context for the psalm's composition. David pleads for Yahweh to vindicate him against Saul (1 Sam. 24.14) in language similar to the psalm.

David continues his lament in **Psalm 36** giving further detail about the wicked (vv. 1-4). They have no fear of Yahweh. Their eyes see only their own flattery and their words are deceitful. David pleads for a continuation of Yahweh's ḥesed, 'steadfast love' which he praises in exuberant language. Those who take refuge in Yahweh 'feast on the abundance of (Yahweh's) house and drink 'from the river of (Yahweh's) delights', the 'fountain of life' (vv. 8-9; cf. Ps. 23.5-6).

With **Psalm 37** there is a sharp change of context. We have heard the words of David to Yahweh as he personally struggles against enemies and seeks to praise Yahweh (e.g. Ps. 35.1-26) and seeks for the community to join that praise (35.27-28). Things now change. Psalm 37, another acrostic psalm, begins with a single voice speaking to an undesignated individual. This continues through v. 11 where there is a shift to mostly third person reflections, many proverbial in nature. Occasionally, the psalmist speaks in the first person (pl. or sg.) but the mood remains reflective (vv. 23-26, 35-36) and in a few verses the imperatives of vv. 1-11 return (vv. 27, 34, and 37) again in the singular. David could be speaking to an individual here or reflecting internally. The laughter of Yahweh at the wicked in v. 13 recalls his laughter at the kings of the earth plotting against Yahweh and his anointed (Ps. 2.4), thus drawing a connection to David. Alternatively, another voice could address David himself. It is not clear. In any case, matters pertaining to the wicked, described in some detail in Psalms 35 and 36, are addressed. The thoughts do not progress in any logical argument. The psalm is largely an anthology or collection of verses on the punishment of sinners and the reward of the just. The basic message of the psalm is conveyed by the overall effect of the collection of statements rather than by any developed argument. This may be the result of the acrostic and proverbial nature of the psalm.

Psalm 37 takes up the sentiments of Ps. 1.6 (cf. 37.28b) and develops them in one way. The material and physical reward of the righteous is seen as imminent (vv. 3-4, 5-6, 11, 19, 23-24, 25-26 etc.), although v. 16 may be an exception. In some ancient communities, especially the Qumran community, the psalm was read eschatologically pointing to a new era when the land would belong again to the true children of Israel (4Q171, 4QPs^a). The interest in the psalm in the possession of the land (vv. 3, 9, 11, 22, 29, 34) could suggest a post-exilic date. While the psalm is meant to have instructional value, it raises questions whether the faithful always receive their needs and the wicked always perish? These questions will only be addressed much later (especially in Psalm 73). In the meantime there is encouragement for the righteous in their struggle (Ps. 37.39-40).

The mood changes again in **Psalm 38**, a psalm of penitence. In line with the theology of Psalm 37, David sees his predicament as an expression of Yahweh's anger and discipline (vv. 1-4). He is in desperate straits with dismayed friends standing aloof and others plotting to take advantage of his predicament (vv. 11-12). His only recourse is to confess his sin (v. 18), plea for Yahweh's aid (v. 21-22) and wait (v. 15). Even though he has protested innocence at other times he is ready to confess the sin he does commit and accept its consequences. His anguish continues in **Psalm 39**. His deliberation to 'guard (his) ways' (v. 1) sounds like a consequence of the confession in 38.18. If so, things have not changed for David. He continues to suffer (39.2-3) and this leads him to musing on the ephemeral nature of human life and seeking his own end (vv. 4-6, 11). His only response is to continue to wait for Yahweh, hope, continue in silence and plead with Yahweh (vv. 7-10). In a point of irony he refers to himself now as Yahweh's passing guest (v. 12). No longer does he speak of dwelling in Yahweh's house his whole life long (Pss. 23.6; cf. 26.8; 27.4-6; 36.8). He now seeks Yahweh's gaze to depart from him, presuming it means judgment whereas it once was a sign of favour (cf. Pss. 4.6; 11.7; 17.5; 24.6; 27.8; 31.16). It is as if he belongs to the wicked (cf. 34.16).

Psalm 40

Waiting for Yahweh has been a theme in recent psalms. The nature of that waiting and its attendant difficulties have been explored (e.g. Psalms 35; 38; 39). David has demonstrated his own waiting (Pss. 25.5, 21; 33.20; 38.15; 39.7) and called others to follow suit (Pss. 27.14; 31.24; 37.7, 34). Now his waiting, which the NRSV translation describes as 'patient', but which could equally be seen as intense or over a lengthy period, has come to an end and he speaks of its outcome and the proper response at its conclusion.

This is an unusual lament psalm. Usually a lament psalm begins with the complaint followed by the thanksgiving. But here thanksgiving and its outcome (vv. 1-10) precede complaint and petition (vv. 11-17). This reversed order and the fact that vv. 13-17 are almost identical with Psalm 70 might suggest that Psalm 40 is a composite of other psalm verses. However, not all the lament is repeated in Psalm 70 and several words tie the thanksgiving and lament sections of Psalm 40 together ('thought', vv. 5, 17; *'āsam*, 'more than ...', vv. 5, 12; *mispār*, 'counted/number', vv. 5, 12; 'see', vv. 3, 12; 'desire/delight', vv. 6, 8, 14; *rāṣôn/rāṣāh*, '[your]will/be pleased with', vv. 8, 13; and 'salvation', vv. 10, 16). Psalm 40 is meant to be read as one. The initial thanksgiving for some past lament serves as a foundation for a further complaint revealing that the way of faith does not just flow in one direction—lament to thanksgiving. Other psalms share this ordering (Psalms 9–10; 27; 44; 89).

Reference in v. 1 to an intense period of waiting picks up the situation at the end of Psalm 39. Yahweh has responded to that prayer with rescue (vv. 1-3). David says Yahweh has drawn him up from a 'roaring pit' (so the Hebrew with possible reference to the waters of chaos) and a 'miry bog'. The imagery is common in the ancient Near East in prayers and myths, such as that telling of Ishtar's descent to the underworld. David had been near death (cf. Pss. 16.10; 30.3, 9), but his feet are now secure (cf. Pss. 17.5; 18.36; 37.31) and a new song of praise for Yahweh as sovereign is in his mouth (cf. Ps. 33.2 and Psalm 30 in general). This has consequences for the community, many of whom will see (*yir'û*) and fear (*yîrā'û*). The play on these words draws attention to this call to trust Yahweh. This is what David prayed for back in Ps. 34.7-11. While it has come only through David's own experience and suffering, it is clearly a gift from Yahweh, the subject of the verbs in vv. 1b–3a. Even David's thanksgiving is a gift.

Verses 4-5 continue to describe the blessing of Yahweh on those who trust. In a similar vein to Psalm 1 the blessing is on the one who avoids certain behaviour, namely turning 'toward the proud' and following 'what is false'. The NRSV reference to 'false gods' is not necessarily implied by the Hebrew. As David addresses Yahweh directly in v. 5 he contemplates the incomparability of Yahweh and the countless number of his 'wondrous deeds and thoughts', terms sometimes connected with the exodus and associated events (Pss. 105.2, 5; 106.22; Mic. 7.15) or with creation (Pss. 96.3; 136.4). The thanksgiving of the individual is tied to that of the nation.

It is only in vv. 6-10 that David turns more fully to his own response to the gifts of deliverance and thanksgiving from Yahweh. Surprisingly, he seems to speak against the offerings authorized within the regular sacrificial system for all four offerings named in v. 6 are regulated in Leviticus 1–4. Such a critical view of the sacrificial system might be seen in connection with prophetic critique from the eighth century BCE onward (cf. Amos 5.21-23; Isa. 1.11-16; 66.3; Mic. 6.6-8; cf. Ps. 51.16-17), although that critique highlights the mixing of pious sacrificial acts with injustice and oppression within society. There is no hint of the latter among those who trust Yahweh in the psalm.

The meaning of v. 6, however, is not readily apparent. The problem lies with the meaning of v. 6b 'but you have given me an open ear' (NRSV). The Hebrew reads literally 'Ears you have dug for me'. The 'but', which the NRSV has, is not there in the Hebrew and possibly comes from the LXX rendering. The 'open ear' is not the alternative to the sacrifices. It may be that v. 6b should be read before v. 6a as something like 'You gave me to understand that you do not desire sacrifice and meal offering,' as the Jewish Publication Society has it. Alternatively, v. 6a and c could be blunt statements regarding sacrifices with v. 6b indicating that Yahweh has opened David's ears. However, there is a brief delay until v. 7 where he hears what is desired and requested. What is a delight to Yahweh is to have his servant say 'Here I am!' and to know that it is the servant's delight to do the will of Yahweh and to have Yahweh's *torah* deep inside.

David's internalisation of Yahweh's *torah* and his delight to embody it is what is emphasized. That is what is written about David in the scroll of the book, possibly a reference to a written document deposited in the sanctuary reminding the deity, in this case, of the donor's thanks and piety in response to deliverance. Such documents were common in the ancient Near East. All this does not mean that the sacrificial system is no longer necessary, but that the internal orientation of the one who comes near to

Yahweh is paramount. The words of rejection highlight this. Moreover, the transfer of words appropriate for sacrifice to the new context serves the same purpose. The word in v. 8 translated in the NRSV as 'will' (*rāṣon*) can also mean 'acceptance' and is used of persons offering sacrifice (Lev. 1.3 etc.; cf. Ps. 19.14). Acceptance applies to the one who offers sacrifice as much as to the offering itself. Some psalms look for both praise and sacrifice (Pss. 56.12; 107.21-22; 116.12-19). This internalisation of *torah*'s prescriptions was also preached by the prophets (e.g. Mic. 6.6-8; Jer. 31.31-34; Ezek 36.26-32; cf. Ps. 51.6, 17).

These verses remind us of 1 Sam. 15.22-23 where Saul is rejected from being king because he 'rejected the word' of Yahweh. The point made in Samuel is that Saul did not obey Yahweh's commands (1 Sam. 15.10). No amount of sacrifice could cover a rebellious and stubborn heart beneath the action. The episode in Samuel underlines the point in the psalm and is most fitting for a psalm of David, who in the Samuel story is just about to receive the spirit of Yahweh in place of Saul (1 Samuel 16).

The outworking of the one who delights to do Yahweh's will finds expression in the proclamation of good news to the great congregation (vv. 9-10). What is in David's heart cannot be kept there (v. 10a) and he now proclaims Yahweh's 'steadfast love', faithfulness, salvation, and righteousness. The mention of the great congregation at the start and end of these verses emphasizes that thanksgiving can only be that if it invites others into its experience. David's task as psalmist is to lead his people in the trust of Yahweh (cf. Ps. 30.4).

There is some uncertainty over how vv. 11-12 are to be read. Major English translations read them as a petition for Yahweh's protection (v. 11) as new difficulties beset David (v. 12). Thus these verses would begin the petition section of the psalm. On the other hand, the Hebrew allows reading v. 11 as a statement of what Yahweh habitually does based on a description of past difficulties in v. 12: 'For evils had encompassed me ...'. In this case, vv. 11-12 would be the final statement to the thanksgiving. The ambiguity reinforces the idea that any plea for deliverance in future situations is grounded in the experience of deliverance in the past and its consequent thanksgiving and proclamation. If the general shape of the psalm with its 'reverse' order of thanksgiving—complaint is a reminder that there is no single movement in prayer from complaint to thanksgiving but a constant movement back and forth, then vv. 11-12 remind us that in this back and forth movement each element builds upon the other.

If v. 11 is read as a petition, thus giving background to the desire that David's opponents be shamed in vv. 14-15, then David seeks from Yahweh the very things he has proclaimed in the great congregation—'steadfast love' and faithfulness. He is beset by evils without and iniquity within. It is instructive that the one who has just demonstrated true thanksgiving and what a truly acceptable offering to Yahweh is, may still find himself beset by iniquities, indeed overwhelmed by them. The mixture of confession and a claim to obedience was also present in Psalms 38–39. In this psalm, both external evils and internal iniquities are beyond counting. David cannot help himself. But we should remember that he has also said that Yahweh's 'wondrous deeds and thoughts' are likewise innumerable (v. 5) and in vv. 1b–3a it was Yahweh who was the one to save. The basis for this new petition lies in his earlier thanksgiving.

David has asked that those who seek his life and look for advantage over him may themselves be shamed by Yahweh (vv. 13-14). He ends the psalm with a general plea for 'all who seek' Yahweh to rejoice and praise Yahweh (v. 16). In this he fulfils his royal role as mediator of the covenant relationship between the people and Yahweh. There is an implicit contrast here, through the use of the same verb *biqqēš*, between those who seek David's life and those who seek Yahweh. David prays that the latter, like him, may become witnesses to Yahweh's greatness (v. 16). Finally David reminds us that this hope for deliverance depends not on his own status or power, for he is lowly and needy among the people. He picks up the language of Pss. 9.18 and 10.2, 9 seeing himself among the needy. Even so, Yahweh still has concern for him, as for all poor and needy. So David asks for Yahweh's help to come soon. The first part of v. 17 counters the feeling of insignificance expressed not so long ago in Ps. 39.4-6 by picking up the thought of the greatness of humankind in Yahweh's eyes in Psalm 8.

In Psalm 40, an individual psalm of thanksgiving and complaint, we see David fulfilling his broader responsibilities for his people. Part of that is in his role as teacher mentioned in Ps. 34.11. David's experience and words are models for all. The pattern in royal psalms (see esp. Pss. 9–10; 89) becomes one for prayer in the community. He takes them beyond the usual pattern of laments deeper into the nature of thanksgiving and its connection to petition and plea. The depth of the relationship with Yahweh that David seeks to convey is embodied in the language he uses. The psalm is full of words relating to the body and its activity ('feet', v. 2; 'steps', v. 2; 'mouth', v. 3; 'ear', v. 6; 'heart', v. 8 [*mēʿeh*], v. 11 [*lēbāb*]; 'lips', v. 9; 'see', v. 12; 'hair', v. 12; 'life', v. 14). When David utters the words in v. 7, 'Here I am' (lit.: 'Here, I have come!') and uses the emphatic pronoun *ʾanî*, 'I', in v. 17, he stands before Yahweh totally vulnerable. Giving all one's life to Yahweh is the essential point of the psalm. Having Yahweh's law within recalls the point made in Ps. 1.2. The delight of the one who was blessed (NRSV: 'happy') in that psalm was the *torah* of Yahweh and constant meditation on it. Now the delight of the one who is blessed (Ps. 40.4) is to do the will of Yahweh and have Yahweh's *torah* in their heart. This was also spelled out as the goal of kingship in the Deuteronomistic law of the king (Deut. 17.14-20). Besides reading the law constantly and observing it so that he may learn to 'fear' Yahweh, the king was not to exalt himself over other members of the community (v. 20), seek personal wealth or power, or oppress the people (v. 16). David exemplifies these things, in the first case in Ps. 40.17 when he equates himself with the 'poor and needy', and in the second case, in a negative comparison with Saul in 1 Sam. 15.22-23, whose problem in that context was both his disobedience and the appropriation of booty dedicated to Yahweh.

Psalm 41

With Psalm 41 we reach the end of Book I of the Psalter. As an individual psalm it can be classified as either a lament associated with illness or a thanksgiving. In favour of the former is that vv. 4-10, the bulk of the psalm, is concerned with complaint and petition. However, David begins the psalm with a note of confidence (vv. 1-3) and concludes it in like fashion (vv. 11-12), with Yahweh having answered the call for help. Which way one reads the psalm depends on how the tenses are interpreted and the timing of the illness in relation to the statements of confidence. Verse 13 concludes both the psalm and Book I with a doxology.

In containing both lament and thanksgiving, Psalm 41 is consistent with the greater part of Book I. But it is more than just another psalm in the collection. It also provides a fitting conclusion to the first book. It begins with another beatitude, *ʾašrê*, 'happy are those' providing a connection with Ps. 40.4, as well as with Pss. 1.1 and 2.12. Book I is thereby enclosed by ʾašrê beatitudes (cf. also within Book I, Pss. 32.1-2; 33.12; 34.8). Other words also provide links between Psalm 41 and Psalms 38–40: 'I said/pray', 41.4; cf. 38.16; 39.1; 40.7; 'to see', 41.6; cf. 40.12; 'to trust' 41.9; cf. 40.3-4; and 'to be pleased/to desire/to delight', 41.11; cf. 40.6, 8.

David begins by pronouncing blessed the 'one who considers' the poor (v. 1). The singular, masculine pronouns and verb forms throughout this section in the Hebrew are hidden in modern English translations for the sake of inclusivity. The ambiguity of the psalm is thereby lost. The singular, masculine pronoun could refer to the psalmist, i.e. David, or be used generically. In the spirit of many of the psalms we have seen in Book I (cf. especially Psalm 1), the ambiguity is deliberate. Blessed is the one who models consideration of 'the poor' for all who follow.

But what does it mean to 'consider' the poor? First, the word 'poor' (*dal*) can mean materially poor, lowly, weak, or helpless. In light of later references to illness, that might also be implied. Secondly, the Hebrew participle, *maśkîl*, can mean 'to make wise, to act prudently, prosper, or have success'. With the preposition ʾ*el*, 'to, toward', it can mean 'to give careful attention to, to study' (cf. Neh. 8.13 in relation to *torah*). It can also imply action as well as thought (cf. Prov. 16.20). It is likely that both careful study and responsive action are embraced by the words. Blessed is the one who both cares for the poor through compassionate action and learns from the situation. The Targum of Psalm 41 conveys this dual sense with its expansion of the verse: 'who considers the affairs of the poor to have compassion on him'. The call to compassion is consistent with the charge on the king (cf. Ps. 72.13) and hence with David as psalmist.

The ambiguity of v. 1a continues over vv. 1b-3. Who is the one whom Yahweh delivers, protects and sustains? Is it the 'poor' or ill, or the one who 'considers' them? But again the ambiguity is instructive. In Ps. 82.3-4 Yahweh chastises the gods for not giving justice to the weak (*dal*) or rescuing them. Yahweh, who does do these things, judges the gods. Ps. 41.1b-3 could, therefore, describe Yahweh's own care for the poor. It is this that David considers. On the other hand, vv. 1b-2 especially could describe the deliverance of David himself, who does the considering. Reference to enemies in v. 2b would well fit this situation. But these need not be mutually exclusive readings. David does consider the poor whom Yahweh cares for and he reflects on his own situation and Yahweh's care for him, especially in times when he is 'poor' even in the sense of ill. At the same time David is called to exercise such care for others as Yahweh does, who even in v. 3b could act as nurse/physician changing the bed of the sick (the Hebrew says: 'all his bed you change in his illness'; cf. NJB and the Jewish Publication Society versions). All who read/hear the psalm and take David as their model in faith are called to such care and compassion. Thus, the beginning of the psalm serves as thanksgiving and instruction in the wisdom tradition of observation and reflection.

David knows that when evil besets him Yahweh will deliver (v. 1, using the same word as in Ps. 40.17). The vocabulary of sustaining and preserving is present in both this section of confidence in Yahweh (vv. 2-3a) and at the end of the psalm (v. 12). The parallel nature of vv. 2-3 with the strong language of illness in v. 3 suggests that what David learns from observing the one who is ill or weak is transferable to other situations. Divine support on the sickbed translates into support in any situation where enemies confront him.

David changes from speech about Yahweh to direct address in v. 2c linking his reflection more closely to his own prayer in vv. 4-10 and 11-12. His reflection on 'the poor' leads into personal petition. In more general terms, reflection connects to and shapes piety. But that was also the case with the (then) unnamed man in Psalm 1 who meditated on the *torah* day and night. The subject of the reflection/meditation and prayer in each case is *'ašrê*, 'blessed'. Both *torah* and other faithful reflection influence the prayer life of the faithful one.

In vv. 4-10 David details his own complaint. Whether it is a current one or one from the past will be dealt with below. The section is enclosed within parallel petitions seeking Yahweh's graciousness (vv. 4, 10). However, while these verses form an *inclusio* containing the identical statement 'Yahweh, be gracious to me', there are differences which signal movement within the lament. In v. 4, David starts with the personal pronoun *'anî*, 'As for me', and after the petition for Yahweh's graciousness and healing, gives the reason 'for I have sinned against you.' In v. 10, he begins with the second person pronoun speaking to Yahweh, *wᵉ'attâ*, 'But you', then after the petition for Yahweh's graciousness and to raise him up, he outlines what might arise from Yahweh's intervention. In these two verses David, in almost covenantal fashion (see earlier comments on Psalm 25 and especially Ps. 33.12), details his own responsibility and then outlines that of Yahweh. The frame for the lament functions as the motivation for Yahweh's action.

The language of healing (v. 4) and lying down (v. 8) suggests that David's problem may be one of illness, thus picking up the introduction in vv. 1-3. However, in seeking healing he states he has sinned against Yahweh (v. 4; cf. Ps. 51.4). This recalls the sense of sin as the cause of troubles in earlier psalms (Pss. 32.5; 38.3, 18; 39.1, 11). But the connection between sin and sickness is not explored in any detail in this psalm. The nature of the illness, of the sin, and any perceived causal relationship are all passed over. What is of most concern for David is the social dimension of his predicament, the rejection of others and what the enemies and friends who oppose him have to say and do.

In his weakened state the enemies hope that evil might come upon him. David's utterance in v. 4 ('I said') is paralleled by that of the enemies in v. 5 ('they say'; NRSV: 'wonder'). There is implicit competition over whose word will have efficacy, David's or that of his opponents. The latter wait for his death and the passing of his name (cf. Ps. 9.5).

A chiastic framework is set up in vv. 5-7 around the words and motives of the enemies:

   A. v. 5—the enemies speak evil (*ra'*) concerning David and seek his death;
   B. v. 6a—they utter lies (NRSV: 'empty words'; Heb.: *sāw'*; cf. Ps. 12.2) when they visit him;
   C. v. 6b—their hearts conceive trouble/sorrow;
   B¹. v. 6c—they tell it outside;
   A¹. v. 7—those who hate him whisper about him and think evil (*rā'â*) concerning him.

At the centre of this arrangement is the trouble/sorrow which enemies plan for David. Surrounding the verses are related words for 'evil'. Verse 8 then details the evil the opponents think although the NRSV changes it to David's thought. They say 'a ruinous thing' (*dᵉbar-bᵉliyya'al*; 'worthless, ruinous thing'; cf. Ps. 18.4, 'perdition') has come upon him and he will not rise again. There may even be in this verse reference to a sorcerer's incantation uttered against David, which in that society would be seen to effect the physical situation of the cursed one. If this is the case then David's request for Yahweh 'to raise him up' in v. 10 directly confronts the curse that he will not 'rise' from his bed in v. 8. Even David's friend (lit. 'man of my peace'; *'îš šᵉlômî*) has 'increased the heel' against him, an obscure phrase but generally thought to imply 'taking advantage' (cf. Ps. 38.11; also the interpretation in John 13.18). The sense of oppression and opposition is compounded by one of loneliness. While the psalm clearly speaks of illness, this lament section is not concerned chiefly with that, but rather with the enemies and once friends who now speak and think against David in his time of difficulty.

Finally, in v. 10 David calls again on Yahweh in words echoing v. 4. He seeks Yahweh's graciousness in raising him up so he might repay those who oppose him. Not only does his petition confront the words of the enemies through the use of the root *qûm* ('to rise'; cf. v. 8) but his desire to 'repay' (Heb.: *wa'ªšallᵉmâ*) forms an ironic word play on the term used for 'friend' in v. 9 incorporating the word *šālôm* 'peace'. What is sought is not personal revenge but divine justice and vindication (cf. Ps. 31.23). The irony is heightened when David describes his friend as one he trusted and with whom he ate. This description only serves to underline the theme of trust in Yahweh in many recent psalms and the image of banqueting in Yahweh's house in the presence of enemies in Ps. 23.5.

But the question remains whether the illness David speaks of in vv. 4-10 is something in the past, and its description here simply a reiteration of the basis for thanksgiving, or whether it is truly the reason for a present lament. The NRSV and other English versions conclude the direct quotation at the end of v. 4. The rest of the lament, vv. 5-10 could, therefore, be a present statement. The flexible use of Hebrew verb forms in relation to tense in poetic language does not help clarify the situation. If we read the verb forms in vv. 11-12 as past thus implying confidence based on what has already happened, and see the use of the perfect of *'āmar* in v. 4 indicating past speech ('I said'), then we could see the whole of vv. 4-10 as a quotation by David of a past lament and petition. On the other hand, it can be argued that the formula 'I said/say', usually introduces actual speech and not reported past speech (cf. Pss. 31.14; 40.7, 10; 75.4; 119.57; 140.6; 142.5 etc.). The petition in v. 10 is, therefore, of immediate concern. The argument can go either way.

In vv. 11-12, David expresses confidence in Yahweh and the assurance of vindication through his own integrity (a legal term indicating innocence of the charge brought) and through the presence of Yahweh. As noted above this could be a statement of past vindication or one of confidence almost in defiance of present difficulties. In either case, David knows Yahweh delights in him and has supported him and made him stand in the divine presence. This is the ultimate statement of assurance and 'victory'.

The psalm ends in v. 13 with a doxology similar to those in Pss. 72.18-19; 89.52; and 106.48. These doxologies respectively conclude Books I through IV within the Psalter. It is suggested that the whole of Psalm 150 functions as the doxology to Book V. In the case of Books I–IV, the doxologies do not connect with the content of the psalms to which they are attached. It is debated whether they originally belonged to the four psalms concerned or were added later to divide the Psalter. If the former is the case the four psalms were probably chosen specifically to conclude the books. The fact that the doxology in Ps. 106.47-48 is quoted in 1 Chron. 16.35-36 as part of Psalm 106 suggests that as early as the time of writing Chronicles, the doxologies were already in their present positions.

The relatively simple doxology following Psalm 41 seeks everlasting praise for Yahweh, the God of Israel. Its placement at the end of Psalm 41 is appropriate as is the placement of that psalm at the end of Book I. The psalm has underlined the utter dependence of David on Yahweh who alone can protect, support and deliver the poor from their enemies. He is even closer than friends who can be fickle in the neediest of circumstances. It is Yahweh who sets David in his presence 'forever'. It is fitting David blesses Yahweh 'from everlasting to everlasting'.

The double ʾāmēn at the conclusion of the doxology, also the case with Pss. 72.19 and 89.52, might suggest a liturgical response. Certainly, Ps. 106.48 suggests that with its 'and let all the people say, "Amen." '. The quotation of that verse in 1 Chron. 16.36 employs the doxology as an actual liturgical response by the people. If the doxologies are linked to such responses then the constant emphasis on David as a model of faith for the people and the one who instructs them in prayer is reiterated.

Psalm 41 may have begun life as a lament in time of illness. Its significance now lies beyond that narrow setting. It has been taken up into the prayers of David, and the prayers of Israel, as instruction in trust in Yahweh, even in the most difficult times when all including friends stand in opposition. The end of Book I of the Psalter, in anticipation of the end of the Psalter itself, speaks of David being taken into the presence of Yahweh forever. Nothing else can one hope for, other than a resounding response of *bārûk* Yahweh, 'Blessed be Yahweh', from the entire congregation. This may have been enacted in the temple liturgy but in this collection of prayers its meaning goes beyond those physical confines.

The psalm keeps its instructional function at the end of Book I. The opening verse gives rise to the question: 'what does David learn from considering the poor?' He learns what has been reiterated throughout the book, that Yahweh remains with him when he is 'poor and needy' (Ps. 40.17). He learns that his restoration depends on Yahweh who sustains the poor. And he learns that his struggle with those who oppose him will likewise depend on Yahweh. Those points were already present in Psalm 1–2 at the start of Book I.

Book II

Book II begins with the first psalms attributed to someone other than David. Psalms 42–49 are a collection of psalms of the Korahites. Psalm 50 is attributed to Asaph. The Korahites, like the Asaphites, are described in the Books of Chronicles as Levitical singers established by David to serve in the house of Yahweh (1 Chr. 6.31-37; 16.4-7). The collections attributed to these groups might have originated in sanctuaries outside Jerusalem. With Psalm 51 we return to Davidic psalms (Psalms 51–70) although Psalms 42–50 are connected to the Davidic collection at the seam by each of Psalms 47–51 being designating a *mizmôr*, a song accompanied by stringed instrument (NRSV: 'a psalm'). In the midst of the David collection Psalms 66 and 67 appear with titles but no personal attribution. Again these are tied into the Davidic collection by designating Psalms 65–68 each as a *šîr*, 'a song'. The collections within Book II, are therefore, tied closely together. Finally, Book II finishes with Psalm 71 with no title and Psalm 72 attributed to Solomon.

The introduction of Korah and Asaph psalms raises a question of whether we can any longer see David as psalmist. While this might be a question in the opening psalm (Psalms 42–43), the military imagery in Psalm 44, the royal Psalm 45 and Zion Psalm 46, together with collection directly associated with David through their superscriptions (Psalms 51–70, minus 66, 67) and the connection of psalms across collection seams through genre terms, all suggest that we are meant to keep reading these as David's psalms. The concluding remark in Ps. 72:20 about David's prayers supports this.

One other point introduced in Book II is the predominance of the divine title *ʾelōhîm*, 'God'. Book I mainly spoke of Yahweh. The use of *ʾelōhîm* continues to Psalm 83 in Book III.

Psalms 42–45

Psalms 42 and 43 are really one psalm with a refrain joining them (Pss. 42.5–6a, 11; 43.5). Together they form a lament built on images of water (streams, tears, deep, cataracts, waves, and billows), thirst and mourning. The lament continues the mood at the end of Book I. A second refrain, occurring in Ps. 42.3, 10, comes from others who constantly ask 'Where is your God?' The play on the personal pronoun related to God is a feature of the psalm. While the adversaries distance themselves constantly asking about '*your* God', David gladly claims his relationship with God speaking in the main refrain about '*my* help and *my* God' (cf. also '*my*' in 42.8, 9; 43.4, and 'the God in whom I take refuge', 43.2). Memory also plays a part in this psalm. As he laments, David remembers how he has faithfully led others in worship (42.4) and, above all, remembers God as creator, and his 'steadfast love' (42.6-8). It is all the more painful that God seems to have forgotten David (42.9). It makes the question of the adversaries all the more real. Nevertheless, David still sees God as his refuge (43.2; *māʿôz*, cf. Pss. 27.1; 31.2, 4; 37.39) and prays for vindication, vowing to return to God's sanctuary which he loves (43.4; cf. 42.4; and Pss. 26.8; 27.4).

Psalm 44 is the first community lament we read, speaking of defeat in battle. It begins with remembrance of the past, specifically when God gave Israel the promised land (vv. 1-3). Like the ancestors David, as leader in battle, does not rely on his own strength but in God (vv. 4-8). The effect of this reliance should be the same for David as for the ancestors, but apparently it is not. Verses 9-16 state the problem clearly. God has rejected the people and they are scattered among the nations. Each of vv. 9-14 details God's rejection ('You have ...') in contrast to David's statement of allegiance in v. 4. The military context is clear but so is the hint at exile, especially that after 587 BCE. Exile is some way off yet, but we already have the sense that David's prayers are relevant to that later situation. While David feels shame (v. 15) God appears guilty. David proclaims the faithfulness of the people, which God would surely know (vv. 17-22). They remember the past (vv. 1-3) and do not forget God now (vv. 17, 20) in contrast to God who has forgotten them (v. 24). In images of waking another from sleep and with an allusion to Gen. 3.14, 19, David calls for their redemption for the sake of God's 'steadfast love' (vv. 23-26).

The mood changes dramatically in **Psalm 45** in what appears to be a psalm for a royal wedding. The superscription lists it as a 'love song'. An unknown singer addresses the psalm first to the king (vv. 1-9), turning then to the queen (vv. 10-15), and returning to the king (vv. 16-17). The whole psalm is in praise of the king. He is victorious in battle (vv. 4-5), exercising justice and equity (vv. 6-7a). He has been anointed by God (v. 7). It ends with possibly God replying that he will establish the king's line and cause his name to be celebrated forever with praise from the people. The reference to anointing and victory reminds of Psalm 2, while his handsome features recall the description of David in 1 Sam. 16.12.

Psalm 46

Psalms 42–43 and 44 both end with matters unresolved. The former concludes with a vow of praise if God will send out light and truth (Ps. 43.4) while the latter ends with a desperate plea for divine assistance (44.26). Psalms 45–48 provide the assurance that is needed. In Psalm 45 there is the assurance of the presence of God's anointed king in his palace. Now in Psalm 46 assurance comes in the form of the description of the city of God as symbolic of God as refuge.

Psalm 46 falls into three sections: vv. 1-3—God as refuge in creation; vv. 4-7—God as refuge as seen in the city; and vv. 8-11—God as refuge who brings peace. A refrain concludes each of the last two sections (vv. 7, 11), although it is absent in the first section, i.e. after v. 3. However, v. 1 does speak of God as refuge, albeit with a different word, and so each section states confidence in God as refuge, and an *inclusio* is formed around the whole psalm on this theme. The psalm is a threefold account of the security provided by God interspersed with statements of confidence.

The psalm is often called a 'Song of Zion' because of the description of the city. Other songs, including Psalms 48, 76, 84, 87, and 122, also focus on Zion. The theme is also found in the prophecies of Isaiah (e.g. Isa. 33.17-22). However, in the case of Psalm 46 we note that there is only mention of the 'city of God' which is not named, and the emphasis of the psalm is not so much on the city itself as on what it represents for the people. Psalm 46 is a psalm about God as refuge. The description of the city serves that purpose. Some 'Songs of Zion', especially Psalms 46, 48, and 76, might be associated with the siege of Jerusalem in 701BCE in the reign of King Hezekiah, and its marvellous deliverance from the Assyrians (2 Kings 18–19 and Isaiah 36–37), or to later threats to Jerusalem. However, these connections are not certain. Moreover, Psalm 46 has affinities to the ancient 'Song of the Sea', Exod. 15.1-18.

David boldly proclaims, on behalf of the congregation, the assurance of God's protection right from the start of the psalm. Verse 1 collects a number of words implying that very notion: 'refuge' ($maḥ^aseh$); 'strength'; and 'help' ($^cezrâ$, implying protection and strength). It is as such that God 'lets himself be found/is found' (NRSV: 'a very present', Heb. $nimṣā'$). Alliteration underlines the point: $wā^cōz$-$^cezrâ$, 'and strength—help'; $b^eṣārōt$—$nimṣā'$, 'in trouble—lets himself be found'. It recalls the earlier thoughts on Yahweh as refuge (Pss. 7.1; 11.1 etc.). The immediate result of this statement is that 'we will not fear'. Fear and anxiety were evident at the end of Psalm 44. Now David urges the congregation not to let such fear conquer them, setting up fear and confidence in God as opposites. In neither case are difficulties foregone (v. 1). It is a matter of how one faces them.

In each section David gives a reason why fear should no longer rule over them. Verses 2-3 turn the old creation imagery of the battle between the seas and the creator god on its head. This theology was possibly part of the earlier tradition of Jerusalem/ Zion before it was conquered by David. Now David describes what could be called an 'undoing of creation' in terms of the tumult of the earth, the mountains tottering, the seas roaring and foaming. Even if that were to happen, there would be no need for fear because 'God is our refuge'. The one who is creator (cf. Ps. 24.1-2) can counter even cosmic disruption. We sense immediately that confidence in God is an offshoot of faith in God as creator. The way David sets these verses up underlines the point. The simple and calm statement that God is refuge is followed by, yet is not challenged by, the mounting up of images of cosmic fury and power.

Another statement of confidence opens the second section. It speaks first of a river 'whose streams make glad the city of God, the holy habitation of the Most High' (v. 4). The water imagery is maintained from vv. 2-3 but the atmosphere has changed from raging seas to a pleasant, delightful river setting. If the psalm has Zion/Jerusalem in mind then we could ask what river is understood. The only water supply to Jerusalem was from the Gihon spring (1 Kgs 1.33; 2 Chr. 32.30) but it is unlikely that this gave rise to the imagery in the psalm. More likely, there is a reference to the mythic tradition of life-giving waters issuing in a controlled manner from the temple or altar where the deity resided. This tradition was widespread in ancient Near Eastern literature. The high god at Ugarit in Syria, El, resided 'at the source of the (two) rivers, in the midst of the fountains of the two deeps'. The tradition survives in biblical texts, e.g. Ezek. 47.1-12 (cf. Gen. 2.10-14; Ps. 65.7-10).

The presence of life-giving water signifies the presence of God in the city, which, as a consequence, shall not be moved (v. 5a). The Hebrew verb, *môṭ*, 'to totter', is used here as it was of the mountains shaking in the heart of the sea in v. 2b. Moreover, God will help (*'āzar*; cf. *'ezrâ*, 'help' in v. 1b) the city when dawn breaks. The latter reference may be a sign of imminent help, i.e. coming at the earliest time battle can be engaged. On the other hand, some psalms suggest that dawn or morning was a time associated with salvation or hope (Pss. 5.3; 30.5; 90.14; 130.6; 143.8).

The result of this is revealed in vv. 6-7. The cosmic gives way to the political. The nations are in an uproar (*hāmâ*, 'to roar' in v. 3) and the kingdoms totter (*môṭ*, 'to totter' in vv. 2b and 5). The same verbs are used in the description of cosmic disruption. Being unsteady on one's feet is an image of destruction (e.g. Pss. 17.5; 18.36; 35.36 etc.). When God utters his voice the earth melts. Then follows the refrain: 'Yahweh of hosts is with us, Jacob's God is our fortress.' 'Yahweh of hosts' evokes the old war imagery of Yahweh (1 Sam. 4.4; 15.2; 17.45; 1 Kgs 18.15; 2 Kgs 3.14), the ark tradition (2 Sam. 6.2, 18) and the Davidic tradition (2 Sam. 7.8, 26, 27). The phrase is used in Ps. 24.10 in reference to Yahweh demanding entry to the city/temple. It is confined in use to 'Songs of Zion' (Psalms 48 and 84). The use of *miśgāb*, 'fortress' (NRSV: 'refuge'; cf. also Pss. 9.9; 18.2) develops the metaphor of refuge, conveying a sense of solidity and inviolability (cf. Isa. 33.16 etc.). The city is a symbol for God's protective presence. Moreover the reference to ancestors of Israel in the 'God of Jacob' evokes the history of God's protection of the people. The quiet strength of the refrain within the city stands in contrast to the terrifying scenes of the nations and the cosmos in uproar outside. Such is the certainty of God 'with us', *'immānû*.

In the final section, vv. 8-11, David addresses the congregation, although it could be read as an address to the nations themselves (cf. Ps. 2.10-12). The refrain (v. 11), however, definitely returns to the voice of the congregation. The focus is eschatological, calling for attention to be given to the marvels of God, the desolations wrought in the earth and especially the end of all wars. The breaking and burning of weapons signifies both victory and the end of opposition (cf. Josh. 11.6, 9; Isa. 2.4 and 9.4).

In this section the warrior image of God is reversed. His victory truly means a rest from all war. God is described as *mašbît milḥāmôt*, 'one who causes wars to cease', with a deliberate play on the noun *šabbāt*, Sabbath.

In this context, the voice of God enters calling the nations and/ or the congregation to 'be still, and know (Yahweh) is God' (v. 10). The meaning of *rāpâ* in the causative form as here is 'to let go, relax, refrain, forsake'. The NRSV 'be still' is, thus, not a call to quiet reflection, but a call to forsake what has gone before. For the nations that means abandoning opposition to Yahweh. For the congregation, it has many meanings: forsaking the fear that has gripped them (cf. v. 2); letting go of trust in their own strength (cf. Ps. 44.3, 6–7); and allowing Yahweh to be their God. Fear will achieve nothing because God is powerful enough for any opposition, the power of opponents is as nothing, and one's own powers are insufficient to save. Concluding that 'we will not fear' in v. 2 was not a call for bravery or heroism, but rather a creedal statement about God.

Yahweh is the one who is exalted, lifted high among the nations and on earth. Opposition turns into praise in this royal context. The invincible warrior is also king. The threefold use of *'ereṣ*, 'earth/land', in vv. 8-10 both emphasizes the extent of Yahweh's rule and, through the ambiguity of land (political domain vs earth), signals that what happens within the congregation's immediate context has cosmic ramifications and vice-versa. It brings together the first two sections of the psalm in this eschatological vision. The congregation responds with the refrain in v. 11. With its word order, *miśgāb lānû*, 'a fortress for us', it echoes the initial statement about God in v. 1, *'elōhîm lānû*, 'God for us', and underscores David's central statement.

The emphasis on God as refuge is fitting following psalms where threats abound. The presence of God's anointed in Psalm 45 and the use of the city as a metaphor for God's protection in this psalm, both bolster confidence in God in the face of many dangers. The uses of the myth of creation as well as the physical strength of the city reinforce the message and question any fear expressed. David gives no promise of the removal of danger or threat, but calls for holding a firm faith in God in the face of such things. In later psalms, the stability of creation will be evidence of Yahweh's reign over all (e.g. Ps. 93.1-2). Here, not even the undoing of creation poses a threat to that, let alone the turmoil among the nations.

The use of the city as a metaphor for God's protection undergirds the connection of this psalm with David, especially in the refrain in vv. 7 and 11. While the psalm may be attributed to the Korahites, it speaks with the voice of David, whose own tradition is intricately connected with that of Zion, especially through the arc tradition. David himself calls for absolute confidence in God. How this will work itself out in the face of the later sacking of Jerusalem and the exile we will have to wait to see.

Psalms 47–49

In language similar in places to Psalm 46, David calls upon the people in **Psalm 47** to clap their hands and shout for joy for Yahweh is king over all the earth. Yahweh has subdued nations (v. 2), is highly exalted, and possesses the shields of the earth, a symbol of the cessation of war. Likewise, in language and imagery building on Psalm 46, David celebrates in **Psalm 48**, another 'Song of Zion', the kingship of God established to the ends of the earth against the threat of the kings of the nations (v. 4). The city again symbolizes the 'sure defence' that is 'our God' (vv. 3, 14). In contrast to Psalm 46, the city is described in more detail (48.1b, 12–13). Both Psalms 47 and 48 employ the old mythic language of combat (47.3; 48.1c ['Mount Zion, in the far north']). Verbal links also exist between Psalms 46–48: 'to be glad' (46.4; 48.11); 'the ends of the earth' (46.9; 48.10); and certain ideas are carried on through synonyms—joy (47.1; 48.2) and exaltation (46.10; 47.9).

With **Psalm 49** the genre changes dramatically to a more reflective wisdom psalm. However, the psalm does pick up and develop motifs from its predecessors. Fear arising from cosmic and national turbulence was addressed in Psalm 46. In Ps. 49.5 David asks why he should fear in times of trouble and later urges others not to be afraid (v. 16). The types of difficulties envisaged are not national or military but those caused by the 'iniquity ... of those who trust in their wealth' (vv. 5-6). Nevertheless, continuity is implied between the sorts of troubles described in Psalm 46 and that now surveyed. In a manner similar to Proverbs and Ecclesiastes, David reflects in Psalm 49 on matters of wealth and wisdom. These things cannot ransom one's life (v. 7) only God can do that according to v. 15. The emphasis in the psalm is on the issue of death. The foolish and the wise both die (vv. 8-10). The difference for those whom David urges not to fear is that while death will shepherd those who are 'self-confident'

(NRSV: 'foolhardy') to the grave (vv. 13-14), God will lead them 'to death' (Ps. 48.14c; NRSV: 'forever'). The whole point of Psalm 49 following Psalms 45–48 is to raise the question of who guides one through life and who is the source of one's confidence and 'fearlessness'.

Psalm 50

The first group of Korah psalms ends with Psalm 49. Psalm 50, a lone Asaph psalm, provides a bridge to the next group of David psalms. A group of Asaph psalms (Psalms 73–83) begins Book III of the Psalter. Asaph, according to 1 Chronicles, was a Levitical priest and one of those David put in charge of music before the tabernacle of God (see 1 Chron. 6.31-48; 15.17; 16.7, 37).

Psalms 42–43 and 44 were laments over individual and community troubles respectively. Psalms 45–48 addressed those troubles calling for confidence and trust. The presence of the anointed king and God's own kingship, likened to the strength of the city, were both points on which confidence could be built. Psalm 50 now looks further into the relation between God and the faithful. It ends with an open invitation to understand what is said and to offer thanksgiving to God. Psalm 51, a prayer of confession, will act as a response.

Psalm 50 falls into four sections. Verses 1-6 provide an introduction by way of a theophany. In vv. 7-15 God addresses the faithful about genuine sacrifice and then, in vv. 16-21, rebukes the wicked. Finally, in vv. 22-23 God calls those who forget God to understand what has been said and then describes the sacrifice that truly honours God. Apart from the theophany the whole psalm is an address by God to the people. Throughout there are references to speech and speaking. The sins of the wicked involve speech as do the sacrifices that are desired by God, thanksgiving and payment of vows. Even the central discussion on the meaning of sacrifice is described in terms of eating, another activity of the mouth.

The focus on speech could suggest a connection to prophetic words. The discussion of sacrifice recalls prophetic questioning of sacrificial practices (Isa. 1.10-17; 58; Jeremiah 7; Amos 5.21-24; Mic. 6.6-8; cf. Ps. 40.6-8), and the gathering of witnesses suggests a trial scene, frequent in the prophets. Alternatively, the background to Psalm 50 could be a festival of covenant renewal (cf. also Psalm 81) with reference to gathering, mention of covenant, sacrifices and allusions to the Ten Commandments. In this case, the aim would be not so much celebration as instruction and reprimand about worship in general.

The psalm opens with a barrage of divine names, *'ēl 'ᵉlōhîm yhwh*, variously translated as 'the mighty one/God, God the Lord' or 'El, God, Yahweh,' etc. (cf. Josh. 22.22). There is no doubt who comes forth and summons the earth in v. 1. However, whereas in other theophanies God or Yahweh comes from a distant place (cf. Deut. 33.2; Judg. 5.4-5; Hab. 3.3; Ps. 68.8), in Ps. 50.2 God shines forth from Zion itself, the very city which symbolizes God's protection, the city whose beauty was noted in Ps. 48.1 as it is in 50.2. God shines forth in the midst of the people, a sign of deliverance to the faithful (Ps. 80.3; cf. Deut. 33.2) but judgment to those who oppose it (Ps. 94.1).

There is a summons for all creation to be present when God judges his people—the earth both east and west, and the heavens which declare God's righteousness as judge (vv. 1, 4, 5). God calls for *ḥᵃsîday* 'my faithful ones,' to be gathered. These have made covenant with God by sacrifice. There is no little irony in this summons. As we will see God rebukes his people over the nature of their sacrifice in vv. 7-15 and then castigates the 'wicked' among them for their behaviour. A question mark accompanies God's calling them 'faithful ones' in v. 5. Likewise, while they have made a covenant by means of sacrifice, some seem to think sacrifice is all that is necessary to maintain the covenant. However, this irony should not be interpreted as a blanket rejection of the 'faithful ones', their sacrifice, or the covenant between them and God as we will see.

In coming with fire and tempest, God will not 'keep silence' (*ḥāraš*). The presence of this word underscores the ambiguity in calling the people 'faithful ones'. The word appears several times in the Psalter. God's silence is like death (Ps. 28.1) or is a synonym for judgment (35.22). In laments it stands for a lack of attention and response by God (39.13; 83.2; 109.1). But in Ps. 50.3 God does not keep silence. One might presume God's coming now signals hope for God's people. It means deliverance as God turns from silence toward them. But as it turns out the matter is not that simple.

The description of the theophany in vv. 3-6 draws heavily on the language of the Mosaic covenant in the Book of Exodus. The fire and tempest are reminiscent of the scene at Sinai (Exod. 19.16-19) and the latter is associated with theophany in Deut. 33.2 and Ps. 68.8. This means that the traditions of Sinai, and the power they have within the community, are transferred to Zion, the city of God. The power of the city as symbol for God's protective strength lies not only in its own attributes as a fortress but with the traditions that are now associated with it.

In v. 7 God begins a lengthy speech that will carry through the rest of the psalm. The first section of the speech, vv. 7-15 is addressed to God's people in general. It starts dramatically with the first and last words of v. 7 echoing the famous *Shema* of Deut. 6.4, although now spoken by God: cf. Ps. 50.7a,c, 'Hear, O my people, ... I am God, your God', with Deut. 6.4, 'Hear, O Israel: Yahweh is our God, Yahweh alone.' Moreover, Ps. 50.7c recalls part of the covenant formula, '... I will be your God' (see Exod. 6.7; Lev 26.12; cf. Exod. 20.2; Deut 5.6). These are powerful words and one hears in them the God of the Sinai covenant speaking to the covenant people. But what a shock the words in v. 7b are: 'I will testify against you.' The covenant God speaks against '(his) faithful one, who made covenant with (him) by sacrifice!' The heavens and the earth, like the gods listed in ancient Near Eastern treaty agreements, are there to witness the charge God has to bring against the people (cf. Deut. 4.26; 30.19; 31.28; 32.1; Isa. 1.2).

The central concern is stated in v. 8. It has to do with sacrifice. But the detailed nature of the rebuke is not yet fully revealed. God does not rebuke them for their lack of attention to sacrifices (v. 8a). Their offerings have been continually before God (v. 8b). On the other hand, God says in v. 9 'I will not take', or 'I need not take', a bull or a goat from them. Is a total rejection of sacrifice envisioned as implied in the prophetic passages noted above? Verses 10-12 could be read in that vein. All creatures belong to God and if God were hungry he would not need to tell the people. The idea of sacrifice providing food for the gods is found in Babylonian texts (*Enuma Elish*, VI.8, 110-120; *Gilgamesh*, XI.156-161). It has the effect of making the deity dependent upon worshippers. But that is not the case here. What is acceptable is a thanksgiving sacrifice (*tôdâ*) and the fulfilment of vows, both related to the answering of prayer in times of trouble (vv. 14-15). These have also been stressed in earlier psalms (Pss. 7.17; 9.1; 22.25; 26.7; 28.7; 30.4, 12; 42.4; 44.8). These two types of sacrifice still involve the offering of animals (Lev. 7.15; 22.21, 23, 29) so God's rebuke does not relate to the act of animal sacrifice itself. Rather, it has something to do with the spirit of the offerings. The offering of thanksgiving and fulfilment of vows brings sacrifice full circle. It is not just a matter of manipulating God through sacrifice, but of genuine prayer and conversion based on a deep relationship. Thanksgiving and payment of vows imply response to the one who has responded to the prayer for help. Verses 14-15 speak about this relationship. God does not simply seek his own satisfaction in sacrifice but a deepening of relationship with the people. That is why the covenant is alluded to for it is the heart of the relationship between God and the people (cf. Ps. 40.6-8). The sacrificial system is not totally rejected, but a superficial understanding of it is, wherein sacrifice is reduced to God's supposed needs and human self-interest. This section on sacrifice picks up what has just been said in Psalm 49. There it was stated that no wealth of one's own can ransom one's life. There is nothing a person can do to redeem another or themselves (49.7-9). In Psalm 50 the point is not the wealth of the sacrifice, nor the mechanics of it, but rather the relationship behind sacrifice. That is what addresses the fear in times of trouble.

The object of God's address changes in vv. 16-21 to the wicked. In previous psalms the wicked have been other nations or foreigners, but here they are clearly people who recite God's statutes and profess themselves as covenant partners. In other words, the wicked here are members of the community whose outward practice of the faith is not in harmony with their other activities. The description of those activities draws on the language of the Ten Commandments citing theft, adultery and false witness against a neighbour (vv. 18-20; cf. Exod. 20.14-16; Deut. 5.18-20). These people resist discipline and dispense with God's word in spite of reciting the statutes and claiming the covenant. Their friends are thieves and their 'portion' ($\d{h}\bar{e}leq$: NRSV: 'company') is with adulterers. This latter term is used in covenant and treaty contexts (e.g. Deut. 29.26; 32.9) thus providing a foil for both the profession of the wicked, who take God's covenant 'on their lips' (v. 16), and the theme of the speech on sacrifice in vv. 7-15.

Verses 16-21 return to the vocabulary of mouth and speech— 'recite', 'lips', 'words', 'mouth', 'tongue', 'deceit', 'speak against', 'slander'—picking up the start of the psalm. The words of the wicked contrast with the lack of words or the silence of God. This had been interpreted as divine complicity and approval (v. 21). They could not be further from the truth, for as far as silence is from speech, so is God's approval from their deceit. God is not 'just like' them and rebukes them. If God had been like them the earlier speech on sacrifice would not have been necessary.

God concludes the speech in vv. 22-23 by addressing both those who forget God, the wicked just mentioned, and those who respond with thanksgiving, a genuine sacrifice. The whole community hears this address, both those who fall among 'the wicked' and those who respond with thanksgiving. Those who forget God should 'understand this' (NRSV: 'Mark this') or God, pictured as a ravenous lion, will tear them apart (cf. Hos. 5.14; Amos 1.2 etc.). There will be no one to deliver them. But to those who bring thanksgiving as their sacrifice, honouring God, God will show them salvation. The contrast between the two groups is sharp, although it is the whole community who hears both promises. Just as the title 'faithful ones' was unclear in v. 5 in terms of to whom it referred, so now the promises of judgment and salvation are held before all. We should compare the possible redemption of the wicked here with that implied in Psalms 1-2.

This psalm has a lot to say about distortion and falsity. It speaks about the nature of genuine sacrifice and the idolatrous images of God that can be generated to support superficial practices. It speaks about the false language and professions of the wicked. In this situation God even speaks in ways that are not clear. But in that very fact lies hope for even the wicked. If they understand, then they too can know deliverance. In what follows in Psalm 51 we will see an example of a faithful response from one who has sinned against God.

Psalm 51

With Psalm 51 it is fitting that we return to psalms attributed directly to David. It has been suggested that this is a prayer of someone gravely ill, but the language of sin and confession outweighs that which could indicate illness, and there are no complaints typical of lament psalms. This is a great penitential psalm which has had a complex history.

The psalm has two main sections, vv. 1-9 and 10-17, each of which has been carefully constructed. The focus of vv. 1-9 is primarily on past sins and circumstances that affect the present and require attention by God. By way of contrast, vv. 10-17 look more toward a future that will arise from God's forgiveness. Everywhere the action of God is determinative for the story, even though talk of human sinfulness dominates. Verses 18-19 are a late addition to the psalm.

Psalm 51

The superscription to Psalm 51 is one of the longer and more specific ones in the Psalter. The psalm is associated with David's adulterous relationship with Bathsheba, and the prophet Nathan's subsequent confrontation with the king. The story is found in 2 Samuel 11–12 and in that context is determinative for the later course of David's reign. A number of verbal connections exist between the psalm and the Samuel account, especially in David's response to Nathan: David confesses he has sinned against Yahweh (2 Sam. 12.13; cf. Ps. 51.4a); David shows great contrition and concern for Bathsheba's child when it is dying (2 Sam. 12.15-17; cf. Ps. 51.17); David depends on the graciousness of Yahweh (2 Sam. 12.22; cf. Ps. 51.1; *ḥānan*, 'to be gracious, merciful'). In *The Midrash on Psalms* it is surmised that David penned Psalm 51 immediately he heard Nathan say 'Yahweh has put away your sin' (2 Sam. 12.13). The association of Psalm 51 with what is arguably David's gravest sin in the Books of Samuel portrays him not only as a repentant sinner but one who brings hope to all other sinners.

David begins the section vv. 1-9 with a petition (vv. 1-2) and ends with one (vv. 7-9). These are connected through common words to form an *inclusio*. The common terms are: 'to blot out', *māhâ*, vv. 1, 9; 'sin', *ḥaṭṭā't*, vv. 2, 9; 'iniquity', *'āwōn*, vv. 2, 9; 'to wash', *kibbēs*, vv. 2, 7. The central part of the section is a confession. Both petition and confession focus on God. David's sin may be what gives rise to the psalm, but he does not linger on that. He addresses God immediately in vv. 1-2, seeking mercy, according to God's 'steadfast love' and 'abundant mercy'. No mention is yet made of his sin and his reason for the petition. God's mercy is seen foremost to flow from God's own nature (cf. Exod. 34.6). The three characteristics of God listed here are matched by three verbs in the petition ('blot out', 'wash', and 'cleanse') and three words for David's sin ('transgressions', 'iniquity', and 'sin'). The generality implied in this variety of words, in singular and plural forms, counters the detail of the sin in the superscription. It seems that while the episode with Bathsheba becomes the context within which the psalm is read, it remains a prayer for all occasions of sin, indeed even about sin in general.

In verses 3-6 David develops this broader reflection. He is aware of his transgressions (plural) and his sin is 'continually' (*tāmîd*: NRSV: 'ever') before him. This word is used many times in psalms. So far it has been used to describe the pray-er's faithfulness or prayer toward God (Pss. 16.8; 25.15; 34.1; 35.27; 40.16).

It was used ironically in Ps. 50.8 in that way. But what is continually before David now in 51.3 is his own sin(fullness). In this statement David both underscores the irony of Ps. 50.8, and is thereby portrayed in Psalm 51 as the truly faithful one, and develops the point made back in Ps. 49.7. The point in v. 3 is reiterated with slight difference in v. 5. This verse is not about conception or sex or the 'passing on' of sin. It is a way of saying that humans are inevitably caught in a web of sin and sinfulness all their lives.

This is one of the two reasons David seeks God's mercy. These reasons are introduced formally in vv. 3-5 by the particle *kî*, 'for'. The other reason (v. 4) is that his sin has been against God alone. This may sound strange given the connection made in the superscription. Did not David sin against Bathsheba and her husband Uriah? But the point made in the psalm is not so much about who is wronged (the most) in any particular sinful act. A theological point is made about sinfulness in general, and sin in its particularities, and the nature of repentance. David did sin against other people and there is need for confession and reconciliation between the parties involved. But in terms of David's redemption and his sinfulness in general, the key to those matters lies in the relationship between David and God. The two are, of course, connected. David's action against Bathsheba and Uriah affects his relation with God. Moreover, it is the relationship with God which names the former as sin. David can only attend to his relationship with others as he addresses that deeper, more intimate relationship with God who desires truth in 'the inward parts' and who can impart wisdom to David in his 'secret heart', i.e. where decision and feelings originate (v. 6; cf. Ps. 49.1-4). The point is already recognized in the Samuel story (2 Sam. 12.7-15a). Elsewhere in the Old Testament, especially in late writings, sin is primarily seen as against God, even when it involves action against another person (e.g. Gen. 39.9; Prov. 14.31; 17.5; and esp. Lev. 6.2-7). In light of this the statement that only God can ransom one's life in Ps. 49.15 makes sense. So, God is justified and blameless in his words and judgment (Ps. 51.4b). There is no sense in which David is deserving of compassion, but every sense in which he is dependent on God.

In a second petition (vv. 7-9), David seeks forgiveness, again using the full range of language of washing and sins (cf. vv. 1-2). He may allude to purification rites such as those in Leviticus 14 and Numbers 19 which involve hyssop, blood and washing. The aim of this petition is that David is restored to a life of joy and gladness (v. 8a), that he, a 'crushed' (from *dākâ*) or broken person (cf. Jer. 23.9), may rejoice again. While the whole of vv. 7-9 forms an *inclusio* with vv. 1-2, there is a smaller *inclusio* within the later verses formed by the two petitions (vv. 7 and 9) around the hope of joy.

The second major section, vv. 10-17, has a complex interlocking structure. It also has an *inclusio*, this time revolving around the words 'heart' and 'spirit' (vv. 10, 17). Further patterns are present within the section. Verses 10-12 are bound together around the word 'spirit'; while in vv. 10-15 a series of petitions (vv. 10-12, 14a, 15a) is each followed by an anticipated result (vv. 13, 14b, 15b). The section concludes with a statement about acceptable sacrifices (vv. 16-17).

Verses 10-12 form a tight unit. In the Hebrew, the second half of each verse begins with the word 'spirit' (*rûaḥ*). Verse 11 in the centre of the sequence contains two negative requests and asks that God's 'holy spirit' (cf. Isa. 63.10-11) not be taken from David. This provides another link with the story of David in the Books of Samuel (cf. 1 Sam. 16.13) but also implies that while as a sinner David is in danger of losing God's holy spirit, his sin itself does not automatically deprive him of the life-giving divine presence or spirit. The outer verses (vv. 10, 12) contain positive requests about the spirit within David himself, although there is some ambiguity over whether the 'spirit' referred to is one granted by God or is David's own spirit renewed in some way. In any case it is clear that the renewing work is that of God, and depends on God keeping David in his presence.

The verb *bārā'*, 'create', a verb restricted to the creative work of God (cf. Genesis 1; Isa. 43.15; 48. 7; 41.20; and 45.7-8) is used in v. 10, thus linking David's forgiveness with the life-giving, ordering work of God in the cosmos. The idea of a 'new' or renewed spirit (cf. Ezek. 11.19; 18.31; 36.26) is also consistent with other aspects of newness in the exilic and early post-exilic prophets (see esp. Isa. 42.9-10; 43.19; 65.17; 66.22; Jer. 31.22, 31). The connection with the Ezekiel passages is particularly strong for each of them speaks of a 'new heart' as well as a new spirit. It is this newness of heart and spirit that will allow David to remain in the divine presence. The joy he desired to hear in v. 8 is that experienced in God's salvation (v. 12).

The consequence of the petition in vv. 10-12 is that David will take up a role of teaching transgressors God's ways (v. 13).

Having been instructed himself by God (Pss. 25.4-5, 9, 12; 27.11) and especially taught wisdom in his secret heart (Ps. 51.6), David now takes up his own teaching role as anticipated in Ps. 34.11. In the context of this psalm we see that repentance and forgiveness lead not only to praise and thanksgiving but to public proclamation. While sin is essentially an offence against God alone (Ps. 51.4) restoration from sin never remains a private affair. References to the transgressors and sinners in v. 13 who will be affected by this response of David, link back to the initial petition of the psalm (vv. 1-2).

David then seeks to be delivered from 'bloodshed' (*dāmîm*) so that he may sing aloud of God's deliverance. The specific meaning of 'bloodshed' is not entirely clear. Several possibilities can be posited and nearly all of them make sense in this context. 'Bloodshed' can refer to a particular crime, particularly murder (cf. Pss. 59.2; 139.19). It can also be used to refer simply to death (Ps. 30.9). Hence, David may be seeking deliverance from those who endanger him, although there is no reference to enemies in this psalm. 'Bloodshed' can also be used to speak of murderers (lit. 'men of bloodshed') but in the sense that they are abhorred by God (Ps. 5.6). They are also associated with deceit or treachery in Ps. 55.23. These will be cast into the pit. David might be seeking disassociation from such types and their punishment in Ps. 51.14. In Ps. 9.12 Yahweh is the one who avenges bloodshed in such cases. Finally, 'bloodshed' can be used as a term for guilt (e.g. Isa. 4.4; Ezek. 18.13) and so David may again simply be asking for forgiveness.

The point coming through in this psalm, and from Psalm 50, is that the forgiveness of sins is not, as might be implied by such words as 'blotting out', simply a matter of removing something undesirable. Rather, it involves a deep renewing of the person which affects many aspects of life. In v. 13, David vowed to teach transgressors God's ways. Now he vows, if Yahweh will open his lips, to praise God publicly (v. 15). This opens up the whole question of the nature of acceptable praise. The discussion begun in some detail in Ps. 50.9-15 is taken up again here. The seeming rejection of sacrifice is stated and then followed by what is an acceptable sacrifice: a broken spirit and a broken and contrite heart. The mention of 'heart' and 'spirit' bring the second main section of the psalm to a close, completing the *inclusio* with v. 10. On the other hand, it suggests that the creation of a clean heart and placing a new and right spirit in David involves his spirit and heart being 'crushed' and 'broken', which sounds anything but newness.

In vv. 16-17 David does not simply present an anti-sacrificial stance. The broken spirit and broken and contrite heart represent a deep understanding of the destructive nature of sin and the meaning of forgiveness. The same verbal root is used to speak of a 'contrite' heart in v. 17b as is used to speak of David's 'crushed' bones in v. 8 (*dākâ*). The one who in an awareness of sin feels 'crushed' by God in body, knows of being 'crushed' in heart in forgiveness. The expression impresses the need for inner transformation in forgiveness, and not just outer offering. In Psalm 49 David stressed the need for the faithful not only to undertake the continual offering of sacrifice to God but to offer thanksgiving as well and to call on God in times of trouble. Now he spells out what thanksgiving and petitionary prayer imply: a real sense of need and brokenness that requires the restoring hand of God.

The final section of the psalm presents a problem. These verses sound out of place following vv. 1-17. They speak of Zion/Jerusalem, not mentioned elsewhere in the psalm. They present a positive view of sacrifice in seeming contrast to v. 16–17, and they move the psalm from the confession of an individual to a petition of the community. Mention of rebuilding the walls of Jerusalem suggests a time of composition after the exile (cf. Neh. 2.11-20). These verses could be secondary and late in composition, perhaps a 'corrective' to the view of sacrifice in vv. 16-17. That may be true in the history of the psalm but it is by no means the case that the verses are out of place where they presently sit.

First, in Psalm 44 there was a hint at possible exile, at least as seen from a later time. The reference to the destruction of Jerusalem could foreshadow that event to come, especially as Ps. 51.18-19 anticipates future action. There are a number of vocabulary links between vv. 16-17 and vv. 18-19 which might suggest an intended connection: 'delight', vv. 16, 19; 'sacrifice', vv. 16, 17, 19; 'please', vv. 16, 18; 'burnt offering', vv. 16, 19. Secondly, the references to the walls of Zion recall the images of the city in Psalms 46 and 48. Finally, in v. 19 the sacrifices mentioned are designated as 'right sacrifices', *zibḥê-ṣedeq*. In Ps. 4.5 the people were urged to 'offer right sacrifices, and put (their) trust in Yahweh'. In Psalm 50 we hear what are not right sacrifices, while in Psalm 51, we hear what they are, namely sacrifice offered by a 'broken and contrite heart'. It could be that the piety suggested in vv. 16-17 is seen as a temporary notion for a time, during the exile, when there was no possibility of sacrifice. More likely, however, the whole thrust of the psalm could be toward a piety in which sacrifice accompanied by an inner trust is what is urged. In either case, vv. 18-19 are not necessarily out of place.

There is also a collectivizing aspect to vv. 18-19 shifting the psalm from David's confession to corporate hope and petition. This move is consistent with earlier psalms where the prayers of David became the prayers of the community of faith. David thus became their model pray-er. One might also see in these verses an eschatological aspect. From the time of David the Psalter looks toward future events which will include the destruction of Jerusalem. The restoration of the city will be the final stage of the renewal of God's people wherein inner piety and trust will be consistent with sacrificial worship. The public and the private, the community and the individual, will be one. Those who through forgiveness are renewed in heart and spirit, with whom God's holy spirit dwells, will inhabit a renewed city offering right sacrifices.

In Psalm 51 David illustrates the proper response to Psalm 50, as one who brings thanksgiving to God, honours God and goes the right way. He seeks release from all that has held him in the past, notably his own sin. Through confession he seeks a new future, a new heart and spirit. But that is not at the expense of the community or its worship, including sacrifice. On the contrary, David's confession as an individual has a corporate dimension in terms of public praise, teaching and prayer. The focus early in the psalm was not so much on David and his sins as on the God who would give him mercy. The focus later in the psalm is likewise not on David's new circumstance but on what that means for the community. Confession is not the end of sin so much as the beginning of praise.

Psalms 52–62

After laments over individual and community troubles (Psalms 42–43, 44), issues of confidence and trust were addressed in Psalms 45–48 urging that there was no need to fear. Psalms 50–51 looked further into the relation between God and the faithful, defining sacrifice as primarily thanksgiving and seeing confession as praise.

In relation to David as psalmist, Psalm 51 creates a problem. It places the psalm in the period of David's reign. Those that follow are mainly associated through their superscriptions with episodes from David's earlier flight from Saul. But this is not the only chronological anomaly in the superscriptions (cf. Psalm 3). It would appear that in its final shape the Psalter gives attention to the presentation of David as faithful pray-er, rather than to strict chronological order. That seems to be the point in the psalms that follow Psalms 50-51, where we return not only to psalms attributed directly to David but to the world of lament.

Psalms 52-55 are joined by the common Hebrew title of 'a *maśkîl* of David'. They are laments concerning enemies and bear similarities to the earlier psalms of the 'poor' in Book I (cf. Psalms 4; 11; 12; 14). Common themes tie the psalms together. Two are associated with specific events in David's life (Psalms 52 and 54) while the superscriptions to Psalms 54 and 55 are identical apart from the event mentioned in Psalm 54.

In **Psalm 52** David mainly addresses the one who boasts of 'mischief' (better 'injustice', cf. Ps. 50.19), loves evil (v. 3), and seeks refuge in things other than God (vv. 6-7). The righteous will witness his end. The psalm fits the situation mentioned in the superscription (1 Samuel 21-22), which describes the betrayal of the priest Ahimelech by Doeg, a servant of Saul. Ahimelech had supported David as he fled Saul. Having spoken against Doeg, David ends Psalm 52 by comparing himself to an olive tree in the house of God, proclaiming the name of God (cf. Ps. 1.3; 23.6; 27.4). While Psalm 52 has some connections to Psalm 51, it provides general connection back to Psalms 49-50 and the matter of trust against the power of the wicked.

Psalm 53 intensifies earlier thoughts on the wicked (cf. Ps. 14.5-6 and 52.5). Its inclusion here brings the two David collections closer together. It gives a theological assessment of the recently mentioned wicked (50.16), and mighty who boast with a deceitful tongue (52.1, 4). They are 'fools' deceiving themselves. David's psalm is applied to the whole people as it ends with hope for deliverance of Israel (v. 6).

Psalm 54 has a similar structure and intent to Psalm 52. David seeks God's help and deliverance from the 'insolent' (vv. 3, 5). The vow of praise (v. 6) is similar to that in Psalm 13 (cf. also 52.11). David, as a faithful one, also promises to give thanks (cf. Ps. 50.23), and a 'freewill offering' (Heb. *nᵉdābâ*). This word occurs nowhere else in the Psalter, and its use here close to Ps. 51.12, where David desires a 'willing' spirit (Heb. *nᵉdîbâ* from the same root), indicates David's proper 'sacrifice'.

The psalm is associated with the episode in 1 Sam. 23.14-28 where David is betrayed by Ziphites while fleeing from Saul (see. esp. 1 Sam. 23.19; cf. also Ps. 54.4 with 1 Sam. 23.16-17).

Psalm 55 concludes this short series of *maśkîl* psalms. It repeats in longer form the petition in Psalms 52 and 54. This time, however, David would escape his trouble if he could (vv. 6-8). What hurts most is the betrayal of a companion (vv. 12-15, 20-21; cf. Ps. 38.11; 41.9; 88.8, 18). The friendship of God stands in contrast to this (cf. Ps. 25.14). While the name of the companion betrayer is not given, the growing distance between Saul and David portrayed in 1 Sam. 16.14-23; 18.10–19.17 comes to mind especially with Saul's frequent deception. David's early life is seen in these psalms to be manifestly one of trust.

Psalms 56–60 form the next series within the second David collection. Each psalm is designated a *miktam*. **Psalm 56** continues the thrust of earlier prayers: David seeks deliverance from those who would destroy him. There is a vow of praise at the end (vv. 11-12; cf. Ps. 54.6-7). Psalm 56 is associated with 1 Sam. 21.11-16 where David flees to the Philistine city, Gath. There are, however, some discrepancies between the texts. In 1 Sam. 21.13 David fears the Philistines but in Ps. 56.4 and 10–11 he claims he is not afraid and trusts in God. In Samuel David feigns madness and escapes (1 Sam. 21.13; 22.1) but in the psalm superscription he is seized. Psalm 56 brings the theme of trust in God to a climax in Book II. Ps. 44:6 stressed not trusting in human effort and Ps. 49.6 spoke critically of those who trust in wealth. But in Ps. 52.8 and especially at the seam between Psalms 55 and 56 there is strong focus on trust in God alone (Pss. 55.23; 56.3-4, 11). **Psalm 57** is more intense than Psalm 56 (cf. v. 1 in each). It is related to David's flight from Saul when he hid in the cave (1 Sam. 22.1-11 and especially 24.1-23). The psalm ends again with the promise of giving thanks and praising Yahweh (vv. 9-11) with the final verse echoing the *inclusio* of Psalm 8.

In **Psalm 58** David cries out against the 'mighty ones' (not necessarily 'gods' as in NRSV). He petitions that they perish (vv. 6-9). Then the righteous will rejoice and people will know that there is a God who judges on earth (v. 10–11). Psalm 58 does not share some of the common vocabulary of Psalms 56, 57 and 59, nor is it specifically linked to David in the superscription. It does, however, add a wisdom connection to the laments with its emphasis on God as judge and reward for the righteous. **Psalm 59** then returns to the individual lament sequence seeking God's help against enemies (cf. Pss. 2.4 and 37.13). God's 'steadfast love' (*ḥesed*) which forms an *inclusio* for vv. 16-17, is the basis for David seeing God as his 'fortress'. Psalm 59 is associated with 1 Sam. 19.11-12 with Saul watching David's house. There are word associations between the texts ('not sinning', Ps. 59.3–4; 1 Sam. 19.4; 'night/morning', Ps. 59.6, 14, 16; 1 Sam. 19.10-11; 'spoken sins', Ps. 59.12; 1 Sam 19.6). The psalm might, however, act as a corrective to the Samuel narrative where David saves himself with Michal's help. In Psalm 59 God saves him.

Psalm 60 is an unspecified national lament. A long superscription associates this psalm with 2 Sam 8.1-14, in which we hear of David's conquest of various West Semitic peoples including the three mentioned in Ps. 60.6-8. However, there is an anomaly between the psalm and the Samuel narrative. The psalm is mostly a lament over God's rejection of his people and their defeat (vv. 1-5, 9-12). The story in Samuel is one of complete victory. The superscription, however, says that the psalm is 'for teaching/instruction'. It could be that the oracle in vv. 6-8, with its connection back to David's victories, is the ensign (*nēs*), a point of rally or safety, referred to in v. 4. So David becomes a teacher as the people cry out in their trouble and reflect on both the story referred to in the superscription and the promise through past victories mentioned in the oracle (cf. Pss. 34.11; 51.13).

Psalm 60 also recalls themes and motifs especially from Psalm 44: 'rejection by God', 60.1, 10 and 44.9; 'God the only one to deliver', 60.11-12 and 44.3, 6–7. Psalm 59 also has common motifs with Psalm 44: being guiltless, Ps. 59.3b-4 and 44.17-21; and the urgent call for God to arise and help, 59.4b-5 and 44.23-26. Thus, Psalms 59 and 60, individual and communal laments, form an *inclusio* with Psalm 44 around Psalms 45–58 embracing themes of confidence (Psalms 45–48), confidence and faithfulness (Psalms 49–51), and individual laments (Psalms 52–58). The theme of national defeat and exile (Psalm 44) returns in Psalms 59–60 but in the context of great confidence and the promise of victory (Ps. 60.6-8).

The small group of Psalms 61–64 opens with a lament but with great confidence in rescue (**Psalm 61**). While it has important links to previous collections (e.g. enemies, refuge: cf. Pss. 43.2; 46.1, 7, 11; 52.7; 57.1 [nb. 'wings', cf. 61.4]; 59.16), the psalm also looks forward. David wishes to abide in God's 'tent' forever (cf. 23.6 etc.). He has received the heritage of those who fear God's name (cf. 60.4) which at the close of Book I he aimed to pass on (Ps. 40.3 and esp. 34. 7, 9, 11). The final prayer for the king, vv. 6-7, even if a late insertion, looks to kingship beyond David. **Psalm 62** is another individual lament but with wisdom aspects (v. 8) and a strong note of confidence (vv. 1-2, 5-6). It calls for trust and refuge in God (vv. 9-10; cf. 52.7) intensifying the thought of Psalm 61 and again looking forward to Psalm 63 through *nepeš*, ('life, self', NRSV: 'soul') and the 'silence' motif (v. 1; cf. Ps. 65.1).

Psalm 63

This short psalm, with its mixture of metaphors and memorable statements of faith, conveys a great sense of confidence and trust, although difficulties giving rise to petitions for help are not far below the surface. Nevertheless, it presents a number of problems: who and how many people are speaking; does it speak of the past or the future; and how do we read the statement on the king?

A number of features are suggestive of structure. The Hebrew *nepeš* (NRSV: 'soul') is used four times with varying senses (vv. 1, 5, 8, 9). The word *kēn*, 'thus, so', occurs at the start of vv. 2 and 4, and *kî*, 'for, because', at the start of vv. 3 and 7. Verse 9 presents a change of subject matter. Finally, there may be an acrostic element in the psalm focussed around the letters *aleph* and *kaph*. Verses 1 and 6 both begin with *aleph* while the following verses, vv. 2 and 7, each begin with *kaph*. In fact, each of vv. 2-5 begin with *kaph*. Moreover, vv. 6 and 11 each contain the root *hll*, 'to praise', closely related to two words which sound similar, *tiśbaʿ*, 'is satisfied' (v. 6), and *hannišbāʿ*, 'who swear' (v. 11). The structure we will adopt is based in part on this data: vv. 1-5, the search for the satisfaction God gives; vv. 6-8, thoughts on God's help; vv. 9-10, the outlook for those who seek the psalmist's life; and v. 11 joy when liars mouths are stopped.

The superscription speaks generally about David's time in the wilderness of Judah. This could relate to when he fled from Saul (1 Sam. 23.14-15; 24.1) although only the references to the wilderness of Judah and thirst connect them. A better relation is with 2 Sam. 15.13–17.23 when, as king, David fled from Absalom who usurped the throne. The psalm has some themes in common with the narrative (wilderness, 2 Sam. 15.23, 28; 16.2; thirst and refreshment, 2 Sam. 16.2, 14; feasting, 2 Sam. 16.2; seeing God in the sanctuary, 2 Sam. 15.25; and combating conspiracies, 2 Sam. 15.31, 34).

David begins by expressing a strong longing for God, picking up the theme in Ps. 62.1 of waiting in silence for God. This time the longing is likened to that of the body for water in a parched land. The use of *nepeš* with its base meaning of 'throat' underscores the metaphor. David's whole being 'thirsts' for God. The use of 'thirst' as an expression of longing has already occurred in Ps. 42.1-3 (cf. Ps. 143.6). Besides thirsting, David 'seeks' (*šāḥar*) God, a verb that has an intensity about it (cf. Ps. 78.34), and in some cases a sense of doing something early. The psalm could be connected to a vigil (cf. v. 6), although our reading is not restricted to that.

Reference to looking upon God in the sanctuary in v. 2 (cf. Pss. 11.7; 17.15) following expressions of thirst is consistent with the association in Ps. 42.1-4. Expressions of thirst and hunger in relation to the quest for God are part of the language of the sanctuary. However, it is unclear in Ps. 63.2 whether looking upon God in the sanctuary is something in the past (so NRSV), an unfulfilled longing ('I have looked for you in the sanctuary to see your power and glory') or a prayer ('O, that I might look upon...'). The latter two would pertain to the present need behind v. 1. Other psalm references to the sanctuary usually imply some hope of a future visit (cf. Pss. 27.4-6; 42.2-3, 5, 11 and 84.1-2).

The statement in v. 3a, that God's *ḥesed* ('steadfast love') is better than life, could imply that David puts little value in his life. But such is not the case in the context of the Psalter where David has been seeking God's *ḥesed* in order to preserve his life in difficult situations. What David speaks of here is the relation between God's *ḥesed* and his own life. The former preserves the latter, especially in difficulties, but this psalm stresses that even while David waits for deliverance God's *ḥesed* sustains him (v. 8). David's praise springs from this deep knowledge. He concludes his thoughts in this opening section of the psalm with a quite different image but one which conveys the 'richness' of God's *ḥesed*. He has likened longing for God to great thirst (v. 1), now, just as when he is satisfied with 'fat' (*ḥēleb* and *dešen* both mean 'fat' [or 'fatty ashes'] and imply the richest of food), so his satisfaction with God leads to praise with joyful lips. God is satisfaction for him at the deepest level, a thought he can only express through words of bodily satisfaction (cf. Gen. 45.18; Lev. 7.25; Ps. 36.7-9).

Verses 6-8 continue the main sentiment but in different language. David returns to an image used early in the psalms, his thoughts in bed. In Ps. 6.6 David spoke of flooding his bed with tears in his distress. Now his bedtime thoughts and meditations (cf. Ps. 1.2) are of God and God's help (cf. Ps. 42.8). Private contemplation is envisaged, reinforcing the emphasis in earlier psalms on inner thanksgiving over against public ritual (cf. Pss. 4.4b-5; 50.7-15; 51.16-17). Following these private thoughts there is an expression of trust and divine help. Verses 7-8 are set out in a chiastic way: God as help—David in the shadow of God's wing—he clings to God—God as support. The two outer expressions of God's help enclose the inner ones which sum up the mutuality of this divine-human relationship. God shelters David in the shadow of his wings, a frequent metaphor for divine protection (Pss. 17.8; 36.7; 57.1; 61.4; cf. Exod. 19.4). The image of Pharaoh under a deity's wings is frequent in Egyptian art. Alongside this is the statement that David 'clings' or 'sticks to' God. The mutuality of commitment is the key to the experience of God's help, and it is commitment within a relationship that allows no substitute.

The psalm shifts tack sharply in v. 9. From thoughts of God on his bed, David considers those who seek to destroy his life (*nepeš*), a formulaic expression for enemies (cf. e.g. Pss. 35.4; 38.12; 40.14 etc.). David reminds readers/hearers that the assurance of God's protection and help, the understanding of *ḥesed* as greater than life itself, is only gained in the midst of dangerous times, when life is threatened. As others seek his life, so his own seeking of God is strengthened, but not in any simple, self-centred way, for what David finds himself seeking is not just his own survival. What lies at the end of his longing is his praise of God. That reverberates through the psalm as David's final goal (vv. 3b-4, 5b, 11a-b and at the centre of the chiasm in v. 7b).

In contrast to the fate of those who seek David's life, the prayer of the psalm is for the king to rejoice in God, and for those who swear 'by him' to exalt. It is unclear whether the swearing is by God or by David as in 1 Sam. 17.55; 25.26; 2 Sam. 11.11; and 15.21, the last of which sees Ittai swearing in the name of David thus reinforcing the connection between the psalm and the narrative, with each interpreting the other. The king is the one who models joy for all. There is, of course, an implication of change of speaker in v. 11a, although David could refer to himself in the third person. The ambiguity at this point strengthens the applicability of the prayer of David for all.

Psalm 63 is linked strongly to Psalm 62 through key words, especially *nepeš* (62.1, 5; 63. 1, 5, 8, 9), *ʿōz* 'power' (62.11; 63.2) and *ḥesed* (62.12; 63.3). These two psalms provide a glimpse of the close inner relationship between God and David which supports his more public petitions like those expressed in Psalm 61 and 64. The community for whom David is a model knows well the nature of the relationship modelled for them.

Psalms 64–71

Psalm 64 concludes the small collection Psalms 61–64. It begins with words similar to Ps. 61.1. In both David seeks refuge (61.2; 64.2). In Psalm 64 David describes the plots (mostly speech and words, vv. 2-6) of the enemies who sought his life in Ps. 63.9. In spite of their sense of security (cf. Ps. 11.11), David is confident God 'will shoot his arrow at them' (64.7). God is David's only defense and his vindication will again have an effect on the faithful (64.10).

The psalms in the next group (Psalms 65–68) are doubly designated 'songs' and 'psalms'. They are mainly thanksgiving psalms with petitions for universal acknowledgement of God's kingship. The first, **Psalm 65**, begins in Hebrew with 'To you silence is praise, O God in Zion' recalling especially Ps. 62.1 and 5. The NRSV 'Praise is due to you' reflects the alternative LXX reading. Psalm 65 is a thanksgiving often associated with harvest festival (possibly Tabernacles; Exod. 23.16; Deut. 16.13-15). It proclaims that God answers prayer (vv. 2, 5), forgives sin (v. 3) and blesses those God brings near (v. 4). Their satisfaction echoes that of Ps. 63.5, which also refers to the sanctuary (63.2). The description of God's bounty in 65.9-13 sees the whole creation break forth in praise as the rains and abundance counter the description of thirst and dryness in 63.1.

The mood and themes of Psalm 65 continue in the community thanksgiving **Psalm 66**, where David calls people to 'make a joyful noise' (v. 1; cf. Ps. 100.1) praising God whose awesome deeds are seen in the exodus (v. 6). God is king over the nations, leading his people through difficult times to safety. David then promises as an individual to offer sacrifices in response. This positive view of sacrifice (also with the king's sacrifice in Ps. 20.3) is in the context of vows and thanksgiving and is not inconsistent with earlier critiques (e.g. Ps. 50.14). David's invitation to all who fear God (vv. 16-19) to hear what God had done for him testifies that God does listen. David is both pray-er and teacher (cf. Ps. 51.13).

Psalm 67 moves to petition while continuing themes from Psalms 65 and 66. There is a hint of a harvest context (v. 6) amidst the petitions (vv. 1-2, 6-7). Verse 1 recalls the Aaronic blessing (Num. 6.25) while the refrain (vv. 3, 5), encloses the call to earth to praise God who judges and guides the nations with equity. Uncertain over the tense of verbs creates a problem. Verse 6a, in the past, stands alongside future petitions. The psalm could anticipate ongoing thanksgiving.

A longer and more difficult psalm follows, **Psalm 68**. It has a number of uncertain words, and difficult points of grammar. Its form is more like that of an anthology of song titles or sayings, than an intended unity, although the themes of exodus, the conquest of Canaan, and the declaration of God's kingship hold it together. There is a mixture of cosmic and historic language, of theophany and exodus narrative. The God who tested the people with burdens (Ps. 66.10-12) now bears them up (68.19). Past events give rise not only to thanksgiving but to petitions for further deliverance and a call to nations to ascribe power to the God residing in the temple at Jerusalem. There is a desire that God's kingship continue to be shown and be acknowledged over earth (cf. Psalm 67). Themes from Psalms 65–67 are maintained in Psalm 68, especially salvation (Pss. 65.5; 68.19-20), abundance (Pss. 65.9-13; 68.7-10) and blessing (both blessing from God: Pss. 65.10; 67.1, 6-7; and blessing of God: Pss. 66.8, 20; 68.19, 26, 36).

The final section of Book II begins with **Psalm 69**, a lament in two halves (vv. 1-13c; 13d-29) in which enemies accuse David falsely. He proclaims his faithfulness and zeal for God's house (v. 9) and awaits God's answer to his prayer (vv. 13, 16-17; cf. Ps. 65:2, 5). As one of the 'lowly' (v. 29) he curses his enemies seeking God's justice upon them (vv. 24a, 27). Repetition between the halves intensifies and unifies the psalm. David vows praise and thanksgiving to God more pleasing than sacrifice (cf. Ps. 50.7-15). The final petition calls the whole earth to praise God and for God to save Zion, implying some present or imminent destruction in Judah and hinting at exile (cf. Pss. 44.11; 51.18; 60.1-3).

In Pss. 68:10 and 69:33 David said that God provides for and hears the needy. In Ps. 69.29 and in **Psalm 70**, verse 5, he prays as one of them. Other themes from Psalm 69 are also developed in Psalm 70. Shame and dishonour were David's concern in Ps. 69:6-7, 19. In Ps. 70:2-3 he prays they will not be his lot (cf. Ps. 71:1, 13, 24). He spoke of those seeking God in Ps. 69:6, 32 and does so again in 70:4, contrasting them with those who seek his life (v. 2; cf. Ps. 63.1, 9). Psalm 70 affirms that God rescues his own.

The brevity of Psalm 70, its similarity of theme to the lament Psalm 69, the fact that it repeats Ps. 40.13-17 with minor variants, that it has similarities to parts of Psalm 35, and that it and Psalm 38 both bear the superscription *lᵉhazkîr*, 'to make known, profess' (NRSV: 'for the memorial offering'), all suggest Psalm 70 may have been placed for editorial purposes. The connections with Psalms 35, 38 and 40 connect the end of Book II to the end of Book I of the Psalter. At the same time while Book II began with laments followed by psalms celebrating God's kingship (Pss. 45–48), so it draws to a close with Psalms 65–68 celebrating divine aid followed by laments.

The penultimate psalm in Book II, **Psalm 71**, although not designated in MT as a psalm of David (but so in LXX), fits his situation well. As an old man David, for whom God has been his hope and trust since youth (vv. 5-6), prays that such trust will still be rewarded in his old age (v. 9) and that not he but his accusers will be shamed (vv. 1, 13). His prayer ends in confidence of fulfillment in v. 24 (cf. 69:6-7, 19; 70:2-3) as David takes up his *kinnôr*, 'lyre', and sing praises to God continuing to tell of God's wonderful deeds (vv. 15-16).

Psalm 72

Book II of the Psalter closes with an intercessory prayer for the king bearing the superscription *lišlōmōh*, 'to/for/of Solomon' raising questions of the role of Psalm 72 in the collection. The psalm was possibly used in a coronation liturgy. The prayers offered for the king reflect broad areas of royal responsibility (justice, fertility, and authority) and indicate how the divine and human realms interact through the king. The psalm has similarities to Egyptian and Neo-Assyrian prayers but they have been adapted to a thoroughly Israelite perception of kingship.

Verse 1 is important, being the only petition addressed to God. Verses 2-17 develop this petition through five sections: vv. 2-4, 5-7, 8-11, 12-14, and 15-17. There is repetition within these sections but also order. Justice for the poor is emphasized in vv. 2-4 and 12-14 while images of fertility are prominent in vv. 5-7 and 15-17. Verses 18-20 are later additions to the psalm related to the closing of Book II.

The superscription associates the psalm with Solomon (also Psalm 127). Many features reinforce the association: the reference to the son of the king, the desire to judge wisely with justice and righteousness, and gifts from foreign places especially gold from Sheba (cf. 1 Kgs 3.3-14; 10.1-12). However, the colophon in v. 20 goes against understanding Solomon as author. The nature of the psalm as intercession for the king, and its inclusion within the 'psalms of David' suggest that we read it as David's prayer for the son who takes his throne, a fitting sequel to the prayer of an aging David in Psalm 71. Reference to 'the king' and 'a king's son' in v. 1 strengthen this connection. The petition is that God may grant *mišpāṭîm* ('judgments, decisions'; NRSV: 'justice'; cf. LXX sg. 'justice') and *ṣᵉdāqâ* ('righteousness/justice') to the king. The prayer is not only that the king may reflect in his decisions and acts the divine principles of justice and righteousness, but that God will guide him in individual judgments and deeds.

In vv. 2-4, David develops the legal language from v. 1 with particular concern for 'the poor'. In praying for his son to defend the poor, David seeks what he prayed for himself (cf. vv. 4, 12; Pss. 9–10; 35.10; 68.10; 69.33). The section creates a *chiasm* with v. 1 through the words 'righteousness' (*zedeq*) and 'justice' (*mišpāṭ*). As the mountains bring *šālôm* (NRSV: 'prosperity') to the people with the hills 'in righteousness', the king's reign becomes an avenue of God's blessing. While the image is basically one of fertility the cosmic connotations of the 'mountains' (cf. Pss. 18.7; 46.2-3; 65.6) is present. *šālôm*, 'peace', will emerge from the cosmic realm. For similar benefits of such a rule see Isa. 32.15-20.

Verses 5-7 develop the fertility language. In contrast to Ps. 65.9-13 it is the king here who, like rain and showers (v. 6), enables the growth in v. 7 of *ṣaddîq*, 'the righteous' (NRSV: 'righteousness') and *rōb šālôm*, 'an abundance of peace' (cf. v. 3). However, while vv. 6-7 are clear v. 5 is not. It reads literally 'May they fear you with the sun, and before the moon, generation after generation.' This is an ancient problem. Who are 'they'? The LXX emends the Hebrew verb slightly to read 'may he live' (so NRSV). This is possible and makes the king the subject of the whole section but the more difficult MT is preferred text critically and is not an impossible reading. The pronoun object 'you' can refer to God as in vv. 1-2, and the subject 'they' to the oppressors of v. 4. If we understand 'with (*'im*) the sun' and 'before (*lipnê*) the moon' in the sense of 'as long as' the sun and moon, i.e. 'for ever' (cf. the moon in v. 7 and Ps. 89.36-37), then the verse implies the perpetual subjugation of the oppressors to God. This matches v. 1 where the king's exercise of justice etc. arises first from God's gift. So here, the eternal fear *of God* by the oppressors whom the king has crushed, enables the king to promote the righteous and peace. What the king establishes is made possible first by God's eternal authority in the cosmos. The use of the sun and moon to speak of the longevity of the king's reign is standard in the ancient Near East.

The third section, vv. 8-11, extends the dominion of the king to all other nations. Its extent ('from sea to sea, and from the River to the ends of the earth') anticipates the Davidic king's authority in Ps. 89.25. Enemies and 'desert dwellers' (*ṣiyyîm*; NRSV reads *ṣārāyw* 'foes' after v. 9b) will bow down and 'lick the dust', a sign of submission (cf. Mic. 7.16-17). Kings from remote places, Tarshish, the isles, Sheba and Seba, will bring gifts also implying tribute and subjugation. Verses 12-14 follow this scene of military and political domination returning to the theme of the poor. Verse 12 begins with *kî*, 'for', introducing the reason for what has been stated. It is because of the king's deliverance of the needy etc. that David can pray for his dominion. But the sentiment of this section is more intense than in vv. 2-4. The king hears the cries of the needy, cares for those without a helper, has pity on the weak, and their blood, i.e. their life, is precious to him. Such cries, help, and pity are what David himself sought from God in his laments. Finally, the king 'redeems' (*yig'al*) their life from oppression and violence (v. 14a). This image of the kin-redeemer has an economic base, and usually refers a family member and ultimately to God. In Lev. 25.25-55 redemption is tied to the Jubilee year and to the exodus. God's people cannot be sold as slaves for they are God's servants whom he brought out of Egypt (Lev. 25.42, 54-55). In Psalm 72, redemption of the poor also becomes the duty of the king. He is called to act rightly like family and, ultimately, like God.

The final section, vv. 15-17, presents translation difficulties but the gist is clear. David again takes up the language of fertility (v. 16). The sequence, language of the poor then fertility in vv. 12-14 and 15-17, repeats the sequence of vv. 2-4 and 5-7 although with extension and intensification. The section begins with the bold statement 'Long may he live!' although it is not clear whether 'he' is the king or the poor just mentioned. The fact that the cry echoes the shout at the enthronement of a new king (1 Sam. 10.24; 2 Sam. 16.16; 1 Kgs 1.31, 34, 39), and that the king is the object of all the desires of the psalm so far, would suggest he is the one for whom the statement is made. It would be appropriate also as our thoughts shift to the reign of Solomon. The great king and psalmist, David, blesses those who follow him.

Thoughts of wealth, continual prayer and blessing follow. While the NRSV translates the verbs as passives, in the Hebrew it is not clear who gives and who receives, who prays, and who blesses whom in v. 15. Arguments can be made each way but it is reasonable to argue that the king distributes the wealth received to the needy and they continually pray for him. David continues his prayer in v. 16 seeking 'abundant' grain (the Hebrew is uncertain) and praying that the people in the cities might also 'blossom' like the grass (v. 16). He concludes with a prayer that the king's name might endure forever with further comparison to the sun (v. 17a; cf. Ps. 45.17). Verse 17b concludes the prayer with a note reminiscent of Gen. 12.2-3 that the nations shall consider themselves blessed in the king. What, in Genesis, takes place through Abraham and the covenant with him, is here established through the king. Even the enemies (v. 9) and others who are possibly subjugated will find the possibility of blessing. This blessing through the king is an extension of the blessing in recent psalms (cf. esp. Pss 66.8, 20; 67.1, 6, 7; 68.19, 26, 35).

The psalm ends in vv. 18-19 with the final blessing on Yahweh. At one level this doxology functions like the others (Pss. 41.13; 89.52; and 106.48) concluding their respective books. But this doxology has several additions which link it closely with Psalms 71 and 72. The wondrous deeds (*niplā'ôt*) and Yahweh's glory (*kābôd*) have recently been mentioned by David (Ps. 71.8, 17) and the blessing of Yahweh's name matches David's prayer for Solomon in Ps. 72.17a. The doxology in Ps. 72.18-19 has been expanded to fit the context of David's reign and prayer for his successor(s). His last words, so to speak, reinforce the point at the start of this psalm, that from God alone comes all that gives life. These words bear close similarity to David's prayer at Solomon's coronation in 1 Kgs 1.47-48. The double 'amen' draws the larger congregation who will read or hear this psalm, into David's blessing of Yahweh.

Book II has the additional editorial statement in v. 20 that 'the prayers of David son of Jesse are ended.' This is not the case as a number of later psalms are attributed to David in the MT mostly in Book V (Pss. 86; 101; 103; 108–110; 122; 124; 131; 138-145). Even if Ps. 72.20 is a remnant of an earlier, shorter Davidic collection its place in the present collection needs explanation. The verb *kālâ* used in Ps. 72.20 (NRSV: 'ended') does not necessarily indicate the end of all David's words. It could indicate a temporary cessation, or, as in Gen. 2.1-2, the completion of everything that can be said even if more words are spoken. In Job 31.40b we are told that Job's words are ended, where, in fact, he speaks twice more (Job 40.3-5; 42.1-6). The end of Job's words signal a transition in the discussion to where others take over. If David is envisaged as an old man at this point handing kingship to Solomon, then it may be that Ps. 72.20 marks the end of his immediate participation in the conversation. Others will now take it up. We will see how the later 'David' psalms fit in this context.

Psalm 72 is a prayer by David for Solomon and all his successors that they each may truly be God's 'son' (Ps. 2.7). It forms a bridge between what precedes and what follows. However, all David prays for will not come to pass under his descendants, for in Psalm 89 the end of David's line will be lamented. The ideal king set forth here will not be realized in any known individual. We have here the beginnings of the hope for a Davidic 'Messiah' in later understandings of that term (cf. e.g. Zech. 9.10c) and as such a critique of those who fall from its aspirations. At the same time with its blessing and double 'amen' it draws the community of faith into David's prayer for the king. The king depends upon such prayers. But their utterance is also a prayer for the coming of such a king.

Book III

Psalm 73

Psalm 73, which begins Book III, is unique in many ways. Its genre is debatable. It relates strongly to wisdom traditions and has similarities to Psalms 37 and 49 in terms of the style of individual reflection and in the issue of theodicy. In the latter regard it has similarities to the book of Job. Psalm 73 poses a dictum about God's goodness in v. 1 and then examines it in light of the psalmist's experience.

It is the first of a series of Asaph psalms (Pss. 73-83; cf. Ps. 50) which constitutes the major part of Book III. As noted for Psalm 50, the Asaphites were Levitical singers and musicians (1 Chr. 16.5-7 etc.) whom, along with the Korahites, David placed in charge of singing and music at the house of Yahweh until Solomon built the temple (1 Chr. 6.31-32). It is appropriate then that the psalms of Asaph appear at a point in the Psalter when the mantle of kingship passes from David to Solomon and that the collections of Asaph and Korah psalms are in Books II and III before reference to the demise of the royal house. According to Ezra 2.41 (cf. Neh. 7.44) Asaphites were among those who returned from Exile.

We will discuss below how this psalm is connected to David, but it is worth noting that its wisdom aspects are appropriate following Psalm 72, a psalm attributed to Solomon, the patron of wisdom. Psalm 73 has similarities to the great prayer of the king in Wisd. 9.1–19.22 and to Solomon's prayer in 1 Kings 3. On his accession Solomon asked God for *lēb šōmēa‘* (v. 9, lit. 'a hearing heart'; NRSV: 'an understanding mind') to judge the people. God was pleased he did not ask for wealth or long life, so vowed to give him *lēb ḥākām wᵉnābôn* (v. 12, lit. 'a wise and discerning heart'; NRSV: 'mind') and wealth as well. Psalm 73 addresses the relation of wealth and power to nearness to God and throughout speaks about the 'heart' (vv. 1, 7, 13, 21, 26). It is appropriate in its place in another way too as it echoes themes and words from Psalms 1 and 2, namely the relative stability of the righteous vis-à-vis the wicked (Ps. 1.3, 4; 73.2, 18) and the happiness or 'goodness' that comes to the one who takes refuge in God (Ps. 2.12; 73.28). So having heard David's 'last words' and as we enter a new phase of the Psalter, we hear again themes from the psalms that directed our reading of the whole, Psalms 1–2.

Psalm 73 is bound together by repeated words and images. Some have a structural function: $’ak$, 'truly, surely', in vv. 1, 13 (not marked in NRSV), and 18; $wa’^anî$, 'but (as) for me', in vv. 2, 22 and 23 (not marked in NRSV), and 28; and $kî$, 'for, when', in vv. 3, 4, 21, 27 (NRSV: 'indeed'). Verses 1-2 and 28 also form an *inclusio* with the common words: 'but (as) for me', 'God', 'good', and 'to [Israel/me]'. The psalm can be divided into v. 1 in which a general premise is stated, vv. 2-12 which describe the wicked, vv. 13-17 as the turning point, and vv. 18-28 in which a resolution is reached.

Verse 1 in the MT reads 'Truly God is good to Israel, to those who are pure in heart.' The NRSV reads 'the upright' for 'Israel' following a common scholarly emendation of the Hebrew. This emendation involves little change to the Hebrew, gives better parallelism in the verse, and fits the individual sense of the psalm better. However, there is no ancient evidence recommending the emendation over the MT. This verse expresses a similar idea to Psalm 1:6 (cf. Deut. 7:12-15; or in reverse Job 4:7-9; 8:20-22; and 11:13-20). It presumes a well-defined world view in which God rewards the righteous and punishes the wicked. Conversely, the righteous are defined by what is presumed to be God's goodness to them.

But a dilemma is created by experience. The psalmist 'almost slipped' when they saw the 'prosperity' (Heb. $šālôm$, 'peace') of the wicked (vv. 2-3). The details of what the psalmist 'saw' (vv. 2-7) and 'heard' (vv. 8-12) are then revealed. The wicked are physically well off. 'They have no pains at their death; their bodies are healthy' (v. 4; NRSV emends) and they have no bodily suffering as other people do (v. 5 with $nāga‘$, 'to strike'). The use of $’^enôš$ and $’ādām$ for 'human' in v. 5 recalls Ps. 8.5 describing the 'weakness' of humans. No weakness is contemplated for the wicked in Psalm 73 (cf. also v. 9). Their pride overflows as 'their eyes swell out with fatness', an image of luxurious living (v. 7a; cf. Ps 104.15). This luxury, however, is both in reality and in the psalm surrounded by pride, violence, malice, and oppression (vv. 6 and 8; cf. Jer. 12.1). Their language is filled with such things as they speak from lofty places, i.e. positions of power (vv. 8-9).

Verse 10 is corrupt in MT and many emendations have been suggested. Even so, MT suggests that people turn to them (the wicked) and 'waters of fullness' are drained for them or 'from them'. That is, the wicked either satisfy those who flock to them or squeeze them dry. Finally, the wicked ask whether God knows what is happening, or even cares (v. 11). Their prosperity leads them to perceive God as superfluous. Ironically, this is similar to the question the psalmist is addressing. The section closes simply: 'Such are the wicked' (v. 12). There is a basic contradiction between this description of the 'prosperity' of the wicked and the statement in v. 1.

Verse 13 begins again with $'ak$ 'truly' (cf. v. 1). Unlike the wicked who have no $'\bar{a}m\bar{a}l$, 'trouble', nor are 'plagued' (v. 5), the psalmist is constantly 'plagued' by the wearisome 'task' ($'\bar{a}m\bar{a}l$) of considering this contradiction (vv. 14-16). The psalmist's 'moral dilemma' is no less real than physical suffering. The psalmist ponders the point of a 'clean heart' and 'hands washed in innocence' (cf. Mal. 3.14–15) which, in Ps. 24.4, were the key 'to standing in the holy place'. But such thoughts would not help the 'circle of (God's) children' (v. 15), who are the 'company of the righteous' or the 'poor' (cf. Ps. 14.5). Rather than 'talking' on ($sipp\bar{e}r$, 'to recount') in this distressed way, the psalmist will, in the end, 'tell' ($sipp\bar{e}r$) of Yahweh's works to this circle (v. 28). This is the first move to 'conversion' for the psalmist, the recognition of community allegiance. The second move comes with v. 17. The psalmist perceives the end of the wicked by going into 'the sanctuary of God'. What this experience was is unclear for the psalmist does not say what they saw there. Moreover, the expression is plural, $miqd^e\check{s}\hat{e}$-$'\bar{e}l$, 'sanctuaries of God'. This could be a(n) unusual) reference to the Jerusalem temple, a plural referring to the parts of a sanctuary complex (cf. Ps. 68.35; Jer. 51.51), or be understood metaphorically as a reference to 'places' where God's holiness is experienced. It might also refer to either the ruined sanctuaries of the old northern kingdom, or various pagan temples. In these latter cases the experience is a negative one, observing what has or will happen to places where Yahweh is not worshipped. If the experience is understood positively then what happened is still unclear—perhaps a theophany, a priestly oracle, or some other experience giving enlightenment. This new 'understanding' ($'\bar{a}b\hat{\imath}n\hat{a}$; NRSV: 'I perceived') contrasts with what the psalmist had 'seen' earlier (v. 3b). The association of other words in Psalm 73 which have to do with temple entrance ('clean heart' and 'hands washed in innocence', v. 13; 'circle/company', *dôr*, v. 15; cf. Ps. 24.4, 6) underpin this new experience as revelatory, whatever form it might have taken.

Finally, the psalmist re-evaluates both the wicked (vv. 18-20) and their own past thoughts (vv. 21-22), and redefines the relationship expressed in v. 1 (vv. 22-28). The language becomes more intimate and direct as it proceeds. The wicked are now seen to be in slippery places (v. 18), destined for ruin (cf. Pss. 1.4-6; 11.4-7; 37.9, 20). They are like a disturbing dream (v. 20), which terrifies for a moment, but, upon awakening, one dismisses the image, *ṣelem*, i.e. as something insubstantial. Such are the wicked.

The psalmist realizes their own former brutishness (v. 21) and ignorance toward God (v. 22, *ʿimmāk*, 'with you'). But *ʿimmāk* is also the answer to the earlier dilemma. The psalmist is continually 'with (God)'. The dual use of *ʿimmāk* forms a bridge in vv. 21-22 between the solution and the earlier doubting. *ʿimmāk* returns in v. 25 in the realisation that 'with God' (NRSV: 'other than you') there is nothing else to be desired. However we understand the sanctuary in v. 17, God now becomes the psalmist's 'sanctuary' or refuge (v. 28; cf. Psalm 27).

Drawing on ancient Near Eastern and Egyptian royal imagery God is said to lead the psalmist by the right hand (cf. Isa. 45.1), and afterward 'receive' (*lāqaḥ*) the psalmist in 'glory' (*kābôd*; NRSV: 'honour'). Whether this refers to the end of the present dilemma or something beyond death is uncertain. *kābôd* can pertain to God and the heavenly realm (e.g. Pss. 19.1; 79.9; 85.9) or be a human quality (e.g. Pss. 4.2; 7.5; 8.6). Likewise, *lāqaḥ* occasionally indicates reception into God's realm (e.g. Gen. 5.24; 2 Kgs 2.11-12; Ps. 49.15). The ambiguity can suggest that the hope for full communion with God breaks into the present situation. Present dilemmas and suffering are not eliminated but they are not the only reality in the psalmist's life. His own heart may fail but God is the strength (so NRSV; MT 'rock') of his heart and 'portion' forever (Ps. 73.26). The solution to the dilemma is in the 'nearness of God', *qirbat-ʾelōhîm* (v. 28). It is all that one can indeed 'have' or 'desire' in heaven or on earth (vv. 25-26), although the ambiguity of the phrase, nearness *of* God or nearness *to* God, remains. The point of realisation of this (v. 23) and the restatement of it (v. 28) are both marked in the same way as the point of danger in v. 2, namely with *waʾanî*, 'but (as) for me'. Verse 1, therefore, must be interpreted in terms of nearness to God, rather than in terms of material or physical well-being.

Only with this final realisation is the divine name Yahweh, with its connotations of a special relation with Israel, used.

Psalm 73 not only begins Book III, it helps shape the direction of the Psalter. As noted it picks up words and themes from Psalms 1–2 and develops the point of Ps. 1.6, exploring how God watches over the righteous, and how the wicked perish when things seem to go so well for them. Psalm 73 also picks up on Psalms 42–43 at the beginning of Book II where David feels far from God. Others taunt him asking 'Where is your God?' (Ps. 42.3, 10). In Psalm 73, God's goodness and nearness are explored in light of the question 'How can God know?' (v. 11). In both psalms God is his refuge (43.2; 73.28) but while in Psalms 42–43 God's nearness will lead David to God's dwelling (43.3-4), in Ps. 73.17 the experience in the sanctuary leads to a new understanding of God's nearness. Finally, the deepening of the psalmist's understanding of the old dictum in Psalm 73 matches the development in thinking about sacrifice in Psalms 49–51. Both developments stand in the context of the relation of wealth to piety (Pss. 49.7-9, 16–20; 73.2-12) and both resolutions involve a change in the heart of the faithful (51.17b; 73.26). These connections with earlier psalms and the movement within Psalm 73 allow David/the psalmist to move from *torah* observance (Psalm 1) toward praise (Psalms 145–150), while at the same time maintaining a balance between the two.

Book III of the Psalter contains several communal psalms and addresses issues of the destruction of the temple and Jerusalem (Psalms 74; 79; 87), the demise of Yahweh's people Israel (Psalms 80; 81; 83; 85), and the Davidic dynasty, its rise and fall (Psalms 78; 89). These issues will constitute major questions for Israel's faith. In this context, Psalm 73 plays a vital role raising questions of the goodness and nearness of God to God's people. As the foundations of faith—temple, Zion, people, kingship—are about to be stripped from the community questions of survival arise. Psalm 73 addresses them discussing the relation between experience and the presence and care of God, an issue which will soon be vital for Israel as a whole. In this sense the initial statement in the MT of Ps. 73.1, 'Truly God is good to Israel ...', is exactly the right one to examine. The verse may have read originally 'Truly God is good to the upright ...'. In its later edited form, however, the subject matter of the psalm is pertinent for the whole nation, the 'circle' of God's children (v. 15).

In one way this is not a psalm of David, but in another the tradition of David's psalms continues. The development of earlier themes in the Psalter and similar language to earlier royal psalms, especially Psalms 18, 20–21, all maintain the connection. The common terminology includes 'pure/clean (of heart/ hands)' (*brr*; Pss. 18.24, 26; 24.4; 73.1) and at God's 'right hand' or lead by the 'right hand' (Pss. 18.35; 20.6; 21.8; 73.23). David's psalms have ended (Ps. 72.20). The wisdom connections of Psalm 73 suggest a connection with Solomon, for whom David prayed in Psalm 72. One may well hear another voice in this psalm but it is one which takes up the mantle of the Davidic tradition.

Psalm 74

Having read in Psalm 73 of the sanctuary as the place of revelation and of the nearness of God, it is a shock to hear in Psalm 74 of both the destruction of the temple and God's distance. This communal lament begins as other laments (e.g. Pss. 10:1; 22:1) but the content sets it apart. Much more than just a building lies in ruins. The continuity of relationship between Israel and God is at stake. As such Psalm 74 is best related in terms of composition to the time of exile when it appears lamentation was a regular part of worship at the temple site (Jer. 41.4-5; Zech. 7.1-3; 8.18-19).

Psalm 74 divides into three main sections: vv. 1-11, the destruction and its immediate consequences; vv. 12-17 recalling God as creator; and vv. 18-23, the final prayer for Yahweh to deliver. Certain motifs and vocabulary tie the sections together, especially 'remember' in vv. 2, 18-19, with vv. 22-23 in parallel, 'do not forget'. The nouns 'enemy' (*'ôyēb*, vv. 3, 10, 18), 'foe' (*ṣōrēr*, vv. 4, 23, and *ṣār*, v. 10) with synonyms 'impious one' (*nābāl*, vv. 18, 22) and 'adversary' (*qām*, v. 23), together with the verbs 'scoff' (*ḥārap̄*, vv. 10, 22) and 'revile' (*nā'aṣ*, vv. 10, 18) form a regular motif.

The first section, vv. 1-11, is framed by questions of 'why?' (*lāmâ*, vv. 1, 11) and the adverb 'forever' (*lāneṣaḥ*, vv. 1, 10), conveying confusion over what has happened and uncertainty over the future. Even as the psalmist questions God, they remind God of divine responsibilities. The congregation God long ago 'acquired' (*qānâ*, also 'created', Deut. 32.6) and which God redeemed, a possible allusion to the exodus, now suffers God's anger. The phrase 'the sheep of your pasture' recalls the language of royal responsibilities in the ancient Near East (cf. Ps. 23; 79.13). Already in vv. 1-3a it is clear that much is at stake in the present disaster for God as well as the people. The psalmist calls God to remember three of the foundations of faith in v. 2—people, Zion, and temple ('where you came to dwell')—and demands God 'direct (his) steps' to the 'perpetual' ruins (v. 3a). The journey anticipated by the psalmist is akin to the theophany described in Deut. 33.2-3; Judg. 5.4-5, 20–21; Habakkuk 3; and Psalm 68, as God comes to deliver his people.

The psalmist describes the destruction of the temple within a chiastic framework (vv. 3b-10) before returning to ask again 'why?' (v. 11). This second question, albeit with some translation difficulties, asks about God's 'holding back' his hand, his 'right hand', a symbol of protection in Ps. 73.23 and saving action in Exod. 15.6, 12. Why does God abandon the congregation to this destruction through inaction? Why is there no hope of rescue or security?

The description in vv. 3b-10 is vivid, even though obscure in places in the Hebrew (esp. vv. 5-6). It opens with the general statement that the enemy has destroyed the sanctuary and the foe 'roared' (like a lion) in the holy place (vv. 3b-4a). Even the silence of the sanctuary is destroyed (cf. Ps. 65.1). The foe and enemy are mentioned in reverse order in v. 10, this time scoffing and reviling God's name. They have set up their 'emblems' (or 'signs', 'ôtōt, v. 4b). The reference could be to cultic or military banners or possibly even to 'omens' as seems to be the meaning in v. 9 where God's congregation receive no 'emblems' ('ôtōt) and there is no prophet or other individual who knows how long the disaster will continue. Of course, we do know of prophets from the time of exile, Jeremiah and Ezekiel among them. The point in Psalm 74 is not that there are no prophets around, but that they either do not receive a word from God as to how long the situation will last or they do not give a hopeful sign of a conclusion to it all.

As noted, the actual description of the destruction is difficult to decipher. Enough is clear, however, to picture the wielding of axes or adzes and other metal implements and the burning of the sanctuary. Even local shrines, which are possibly referred to by 'all the meeting places of God' in v. 8b, were burned. We could compare the description of God's act of judgment in Isa. 10.33-34.

The shock of the first section is countered strongly by vv. 12-17. The hopelessness of vv. 1-11 is met by what sounds like a hymn of praise to God. It certainly is praise but praise uttered in the context of lament. As such it performs a number of functions. It brings God's role as divine king, the one who can work 'salvation in the earth', to the fore. It describes God's royal role in terms of creation, employing the old myth of the battle of the creator God with forces of chaos in the guise of a sea monster. This is familiar from the Babylonian story *Enuma Elish* and in a different guise from the Ugaritic tales of Baal, but also in the biblical tradition from Isa. 51.9-10; Job 26.10-13; Pss. 65.7-8; 89.8-11; 93; 104.1-9; and 114. As a story of primordial conflict it portrays God as one able to meet the destructive activities of the enemy in the temple. The hymn also has a number of aspects which recall Israel's own story of beginnings in the exodus—the division of the sea, the food in the wilderness, the cutting of openings (v. 15; *bāqa'*, 'to cleave, split; cf. Exod. 14.16, 21). But in bringing such stories to mind and subtly relating the myth to the exodus story, so that the myth is grounded in history and past events seen in mythic perspective, the psalmist both tells what is 'really' happening in the destruction of the temple and highlights the unseen implications of God's present inactivity. Verses 12-17, therefore, function as a strong motivation for God to 'remember', i.e. respond in action. The frequent use of the emphatic pronoun *'attâ* ('you': seven times in vv. 13-17) with *lekā*, 'to you' twice in v. 16 underscores God's responsibility. God is capable of halting the destruction by the enemy and is the only one who can indeed redress the wrong, a wrong which ultimately is an attack on God's rule. If the people are to have hope in this circumstance then it lies with God and all the poet can do is sing the myths and stories of old which proclaim that point. In vv. 16-17, arranged in a chiastic pattern (day and night—luminaries—fixing boundaries—summer and winter), there may also be an allusion to the end of the flood story in Gen. 8.22.

One important point in this whole section, at least for the reading of Psalm 74 within the Psalter, is the fact that in v. 12 we have the only 1st person pronoun in the psalm, '*my* king'. The psalmist says this of God. If we hear in the psalms the voice of David, then the shift in focus to divine kingship both signals an emphasis to come, especially in Book IV, and points to another important aspect of the Davidic legacy, acknowledgement of God's kingship as the source of hope and praise in the face of devastating events in one's life.

The final section reiterates the call for God to 'remember' and the language of 'enemy/foe' and 'scoff/revile' (vv. 18, 22; cf. vv. 2, 10).

Eight imperatives addressed to God, both positive and negative, govern the section. In the description of the destruction it was God's 'name', which dwelt in the temple (v. 7), that was reviled by the enemy (v. 10). The theme of God's 'name' returns with mention of the 'impious' reviling it (v. 18) and the hope that the poor and needy will eventually praise it again (v. 21). It is clearly God's reputation that is at stake. The section is also set up in a chiastic pattern around the description of the enemy and God's people: enemy/impious people/wild animals—your dove/your poor—downtrodden/poor and needy—the impious/your foes/your adversaries. The outer verses on the enemy etc. (vv. 18, 22-23) are both introduced by 'remember' (// 'do not forget' in v. 23). The use of the possessive pronoun 'your' with both 'dove' (v. 19) and 'foes' (v. 23) also both highlights God's commitment to his people and stresses God as the one ultimately under assault. The call for God to 'have regard for the covenant' (MT, v. 20a) at the centre of this chiasm makes the same point.

When the psalmist refers to God's people using the phrase 'the life of your dove' (v. 19a; NRSV: 'soul') a number of references are possible. It may be simply a reference to the vulnerability of birds in general (Pss. 11.1; 102.7; 124.7) hence highlighting the cost of God's inactivity for the poor, or it might be an allusion to the use of doves in rituals associated with agreements in both the ancient Near East and Israel (cf. Gen. 15.9), hence underpinning the reference to covenant in v. 20, although which covenant is implied remains unclear. What God is asked to do in v. 22 is precisely the responsibilities of a covenant suzerain.

The use of *dak*, 'crushed' (NRSV: 'downtrodden') in v. 21, recalls both the description of the poor in Pss. 9.9 and 10.18 and the description of the one broken by God who now offers an acceptable sacrifice (Ps. 51.8, 17). The battle cry for God to 'arise' in v. 22 is, therefore, fitting from one who claims response from God (cf. Ps. 44.26; 82.8). The last word in the psalm, 'continually', reinforces the uncertain length of the destruction and its consequences, a point already stressed in v. 1 ('forever') and throughout the psalm (vv. 3, 9, 10, 19, 22-23). This is why the motivation for God to act must come from stories of long standing (vv. 2, 12-17) and why in vv. 16-17 God's rule over time and the seasons is stressed.

Israel's story is collapsed in time as we move from Book II to Book III. From mention of Solomon we have moved quickly to the destruction of the temple. But the aim seems not to stick strictly to the historical sequence in these psalms. We will meet in Psalm

79 another description of the temple's destruction and only in Psalm 89 is there mention of the demise of the Davidic dynasty. The history is presented theologically not just chronologically.

The problem in Psalm 74 is the enemy's attack on the temple and its theological consequences. God's name, i.e. reputation and authority, is at stake. But this attack has created a problem between God and God's people. If God has been their king 'from of old' God has both the power and reason to act. But God does not and there is no immediate mention of Israel's sin that might explain that fact (cf. later Ps. 79.8). Just as Psalm 73 dealt with a conflict between experience of the world and Israel's faith confession, so in Psalm 74 there is a conflict between the immediate experience of the destruction of the temple and what they have professed 'from of old', namely that God is 'my king' (Ps. 74.12). The destruction of the temple implies a breakdown in the relationship with God, in perceiving the nearness of God. That is what was addressed in Psalm 73. While the question of the wellbeing of the wicked gave rise to the individual psalmist's dilemma in Psalm 73, a matter extended to Israel in v. 1, the dilemma described in Psalm 74 raises an even greater and more urgent question. Psalm 73 suggests a possible solution for Psalm 74. Resolution of the dilemma will be in a reappraisal of what it has meant to call God 'my king from of old'. That will follow. The question of sin will not be irrelevant, but the focus will be on the kingship of God.

Psalms 75–77

After the desperation of Psalm 74 the note of thanksgiving in v. 1 of **Psalm 75** provides some hope. It is underscored in the clause 'your name is near' which combines emphasis on God's name from Ps. 74.7, 18, so reviled there, and the nearness of God in ways counter to experience from Ps. 73.28. Further hope is generated when thanksgiving quickly turns to a divine statement of impending judgment upon the wicked (75.2-5). The language of boasting even recalls the speech of the wicked in Ps. 73.11. Only with the God of Jacob (75.9) is there judgment 'with equity' (v. 2) and deliverance or 'lifting up' (v. 6). Psalm 75 bears a close relationship to Hannah's song in 1 Sam. 2.1-10, establishing those who pray it as among the righteous.

Psalm 76, a 'psalm of Zion' with similar themes and vocabulary to Psalms 46 and 48, continues the praise of the God of Jacob (76.6) from Psalm 75. It defies the disaster of Psalm 74 by proclaiming Salem//Zion as God's abode, the place where God broke 'the flashing arrows, the shield, the sword, and the weapons of war' (76.3). The community has known God's deliverance in the past (vv. 5-6, 8-9) and it leads to the proclamation of the greatness of God's name (v. 1; cf. 75.1 and 74.7, 18), to the praise of God's strength and might above all human might, even above the 'majestic mountains' (v. 4), and to the confession of the incomparability of God (v. 7) who judges the whole earth (vv. 8-9; cf. 75.2, 7). Even human rage will only lead to praise of God (v. 10). Thus, the psalmist calls for vows to Yahweh with hope in the one who cuts off the spirit of princes and inspires fear in kings. Psalm 76 addresses the despair of Psalm 74, with vv. 8-9 sounding like a direct response to 74.19-21.

Psalm 77 returns to lament, thus making a break with Psalm 76. The specific trouble is not detailed, but the agony of the psalmist is evident (vv. 1-4). The psalmist considers the 'days of old' (v. 5) and asks a series of questions whether this disaster will go on 'forever' (vv. 7-9). The language is reminiscent of Psalm 74 as is the recall of the deeds of Yahweh, the wonders of old and mighty deeds (Ps. 77.11-12). The mythological language in vv. 16-20 also recalls that of Ps. 74.12-15, although in Psalm 74 the language focused more on creation with a hint of the exodus in v. 15 while here the reference is more clearly to the exodus itself. This will lead naturally into Psalm 78 with its reference to 'dark sayings of old' about exodus (Ps. 78.2). Psalm 77 reminds that while there is cause for confident praise of God, it too becomes part of an urgent plea for deliverance in the context of disasters such as described in Psalm 74.

Psalm 78

The psalmist now utters 'dark sayings from of old' (v. 2) recalling God as king 'from of old' and God's 'wonders of old' in Pss. 77.11 and 74.12 respectively (cf. also Heb.: *qedem/miqqedem* in 74.2 [NRSV: 'long ago']; 77.5). This suggests that Psalm 78 is a response to the earlier laments. However, the 'dark saying', or more properly 'riddle, perplexing saying' (Heb.: $ḥîdôt$), is all the more perplexing since the new sanctuary and dynasty promoted in Psalm 78 are themselves questioned in Book III with the destruction of the sanctuary in Psalm 74 (repeated in Psalm 79), and God's rejection of the Davidic dynasty in Psalm 89. There is a 'riddle' in the placement of Psalm 78 as well as within its verses. It is well titled a *maśkîl* (from *śkl*, 'to be wise/skilful') implying some didactic purpose even though the form of Psalm 78 is not easily defined. While its focus is historical recitation, it is also proclamation for present and future generations, and may have had catechetical or liturgical functions in its own history (cf. Psalms 105, 106 and 136; Exod. 15.1-18 and Deuteronomy 32).

Psalm 78 falls into four major sections: vv. 1-8, an introduction; vv. 9-39, the rebellion and forgetfulness of the Ephraimites; vv. 40-64, the continued sin of the people in the wilderness and the promised land; and vv. 65-72, God's rejection of Ephraim and choice of Judah, Zion and David. The positive view of Judah along with connections to Hosea, Amos and Psalm 49, suggests an original date for Psalm 78 prior to or during the exile at the latest. In its present context in the Psalter, however, it carries new meaning.

The purpose of the psalm is set out in vv. 1-8. This section divides into vv. 1-4 and 5-8, both of which mention sayings or *torah* (cf. the synonyms *'ēdût*, 'testimony', v. 5, and *miṣwōt*, 'commandments', v. 7) recounting the wonderful deeds of God shown to 'our' ancestors to be told to future generations. Verses 1-4 form an invocation to 'my people' to listen to the teaching of the psalmist who speaks by way of *māšāl*, 'parable or proverb', and *ḥîdôt*, 'riddle, perplexing saying'. These terms suggest some deep and difficult lesson hidden in the past events to be learned again by later generations. The purpose is outlined further in vv. 5-8 where it is traced back to the decree established by Yahweh. It was given so that the people may have hope and not forget God's works unlike their ancestors. The intent in vv. 1-4 thus carries on God's intent in the *torah*. It is little wonder that the opening statement, 'Give ear, O my people, to my teaching', echoes God's own statement in Deut. 5.1 at the start of the Decalogue. The use of 'my people' already sets both the psalmist among this people, and as representative of God to the people, i.e. in some prophetic or royal role.

The first main section of the psalm begins abruptly in v. 9 with reference to the tribe of Ephraim, one of the main tribes of the northern kingdom, Israel. It took its name from Joseph's younger son (Gen. 41.51-52). Verse 9 could refer to any of three possible episodes, the defeat by the Philistines (1 Samuel 4–6), the defeat of Saul (1 Samuel 31) or the final defeat of the northern kingdom in 722 BCE (2 Kings 17). The reference to Shiloh in v. 60 favours the first episode. In the present form of the psalm, the reference to Ephraim introduces a major focus, namely the rejection of Ephraim who, counter to the point of God's decree, had forgotten what God had done in the past and broken the covenant (vv. 10-11; cf. v. 7).

Verses 12-16 describe the past deeds of God, namely the escape from Egypt and God's leadership and abundant provision in the wilderness. In spite of this Ephraim rebelled again and tested God (vv. 17-20). In the Pentateuch account of the wilderness wanderings Israel complained for lack of water and food (cf. Exod. 15.22-17.7; Num. 11; 20.1-13), but in Psalm 78 the sin of the people is to question God's care even after it has been clearly demonstrated. Their unsteadfast heart and faithless spirit (cf. v. 8) are not a lack of courage and trust in the face of danger, but a questioning of God's compassion having just experienced it.

Verses 21-22 open the next subsection, vv. 21-30, describing Yahweh's anger against Ephraim. The section also closes with an expression of God's anger (v. 31) making an *inclusio*. Verse 23 sounds like the beginning of a theophany in which God usually comes to combat enemies and save his people (e.g. Judg. 5.4-5; Hab. 3.3-15). But in Psalm 78 God is angry with Ephraim. We might expect some punishment for them but what God rains down is not destruction but manna and grain in abundance (vv. 24, 27). God's action embodies both great care for and frustration with the people.

In spite of this unexpected and undeserved abundance the people sin still further (vv. 32-39). God's anger is vented again but this time it is met by repentance. The people remember God is their rock and redeemer, but it is not a memory that negates their former forgetfulness (v. 11). Their repentance is mere flattery and lies (v. 36). Still, God, is compassionate, forgiving them and restraining his anger, remembering that they are flesh (v. 38). It is God's memory that sustains the people, not their own duplicitous recall.

As Psalm 78 unfolds we see each succeeding generation rebel and test God, not remembering their redemption in earlier times. The point of vv. 5-8 has been lost. The repetition of key words conveys this forgetfulness.

	verses 9-39	**verses 40-64**
to turn (*hāpak*)	v. 9	v. 57
to keep (*šāmar*)	v. 10 (covenant)	v. 56 (decrees)
to rebel (*mārâ*)	v. 17	vv. 40, 56
to test (*nissâ*)	v. 18	vv. 41, 56
anger (God's) (*'ap*)	vv. 21, 31, 38	vv. 49, 50 (58)

In vv. 40-55 Ephraim rebels in the wilderness. They are reminded of the plagues (vv. 43-51), the escape from Egypt, guidance in the wilderness and the possession of the promised land (vv. 52-55). Matters of memory, e.g. the plagues, are mixed with 'present' events such as the wilderness wanderings. The point appears not to be to produce a chronological record of the past deeds of God, but to illustrate the interplay between memory of events past and 'present'. Even the 'past' events function on more than one level. The plagues in vv. 43-51 serve not only as one of God's great deeds from the past but as a reminder of God's punishment of those who oppose his purpose (cf. the lists of plagues in Exodus 7–12 and Psalm 105).

While vv. 40-55 end with another example of God's graciousness toward the people in the apportionment of the promised land among Israel's tribes, vv. 56-64 record again how they have rebelled and tested the Most High God. This time the sins occur in the land and are briefly defined as idolatry (v. 58). God is again angry (vv. 59-64) abandoning his northern sanctuary at Shiloh (see 1 Sam. 4.1b-11). But there is a difference here. There is a sense of utter abandonment as even the widows do not even make lamentation (v. 64). Where is God's compassion?

The parallel structure between vv. 9-39 and 40-64 suggests that God's choice of Judah, Zion and David in vv. 65-72 is precisely that expression of compassion. Verse 64 ends in hopelessness and what follows is quite unexpected. Having delivered his people to captivity and the sword (vv. 61-62), God arises suddenly as if a drunken warrior rising from sleep to put his adversaries to rout. The image is one of uncontrollable power and the enemies, although undefined, may well be God's own people Ephraim (v. 67). In their place God chooses the tribe of Judah, Zion as the place of his sanctuary, and David to shepherd 'his people Jacob' (v. 71), the latter phrase recalling the use of 'my people' back in v. 1.

The choice of David is given most space in these verses and becomes the focus of the psalm. David is given two significant titles. He is first described as God's 'servant' (v. 70). The term is frequently used by the psalmist to refer to themselves (e.g. Pss. 19.11, 13; 27.9; 31.16; etc.) but is also used when speaking about David in the superscriptions to Psalms 18 and 36 and later in Pss. 132.10 and 144.10. It is used four times in Psalm 89 referring to David (vv. 3, 20, 39, 50). The term 'servant' is also one of honour among the Deuteronomists, in Second Isaiah and Ezekiel. Secondly, David is chosen to be 'shepherd' to God's people (v. 71). This term when used positively is reserved for God in the Psalter (Pss. 23.1; 28.9; 80.1) and Israel is occasionally referred to as God's 'sheep' (Pss. 74.1; 78.52; 95.7; 100.3). In Ps. 78.71 David is chosen to undertake the same shepherding task God had in the wilderness (vv. 52-53). A reason for this choice is only given in v. 72. David leads Israel 'with upright heart ... and ... with skilful hand.' In this he stands in contrast to the ancestors in v. 8.

At one level Psalm 78 is about the rejection of the northern kingdom and God's choice of Judah, Zion and the house of David. In spite of God's compassion, continuous rebellion led God to reject the tribe of Joseph in favour of Judah. However, the northern kingdom is only sparingly mentioned by name or location (only in vv. 9, 60 and 65). For the majority of the psalm the people are referred to generally as 'my people' (v. 1), 'Israel//Jacob' (vv. 5, 21, 31, 41, 55, 71), the 'ancestors' (vv. 3, 5, 8, 12, and 57) or by an unspecified 'they' etc. Thus, the psalm also speaks at a more general level to an Israel beyond the north, a unified Israel. The replacement of Ephraim by Judah and Shiloh by Zion also implies a single avenue of relationship with God. Therefore, Psalm 78 not only speaks about the Ephraimites but addresses those in Judah who follow. They too need to hear the 'riddle' within the psalm and learn the lesson passed down from the ancestors. The lack of a final word about Judah leaves the story open to the future where rebellion and hope will continue to shape the drama of Israel.

The psalm also speaks about the nature of the rebellion of Ephraim. The result of the psalm mixing memory of past events with present experience is twofold. First, Ephraim's rebellion did not arise through a lack of experience of God's compassion. They knew too well God's compassionate and forgiving nature yet still denied that in their behaviour. The psalm speaks about a deep level of memory that shapes action. It is thus in the realm of the heart that David is finally contrasted to both the ancestors and the generations which preceded him (see vv. 72 and 8, 18, and 37). Hope rests on memory which learns from both past events and from God's *torah* and covenant. What is to be passed on from one generation to another is a way of recounting the past that draws out its deep lessons about human rebellion and divine grace so that the lives of future generations are transformed. David is portrayed at the end of the psalm as the custodian of this memory, the one who embodies the divine guidance in his life.

But another riddle is attached to Psalm 78. Within the Psalter as a whole Psalm 78, with its tale of the rejection of the northern kingdom in favour of Judah, sits between the account of the end of David's reign and the accession of Solomon (Psalm 72) and the later demise of the Davidic dynasty (Psalm 89). This is appropriate both historically and theologically. But we also have in Book III Psalms 74 and 79 which tell of the destruction of the temple in Jerusalem, Psalm 77 which laments God's spurning his people, and Psalm 89 which will lament the end of the Davidic dynasty. In what way can one read Psalm 78 in this context?

First, the present placement of Psalm 78 suggests that it is an answer to the problems raised in Psalm 74 and 77. Recovery of the community through the compassion of God is possible. Even the demise of either or both the Jerusalem temple or the Davidic dynasty will not negate the hope of those who do 'not forget the works of God, but keep his commandments' (v. 7). Secondly, Psalm 78 sets David in an important position. He embodies God's leadership of the people. However, in the rough historical frame of the Psalter we have moved beyond David's period (cf. Ps. 72.20). Related to this question is the identity of the speaker. The use of the term 'servant' for David in Ps. 78.70 is a clue to the identity of the one imagined speaking in vv. 1-4. Both the unnamed speaker at the start and David at the end of the psalm embody the lessons of the psalm, as well as identify fully with the community (note the shift in pronouns from 'I' to 'we' in vv. 1-3). It may be possible that we have in Psalm 78 the first move toward *David redivivus*, picking up on the reference to David and his descendants in Ps. 18.50 and anticipating further development in Psalms 89, 132 and 144.

Psalms 79–88

The confident statements about Zion and God's servant David at the end of Psalm 78 are negated at the start of **Psalm 79**. Jerusalem lies in ruins, the temple has been defiled and God's 'servants' have become food for the birds. Common terms (nations, servant, blood, Jerusalem, neighbours, taunt) in vv. 1-4 and vv. 10-13, providing an *inclusio* for the psalm. These verses express concern for the future of God's people. In vv. 5-9 the familiar lament of 'How long, O Yahweh' is heard (v. 5; cf. Pss. 6.3; 13.1-2; 74.10 etc.). This section asks God whether the sin of people will affect God's response as a saving god (v. 8; cf. Ps. 78.18-19).

God's reputation and faithfulness are as much at stake as the people's future.

Any of the attacks on Jerusalem could be behind this psalm but the severity of this attack and connections with Jeremiah (e.g. vv. 2-3, cf. Jer. 7.33; 14.16; v. 6, cf. Jer. 10.25 etc.) suggest foremost the destruction of 586 BCE. Thus, both Psalm 74 and 79 speak of the same event. Psalm 79 is more concerned with human suffering, the role of sin and God's honour, while Psalm 74 deals with the cosmic significance of the destruction.

The psalms telling of temple destruction (Psalms 74 and 79) surround Psalm 78 describing the failure of the northern kingdom and the divine election of Judah, Zion and David. The positioning of Psalm 78 suggests that the destruction described in Psalm 74 is not the end of God's dealing with Israel, despite the historical anachronism. On the other hand, the placement of Psalm 79 argues that Psalm 78's positive end did not conclude the matter either. Psalm 79 begins a second sequence of psalms (Psalms 79–82) leading from lament through divine pronouncement (Psalm 81) to God's sovereignty in the divine council (Psalm 82), a sequence similar to that of Psalms 74–76. The cycle of lament and hope will continue, even in the gravest situations. Several terms and expressions associated with God connect Psalms 79 and 78 confirming the forward movement, namely 'wrath', 'memory and compassion' and 'shepherd' (cf. 79.5, 8–9, 13 with 78. 38–39, 52, 59).

Lament continues in **Psalm 80** picking up the shepherd imagery (cf. Pss. 78.52 and 79.13) but deepening the sense of despair. The $\bar{e}d\hat{u}t$ 'testimony' in the superscription (NRSV: 'covenant') may allude to the 'decree' (NRSV) in Ps. 78.5. God's wrath and Israel's scorn continue. The psalmist pleads for the deliverance of the community (vv. 3, 7, 19). Like Psalm 79, Psalm 80 ends with a plea to God (80.18). While references to Joseph etc. (vv. 1-2) suggest a northern origin, Psalm 80 has been edited to incorporate Jerusalem temple theology (cf. the reference to the cherubim of the ark, v. 1, and the similarity of the refrain and v. 18 to Num. 6.24-27). The destruction of both the northern kingdom and Jerusalem are incorporated in this one lament. The intent that Psalm 78 should speak to all Israel is carried forth.

The call to praise God at the start of **Psalm 81** suggests a festal context. God has made a 'decree', $\bar{e}d\hat{u}t$ etc. (v. 5; cf. Ps. 78.5 and 79 [superscription]) in Joseph. But then the psalmist hears an unknown voice responding to a call for help, probably that in

Psalms 79–80. The voice is soon revealed to be God's (vv. 6-16). This divine response is complicated by the people's continued rebellion. While God has fed them with tears (80.5) his desire has been to fill their mouth with 'the finest of the wheat' and 'honey from the rock' (81.10, 16). Psalm 81 is an initial divine decree following the lament of Psalm 79–80, just as Psalm 76 responded to Psalms 74–75.

The divine response moves in a new direction in **Psalm 82**. Instead of hearing of further divine action against the nations, we are ushered to the divine court where God sits in judgment in the midst of the gods (v. 1). In their rule on earth the gods have shown partiality to the wicked and not given justice to the lowly (vv. 2-3). Corruption in heaven leads to injustice on earth (v. 5c), so now God's just judgment in heaven becomes the foundation of a call for his judgment on the nations of earth (v. 8). They have destroyed God's temple, Jerusalem and his people (Psalms 79-80). The 'strange god among' Israel in Ps. 81.9 is, in Psalm 82, stripped of divine status by God who reigns over all.

At the start of **Psalm 83** we hear the cry of desperation that lies behind the petition (Ps. 82.8; cf. Ps. 50.3a). In vv. 5-8 a list of enemies, who continue to conspire against Israel and God, is given. God is asked to do to them as he had done to others in the past (vv. 9-12; alluding to Judges 4–8). The psalm ends (vv. 18) assuming that such enemies may yet know Yahweh as the Most High over all the earth (cf. Ps. 82.8). Psalm 83, despite possible northern origins (see vv. 5-8), may have been edited in the context of the larger Book III. Its lament reaches well beyond the historical bounds of the northern kingdom.

The mood changes again in **Psalm 84** as we begin the second group of Korah Psalms, Psalms 84–85, 87–88. Psalm 84 bears many similarities to the opening psalm of the earlier Korah collection (Psalms 42–49). The psalmist longs for the dwelling of Yahweh. The birds even have a home there (v. 3). The psalmist rejoices in Yahweh's care for those who 'walk uprightly' or in Yahweh (vv. 11-12). While the psalm could be prayed at the gates of the temple it could also be prayed by one who longs for Yahweh's dwelling from some distance, in time or space. In this vein v. 5 speaks of those in whose hearts are 'the paths of pilgrimage' ($m^esillôt$; NRSV adds 'to Zion'). Either physically or metaphorically they are turned toward Yahweh's dwelling. If the psalm is read as a distant prayer then it is not out of context in its present position. It more closely parallels Psalms 42–43 and lends itself even to times when the temple is either non-existent or inaccessible. The reference to the 'anointed' in v. 9 could then be either to the king or high priest, or quite possibly be an expression of hope in a new king to come.

Psalm 85, which may have been composed for an agricultural festival (see v. 12), speaks in its present context more generally of hope for deliverance. The reference to forgiveness in the past (vv. 2-3) could recall Psalm 78. Verses 4-7 then plead again for restoration. The NRSV translates the difficult phrase in v. 1, *šabtā š^ebît/s^ebût*, as 'restored the fortunes' and so presumes such an interpretation. Alternatively, the phrase could be understood eschatologically seeking some final deliverance. Whichever the case the psalmist waits hopefully for Yahweh to speak (vv. 8-9; cf. the silence of God in Ps. 83.1). At the end of the psalm, Yahweh comes with his entourage of steadfast love, faithfulness/truth, righteousness/justice and peace. Yahweh comes even as the one who walks uprightly turns, at least metaphorically, toward Yahweh (Ps. 84.5, 11). Finally, a point of ambiguity is evident. The NRSV translation of v.10, 'steadfast love and faithfulness will meet; righteousness and peace will kiss each other', is a beautiful poetic vision. However, the verbs used (*pāgaš* in Niphal and *nāšaq*) imply general encounter and in the latter case, the possibility of conflict. The meeting of justice, truth, faithfulness and love is not always a smooth encounter.

The quiet confidence of Psalms 84–85 continues in **Psalm 86**, which stands out as a psalm attributed to David in the midst of a Korah collection. In terms of content, the psalm is often seen as a recapitulation of the earlier Davidic collections (Pss. 3–41 and 51–72; cf. e.g. v. 2 with Ps. 25.20; v. 4b with Ps. 25.1; v. 6a with Ps. 55.1 etc.). Stress on the psalmist as Yahweh's 'servant' in vv. 2, 4 and 16 also recalls the designation of David as such (cf. esp. Ps. 78.70; and 18.1; 36.1; and later Psalm 89). The servant is mentioned in vv. 1-7 and 14-17 where we have petitions to Yahweh, who exhibits graciousness and steadfast love (vv. 2, 5, 15), to preserve and strengthen against the insolent. In vv. 8-13 David proclaims Yahweh as great recalling the picture of Yahweh among the gods (v. 8; cf. Psalm 82) and the nations coming to Yahweh's abode (v. 9; cf. Isa. 2.2-4; Mic. 4.1-3). It is an expression of the trust in Yahweh in time of difficulty already claimed in v. 2. This trust is built on creedal elements in vv. 10 and 13 which echo statements in the two petitions (vv. 5, 15; cf. Exod 34.6-7, 10). As the words of Yahweh's servant David, mentioned in Ps. 78.70, the whole psalm echoes earlier Davidic prayers and praise and draws later Israelites into the great king's trust in Yahweh.

Picking up the theme of Ps 86.9, **Psalm 87** anticipates the nations becoming citizens of the 'city of God', which stands gloriously upon the 'holy mountain'. Although the psalm is somewhat enigmatic in content, enough is clear to see that in this Song of Zion (cf. Pss. 46, 48, 76, 84, 122) Yahweh even registers the peoples as citizens of the city. It remains unclear, however, whether these peoples are foreign nations, diaspora Jews and/or proselytes. But within the context of Book III, especially with its description of the temple's destruction in Psalms 74 and 79, an eschatological reading of Psalm 87 is suggested. The list of nations in the psalm is a catalogue of ancient and exilic enemies of Israel. Their flowing into Zion counters the outflow of the fear of God from the city which it took to quell the assembled nations in the earlier Korah Psalms 46–48. At the same time Psalm 87 is the anticipated completion of the longing for both sanctuary and renewed land expressed in Psalms 84–85. But this longing is always in the context of the sin of Israel and the action of enemies which need to be faced. The promise of future peace and security will stand but only in the context of real disaster.

Book III is full of ups and downs, of shifts between hope and despair, darkness and light. **Psalm 88**, the most desperate of laments, plunges us from the heights of Psalm 87 into the language of death (vv. 3-7, 10-12), both physical and social (vv. 8, 18). A life threatening illness could be behind the psalm but the variety of imagery (undefined troubles, forsaken, overwhelming waves, captivity, cast off, being surrounded, flood) suggests we look to a more general context. The psalmist faces a 'death like' situation whatever its nature. Descriptions of the psalmist's plight (vv. 1-7 and 13-18), surround a central section (vv. 8-12). There is scarcely even a petition in the psalm, except that the psalmist's prayer be heard (v. 2; cf. vv. 9b, 13). A series of rhetorical questions (vv. 10-12) casts doubt on the efficacy of Yahweh's 'wonders', 'steadfast love', 'faithfulness', and 'saving help'. The psalm ends with cry that all is in darkness (v. 18). In fact, darkness pervades the psalm (vv. 1, 6, 9 and 12), in contrast to the assurance that Yahweh is 'sun and shield' withholding nothing from those who trust and walk uprightly (Ps. 84.11-12).

Contrast is at the heart of the function of Psalm 88 in its present context. The Asaph psalms (Pss. 73–83) juxtapose hope and lament portraying anguish over the destruction of Jerusalem (Psalms 74, 79) alongside the seeming unending graciousness of Yahweh (Psalm 78). The repeated cycle of lament leading to hope (Pss.74–76 and 79–82) underscores this but this sub-collection concludes with another lament asking again that the enemies of Israel may know Yahweh's sovereignty (Psalm 83). The Korah psalms (Pss. 84, 85, and 87) extend this hope with longing for Yahweh's dwelling and restoration of the land. However, the darkness of Psalm 88 throws a pall over this hope returning us again to the hardness of Israel's existence. We are left balancing hope with uncertainty, the reality of the latter of which cannot be underestimated. As we will see in Psalm 89, the very promise of Yahweh to David, presumed at the end of Psalm 78, will itself be threatened by Yahweh's own inaction. The matters that are the subject of the rhetorical questions in Ps. 88.10-12 will be tested, and all this in spite of a reiteration of David's own prayer in Psalm 86.

Psalm 89

Psalm 89 concludes Book III of the Psalter. While attributed to one Ethan the Ezrahite, a wise man of renown according to 1 Kgs 4.31, it is a psalm about Yahweh's promise of eternal faithfulness to the dynasty of David, a promise which has been broken.

The psalm breaks into five sections. Verses 1-4 introduce the subject of the psalm. This is developed in two sections, first a hymn of praise to Yahweh in vv. 5-18 and then a recall of Yahweh's promise to David and his descendants in vv. 19-37. The shift from present words about Yahweh to Yahweh's own past words after v. 18 suggests a break at that point. Finally, in vv. 38-48 the psalmist laments how things have gone wrong and petitions Yahweh in vv. 49-51, in language recalling the introductory verses, to remember his servant. Verse 52 is the benediction which concludes Book III of the Psalter. The psalm contains elements of thanksgiving and lament. The fact that the thanksgiving precedes the complaint and petition, contrary to most individual laments, and thus becomes the basis for lament, gives the petition particular power and an open-endedness seen only in a few other laments (e.g. Pss. 44; 74; 88).

There are a number of possibilities for the date of the final composition. The focus on the present situation of the king and lack of reference to the temple's destruction could suggest that some pre-exilic national defeat has occasioned the psalm.

Connections to kings Jehoiachin, Hezekiah or Josiah and others are possible. On the other hand, the disaster described in vv. 40-44 is so great that it is hard not to associate it with the destruction of Jerusalem in 587 BCE. Finally, the lack of reference to the temple might suggest that it has been rebuilt, setting the psalm after 515 BCE. The latter suggestions do not preclude some earlier sections within the hymn. The lack of specificity may even have allowed the psalm to work in more than one context.

The psalm opens with a strong word of praise. The psalmist will sing of Yahweh's $ḥ^a sādîm$ ('acts of steadfast love'; NRSV sg.) and $'^e mûnâ$ ('faithfulness') forever and to all generations. *ḥesed* and $'^e mûnâ$ are, either in the psalmist's belief (MT; NRSV: 'I declare') or as declared by Yahweh (LXX: 'you said'), established forever, 'as firm as the heavens' (v. 2). The parallel use of Yahweh's 'steadfast love' and 'faithfulness' sets the theme for the psalm. These words appear seven and eight times respectively in the psalm, six times together (cf. also Pss. 85.10; 86.15 and 88.11). The rhetorical question in Ps. 88.11, whether Yahweh's 'steadfast love' and 'faithfulness' can be declared in death, is developed fully in Psalm 89 in relation to the Davidic dynasty.

Verses 3-4 quote Yahweh's promise regarding the covenant established with his 'chosen', his 'servant David', the language recalling Ps. 78.70. This promise is, like the psalmist's declaration of praise in v. 1, 'forever' and 'for all generations'. In quoting Yahweh's own words the psalmist's declaration stands on firm ground. The words of Yahweh lead naturally into a hymn of praise (vv. 5-18) for Yahweh as wonder worker, faithful and incomparable among the $b^e nê$-$'ēlîm$ ('children of the gods'; NRSV: 'heavenly beings'). The language in vv. 6-7 recalls the scene in Psalm 82. The hymn describes Yahweh's victory over Rahab in creation ending with a statement of Yahweh's sovereignty (v. 13), the foundations of which are 'righteousness' and 'justice'. His courtiers are 'steadfast love' and 'faithfulness', the eternal characteristics of Yahweh and that which the psalmist praises (v. 14; cf. Ps. 85.10-11). All of this has its parallels in ancient Near Eastern myth.

The hymn concludes with the blessedness (NRSV: 'Happy') of those who walk in the light of Yahweh. What is celebrated in the heavens has its counterpart in the lives of Yahweh's people on earth. The darkness of Psalm 88 is nowhere contemplated in this praise (v. 15). All that has been said in Psalm 89 so far contradicts the anguish of Psalm 88. The shield, i.e. protection, and the king of these people belong to Yahweh, the Holy One of Israel (v. 18). Although we do not know it yet, these traditional affirmations anticipate in word and idea the lament to come.

In vv. 19-37 Yahweh speaks again, but now to his 'faithful ones' (MT pl., NRSV translates as sg.). Already, therefore, there is a hint at the addressee in the psalm being broader than just the Davidic king. The promise Yahweh makes is fulsome and positive. Yahweh's hand will 'be established' with David (v. 21, *kûn*; NRSV: 'remain'), using the same verb as will later refer to the eternal establishment of the moon (v. 37a). No enemy will outwit David (v. 22) and Yahweh will crush David's foes before him (v. 23). Yahweh's steadfast love and faithfulness, which go before Yahweh in the heavens (v. 14b), will be with David (v. 25). A correspondence is being established between the statements of praise called for in the heavens and what is promised David on earth. This correspondence was anticipated already in vv. 1-4 where Yahweh's promise was said to be forever just as the psalmist promised to sing of Yahweh's steadfast love forever. The correspondence is detailed:

the Lord's hand/arm is strong (v. 13)
   the Lord's hand/arm will be with David and strengthen him (v. 21)
the Lord defeats his mythic enemies [Rahab] (vv. 9-10)
   the Lord promises to defeat David's foes (vv. 22-23)
steadfast love and faithfulness go before the Lord (v. 14)
   they shall be with David (v. 24)
the Lord rules/stills the raging sea (vv. 9-10)
   the Lord will set David's hand on sea/river (v. 25)
the Lord rules in heaven and is great and awesome above all around him (vv. 5-7)
   David rules on earth but will be the highest of kings (v. 27)
Israel's horn is exalted by the Lord's favour (v. 17)
   David's horn will be exalted in the Lord's name (v. 24)

The reign of David and his descendants is intricately bound to the reign of Yahweh over creation. David and his successors are Yahweh's agents, but this is more than simply authorisation for the dynasty. It ties the question of the sovereignty of Yahweh firmly to the fortunes of the Davidic line. The creation language throughout the correspondence implies this. Unlike Psalm 72, only the king's military activity, which corresponds to Yahweh's victory over chaos in creation, is mentioned in Psalm 89. Any defeat of the Davidic king calls not only human but divine sovereignty into question. However, this raises the question of the frailty of the Davidic kings. The problem is dealt with directly. While David's royal status is stressed, he remains, nevertheless, one 'found', 'chosen from the people' (Ps. 89.19c-20a). His humanity is underlined. But even if David's descendants forsake Yahweh's law, effectively failing the law of the king in Deut. 17.18-20 or not living up to the aspirations of Ps. 1.2, Yahweh vows not to violate his own covenant (Ps. 89.34). The faithfulness of Yahweh in the face of human waywardness demonstrated in Psalm 78 up to David's time is promised even beyond that. Human sinfulness will not nullify the divine promise.

The enduring witness of the sun and moon (vv. 36-37) in part provides a point of comparison for the everlasting nature of the line of David in the promise of Yahweh. They represent the heavenly bodies, which have been firmly established (v. 2). They are also a reminder of the sovereignty of Yahweh over the heavens (v. 17). The imagery may also call upon ancient Near Eastern treaty traditions in which deities associated with the sun and moon, among others, are called upon to act as witnesses to the agreement.

The promise of Yahweh in Psalm 89 recalls other texts, notably 2 Sam. 7.8-17 (// 1 Chron. 17.7-14) and Isa. 55:1-5. While the essence of the promise is similar in regard to the dynasty of David and some relationship between them cannot be ruled out, a different purpose is at work in Psalm 89. The promise to the dynasty in the psalm is made foundational on a cosmic scale.

Having set up this close correspondence with an eternal promise on Yahweh's part, the complaint in vv. 38-48 comes as a shock. A series of accusations are made against Yahweh which relate specifically to the promise. In vv. 38-40 Yahweh is 'full of wrath against his anointed' (cf. v. 20), has 'renounced the covenant with (his) servant' (cf. v. 34), and has defiled the king's crown. The accusation is detailed in terms of the conquest of the city (vv. 40-45), hence suggesting the time to exile, although further allusions connect this section also with the promise. Yahweh has strengthened the hand of enemies who rejoice (v. 42, cf. vv. 21-23, 25), has thrown David's throne to the ground and cut short his days (v. 45, cf. v. 29). In short, the promises founded in Yahweh's own kingship are not operative in the life of king and people.

The lament itself is expressed in vv. 46-48 with reference to the frailty of humankind. Sounding a little like Ecclesiastes there could be a touch of cynicism in these verses although it is more likely the point is to highlight the eternity of the divine promise.

The lament widens the relevance of the psalm beyond the king with reference to 'all mortals' in v. 47 and the general question in v. 48. Moreover, although the Hebrew of v. 47 presents some translation problems, the personal reference by the psalmist (NRSV: 'my time'; MT $'^{a}ni$, 'me') suggests the possibilities that the psalmist stands in the line of David or that the psalm is appropriated beyond even David's line. That is, the fate of the royal house is representative of that of the people as a whole.

The lament continues in vv. 49-51 while developing the petition for Yahweh to 'remember' already briefly mentioned in v. 47. These final verses are important. The vocabulary of vv. 1-4 ('steadfast love', 'faithfulness', 'swore to David', 'servant', and 'anointed') is repeated creating an *inclusio*. This is reinforced by the return of the 1st person singular pronoun (v. 50b; cf. v. 1a). This *inclusio*, however, does not bring us quite back to the starting point for while there are connections across the psalm, there is also tension between the start and the unresolved ending. The only hope for the psalmist is to cling tenaciously to the possibility of Yahweh's steadfast love and faithfulness being everlasting as is proclaimed. This confidence may even be present in the addition of v. 53, the concluding doxology for Book III. Its blessing upon Yahweh counters the unanswered petitions of vv. 50-51.

The superscription attributes Psalm 89 to Ethan the Ezrahite, thus removing it in a sense from David. David remains throughout a figure of the past (vv. 3, 49), albeit a faithful, mighty, and chosen one. However, there are times when the psalmist speaks personally and assumes the role of inheritor of the promise to David (e.g. vv. 47, 50). While the psalmist may not be David, they stand in his line.

The situation is developed further with the use of the collective pronoun 'our' in vv. 17-18. In fact, vv. 15-18 are spoken on behalf of the community. Other features of the MT suggest a collective interpretation but are lost in translations. These include in v. 19 where the vision of Yahweh's promise is spoken to $h^{a}sîdêkā$, 'your faithful ones' (NRSV: sg.) and in v. 50 where Yahweh is called to remember $'^{a}bādêkā$, 'your servants' (NRSV: sg.). More broadly, v. 27 is the only place in the Hebrew Bible where 'firstborn' is used of the king. Elsewhere it is used of all Israel (e.g. Exod. 4.22; Hos. 11.1). All of this suggests that Palm 89 is not meant to be appropriated only by the royal household but by a wider community. The parallelism of vv. 50-51 would, therefore, suggest a collective interpretation of 'your anointed' (cf. Hab. 3.13a).

The call to remember (v. 50) is a call for Yahweh to act in the present as in the past; in this case to act on the promise to David. Divine remembering is a way of actualizing Yahweh's presence as it has been experienced in the past. The experiences behind Psalms 74, 79 and now 89 in particular threaten not only Israel's existence but call into question all they have known and experienced about Yahweh. It is little wonder that the call for Yahweh to remember his past ways (or in reverse not remember Israel's sin) is particularly frequent in Book III and onwards (Pss. 74.2, 18, 22; 78.39; 79.8; 88.5; 89.47, 50). It can be argued that the stress laid on the covenant with David in Psalm 89 (vv. 3, 28, 34, 39) is a way of both relating this royal covenant to the Sinai one and its theology, and of transferring emphasis to it. Such a shift would fit the post-exilic references to the covenant with David (2 Sam. 23.1-7; Isa. 55.1-5; Jer. 33.19-22; 2 Chr. 13.5; 21.7).

This shift in Book III is matched by another which seeks to address the calamities and failures of the period of the divided monarchy. We noted before the early emphasis in Book III on the destruction of the temple in Psalm 74 and repeated in Psalm 79. Now in Psalm 89 the continuity of the Davidic dynasty seems lost. If Book II of the Psalter led us to the transition from David to Solomon, Book III deals with the historical realities of the period after Solomon in a quasi-historical fashion, with references to the destruction of the temple (Psalms 74; 79) enveloping the earlier story of the northern kingdom Israel (Psalm 78). At both ends of the book a psalm of national disaster is preceded by an individual psalm of distress. The book ends with two psalms without resolution (Psalms 88; 89) implying that the solution to the national dilemma is not yet fully clear. On the other hand, hints at a resolution have already been given. In Psalm 73, the first psalm in the book, the resolution of the problems of experience and faith lie in a new understanding of God's goodness to Israel and of God as refuge, as well as an emphasis on the telling of God's works (Ps. 73.20). Psalm 78 does this last thing in a way that focuses attention on the Davidic dynasty. However, by surrounding Psalm 78 with psalms of later disasters, it is suggested that lessons to be taken from God's past works have to be understood in a new context. The old hopes of the Davidic monarchy expressed in various ways in Psalm 2–72, reflected in part in Ps. 89.26, need to be modified in light of new national experiences. However, the hope bound up with the election of David itself, as highlighted in Psalm 78, is still relevant for the future. Whether this election will be reshaped in messianic terms or in some other form of restoration of the Davidic dynasty is yet to be seen. Book III of the Psalter helps those faithful who struggle with the relation between hope, faith and divine promise on the one hand and historical experience on the other. The resolution is not yet fully expressed but the issues have been raised.

Book IV

Psalm 90
Although Psalm 90 has a number of translation difficulties, it clearly provides both a link back to earlier psalms and a new direction for the Psalter at the start of Book IV. The superscription attributes the psalm to Moses, the only psalm to do so. We also note that Moses is referred to a total of seven times in Book IV and only once elsewhere. This focus is significant. Outside the Psalter Moses is associated with major poems in the Hebrew Bible, especially Exod. 15.1-18; Deut 31.30-32.43 and 33.1-29. Some of Psalm 90's language bears similarities to the poems in Deuteronomy. Moses is designated 'man of God' in Deut. 33.1 as he is in the superscription to Psalm 90 (cf. Josh. 14.6; Ezra 3.2). In terms of the psalm's content, the attribution to Moses reminds us that Moses was the only one who interceded with God for the people and told God to 'repent' (šûb) and 'have compassion' (nāḥam) (cf. the same verbs in Exod. 32.12). In addition, Moses clearly suffered under divine wrath as does the psalmist and their audience (cf. Deut 3.26; 32.51-52). The attribution of the psalm to Moses, for whatever reason, takes the psalm in the reader's mind back to a time before the Davidic covenant, indeed to the earlier covenant of Sinai. It may even suggest a time of waiting and hope, even as Moses failed to see the fulfilment of his leadership of God's people (Deuteronomy 34).

The psalmist speaks in the 1st person plural throughout the psalm, drawing the community into the prayer. While it has some elements of lament (e.g. the final petition in vv. 13-17), other elements are missing, replaced by doxology (vv. 1-2) and a central complaint couched in wisdom like reflections (vv. 3-12). The rhetorical question and wisdom petition in vv. 11-12 are at the heart of the psalm. The occurrence of the word *'ᵃdōnāy*, 'Lord', in the first and last verses of the psalm provides an *inclusio* and a sense of completion in God. The mixed form of the psalm may have some Sumero-Babylonian and Egyptian parallels but in its present context, it seems to have mostly didactic and reflective purposes. The contents of the psalm do not dictate an exilic date for its composition but it is certainly not out of place in that period.

Verses 1-2 consist of the praise of God in the form of an extensive chiasm: 'Lord, you'—'all generations'—mountains—'were brought forth'—'you formed'—'the earth and the world'—'from everlasting to everlasting'—'you are God'. The focus is on the one called $^{a}dōnāy$, 'Lord', later named Yahweh in v. 13, being God, a statement founded in the traditions of creation. This one is described as a 'dwelling place' (v. 1, $mā'ôn$; sometimes translated as 'refuge'). An important shift takes place here. $mā'ôn$ is rare in the psalms and has only been used so far in Pss. 26.8; 68.6; and 71.3. In the last it implies the sense of refuge but in all three it refers to a physical place, especially the temple in the first two. Synonyms such as $miškan$, 'abode, dwelling' (Pss. 43.3; 74.7; 78.60; 84.1) or $sukkô$, 'thicket, booth, refuge' (Ps. 76.2) have also been used in a physical sense. However, in Ps. 90.1 and in 91.9, $mā'ôn$ (translated 'refuge' in the latter in NRSV) is applied to God (cf. Deut. 33.27 where the MT reads 'the eternal God is a dwelling place'). Our attention is shifted from places where God dwells, to God being the one in whom the community dwells; it is a fitting word when all other institutions of the faith have been decimated.

The grandeur of the initial statement about God is countered in vv. 3-6 by reflection on the brevity of human life. This recalls similar questions in Ps. 89.46-48. The situation in Psalm 90 is further complicated when human sinfulness is brought into the equation (vv. 7-10). Moreover, it is God who 'turns' humans back to dust (v. 3) and 'consumes them by his anger' (v. 7). The MT of v. 5a gives rise to a number of interpretations but the sense of humans being 'swept away' and becoming 'like sleep', so MT, is firm and implies a transitory and vulnerable existence. No enemy is mentioned in this psalm as is usually the case in laments. Here the community's adversary is the one who is God, their 'dwelling place'.

There is need in this complex situation for seeking wisdom and understanding. It is little wonder that the section ends in vv. 11-12 with a question and a petition. The petition is not for relief, which will be the concern of the next section, but for learning: 'so teach us to count our days, that we may gain a wise heart.'

Of course, even in this contemplation of human frailty before the eternal nature of the divine, there is already evidence of some learning and the gaining of wisdom. First, the section does not relate sin to the brevity of human life in a simple causal fashion. Rather the two are juxtaposed with the brevity of life discussed before any mention of sinfulness and divine wrath. Humans may come to the end of their life 'in (God's) anger' (v. 7) but that is a statement of extent not cause. Secondly, the statement of God as 'dwelling place' in v. 1 is not negated by the knowledge of human limitation, for both the petition for wisdom in v. 12 and that for relief in vv. 13-16, presume the sovereignty of God acts even in the brief lives of the pray-ers. Indeed, it could be argued that knowledge of divine wrath is the very thing that brings hope to the community because it is that knowledge that leads the community to respond to God as dwelling place, even if only for the brief time at their disposal.

This sense of acceptance of the brevity of life and of the recognition of God's presence even within that brief span has been the usual understanding of these verses. A lot depends on how we understand the verbal phrases 'who knows' in v. 11a (NRSV: 'who considers') and 'to count our days' in v. 12a. The former could be a negative statement, i.e. 'no one can know' (cf. Prov. 24.22; Eccl. 2.19), or on the other hand anticipate a positive answer (e.g. 2 Sam. 12.22; Joel 2.14 and Jonah 3.9). The petitions in vv. 12-17 suggest that the question in v. 11a is genuinely an open one. The verbal phrase 'to count our days' in v. 12a, could mean, on the basis of Akkadian and Ugaritic prayers and omen texts relating to the length of suffering of the pray-er, that the psalmist contemplates not the brevity of life in general so much as the length of the present distress. This would fit the question of 'How long?' which follows. But over against this there is still the statement in v. 7, which sees life determined by the wrath of God. There is also the general propensity of laments to maintain hope in the midst disaster. It is not beyond bounds that in Psalm 90 the psalmist contemplates both the brevity of life and the general implications of that as well as the immediate matter of the length of the present dilemma. If the present dilemma is read as the exile then counting one's days has a particular pertinence.

Further contrast is made in vv. 13-17 as the psalmist turns quickly to seek a 'turning' from God (v. 13, šûbâ, also 'return, repent') and asking 'How long?' Contemplation of the brevity of life in comparison to the eternity of God has neither dulled the psalmist's brazenness to demand things of God nor their trust that to do so is a worthwhile task. If the counting of days in v. 12a is a matter of the length of present suffering, then the psalmist's question of 'How long?' is clear and consistent. However, if there is some level of contemplation on the fleetingness and vulnerability of human life then there is no little irony in the question. Even in the brevity of their life, God's servants will seek compassion, be satisfied with God's 'steadfast love' (*ḥesed*) and rejoice all their days. Only what is everlasting can satisfy in such a short life. They seek joy that will at least match the time of 'evil' they have seen (v. 15).

In this section there are a number of connections both within the psalm and without. The reference to 'the morning' recalls vv. 5-6 in the earlier section. The demand for God to 'turn' recalls that same section of Psalm 89 that the second section of Psalm 90 reflected, namely 89.46-48. The link between the end of Book III and the start of Book IV is made firmer by reference to satisfaction with God's 'steadfast love'. It was precisely that entity that was questioned in Psalm 89. Thus, there is a level of resolution in Psalm 90 to the problem faced in Psalm 89. At the same time the reference to 'servants' (pl.) in 90.13 broadens the question beyond the one servant, i.e. the Davidic monarch. A broadening of the use of 'servant' and 'anointed' had already started in Psalm 89, especially in vv. 50-51.

Psalm 90 ends with a petition for $^{\text{}a}dōnāy$ to prosper the work of the community. We have already noted that the occurrences of $^{\text{}a}dōnāy$ in vv. 1 and 17 create an *inclusio* around the psalm. That is strengthened by reference to the work of human hands in v. 17 and the work of God in creation in v. 2a. The comparison ties the two together, while the contrast maintains the theme of vv. 3-12. The eternal and everlasting nature of God's work finds manifestation in the limited and fleeting toil of humans. This is the nature of God's dwelling with his people and the thing which gives human work its value. Just as in Psalm 73 at the beginning of Book III where the psalmist concluded that goodness was in the nearness of Yahweh, so now, in acknowledging the fleetingness and vulnerability of human life, as well as the pervasiveness of the people's iniquities and secret sins, the psalmist concludes that to know God's work, glory and favour, and to have our work prosper is a wonder.

This psalm is not a mournful reflection on the brevity of human life and a resignation to the inevitability of death. While it has both elements of the wisdom tradition reflecting on the human lot in life and those of the lament, its main function at the start of Book IV is one of generating hope. It calls the servants of Yahweh to entrust their brief experience of life to the one who grants life and who as God is their dwelling place.

Seen in this vein, the psalm creates a number of tensions and contrasts with previous prayers. In the election of the tribe of Judah, Zion and the house of David at the end of Psalm 78, great hope was placed in central institutions—social allegiance, city and temple, kingship. But other psalms in Book III proved that these can fail. The temple can be destroyed (Psalms 74, 79), city walls can fall (Ps. 89.40), and kings can lose divine support (Ps. 89.43-45). Psalm 90 calls on Yahweh's servants to recognize another place of confidence, and to put trust in the one behind the election. It reminds us that entrusting our brief and frail time to God is itself an act of faith. Gaining a wise heart involves above all understanding that God is our dwelling place. Even if the act of 'counting our days' in v. 12 is in part a matter of seeking how long suffering will last, and in this context the suffering of exile, then it is also calling upon those who suffer to continue to seek the favour of Yahweh and ask that the work of their hands might participate in the divine work in creation. It is also a plea that wrath will not be the only thing which defines the divine-human relationship. Sin is certainly a factor in that relationship, and it can have dire consequences, but it need not determine all.

As we commence Book IV of the Psalter Psalm 90 forms a bridge to a new understanding of faith. It takes us back to a time before that of David and his covenant with Yahweh. Through its superscription, notable in a book of the Psalter which has a prevalence of psalms without superscriptions, it introduces a 'Mosaic' emphasis which will remain strong through the book. Psalm 90 prepares for a deepening of faith which will help Yahweh's people move beyond the laments that have dominated their life to date. Their focus will be on Yahweh as king.

Psalms 91–104

Psalms 91–92 develop themes raised in Psalm 90. **Psalm 91** speaks to those who live in 'the shelter of Most High' and who proclaim Yahweh as refuge. It is about those for whom Yahweh is a dwelling place ($mā\ ̔ôn$ is repeated in Ps. 91.9 from 90.1). It assures them that Yahweh hears the call in Psalm 90 and will deliver them (91.14-15). In contrast to the brevity of life lamented in Ps. 90.4-6, 9-10, Yahweh will satisfy them with long life (91.16a). As further assurance, **Psalm 92** gives thanks declaring Yahweh's steadfast love and faithfulness and countering the questions of Psalm 89. A brief connection is made in v. 1 to Psalm 91 ('Most High', cf. 91.1 and the divine 'name', cf. 91.14) and more substantial ones back to Psalm 90 through the realisation of several aspects of the petition in Ps. 90.13-17 (see the common terms/phrases 'gladness' and 'joy' in 92.4, cf. 90.14-15, and Yahweh's 'work' in 92.4-5, cf. 90.16). The image of the briefly flourishing grass is picked up from 90.5-6 in 92.7, albeit in a negative way. The righteous are compared to an evergreen tree planted in the house of Yahweh. The reference to the righteous dwelling with Yahweh in a tangible location (vv. 12-14; cf. Psalm 1), in contrast to Yahweh becoming their 'dwelling place' as in Ps. 90.1, raises the question of whether a future promise about the temple's reconstruction is indicated.

Psalm 93 introduces the sequence Psalms 93–100 which is central to Book IV. It affirms Yahweh's kingship over all creation. The clause Yahweh $mālak$, 'The Lord is (has become) king' echoes through these psalms (Pss. 93.1; 96.10; 97.1; 99.1; note also 95.3; 98.6; 99.4). Yahweh's establishment of the world (93.1c) is the foundation of kingship. He is more majestic than the many waters, the symbol of the forces of chaos (v. 4). Moreover, his kingship is everlasting (v. 2), as too are 'his decrees' and the 'holiness' that befits his house (v. 5). This is a statement of trust and confidence that Yahweh will provide peace, security and order in the world. The reference to Yahweh's 'house' ($bayit$; also = 'temple') is again perplexing. In what way does this 'house' relate to the destroyed structure of Psalms 74 and 79?

With **Psalm 94** the mood changes briefly. It takes up the plight of the afflicted and seeks Yahweh as the God of vengeance to judge the wicked and plead for the orphan etc. The reference to the foot slipping (v. 18a) and the apparent success of the oppressors (vv. 4-7) recalls the dilemma of Psalm 73, but here the psalmist is confident that Yahweh will not forsake his people (v. 14-15). Yahweh's steadfast love holds him up (v. 18b). The theme of Yahweh's kingship is not explicit in this psalm but the petition for justice and the concern for the widow and orphan suggest a royal context. What is at issue in Psalm 94 is human pride and arrogance (esp. v. 7). Yahweh's 'majesty' in 93.1 ($gē'ût$), however, forms a counterpoint to 'the proud' ($gē'îm$) in 94.2-7. Confidence in Yahweh's sovereignty justifies the call on Yahweh to intervene for the people. So while Psalm 94 dampens the enthusiasm of Psalm 93 somewhat, it nevertheless builds on the latter's central assertion. That is made explicit through shared common vocabulary: e.g. *dky* 'roaring' in 93.3 and *dk'* 'to crush' in 94.5; *nś'* 'to lift up, rise' in 93.3 and 94.2; *mwṭ* 'to totter' in 93.1 and 94.18 (NRSV: 'be moved' and 'slip') etc.

The fact that Psalm 94 is followed by another psalm, **Psalm 95**, which proclaims that Yahweh is 'a great king above all gods' (v. 3) further anchors Psalm 94 in place. Following the petition of Psalm 94, Psalm 95 is an invitation to the community to give thanks and praise to Yahweh as king. The last part of the psalm (vv. 7b-11) reads as a response from Yahweh that 'you' (pl.) would listen to Yahweh's voice and not be like those in the wilderness who tested Yahweh. This echoes the use of the wilderness period as one of rebellion against Yahweh in Book III (cf. Pss. 78.17-31; 81.10-13).

Psalms 96–99 form a set of four hymns of praise with an alternating correspondence. Psalms 96 and 98 each begin with a call to the people to 'sing to the Lord a new song' (96.1; 98.1). The reasons given for the summons are, in the case of Ps. 96.4-6, the greatness of Yahweh the creator above all other gods who are but idols, and in 98.1b-3 that Yahweh has remembered his steadfast love (contra the question in Psalm 89) and made his victory known. A longer summons for all creation to praise Yahweh follows in each case (Ps. 96.7-13a ; 98.4-9a), and a second reason, 'for he is coming to judge the earth' (96.13; 98.9). The seemingly unrestrained praise of Psalms 96 and 98 is interspersed with more measured praise of Yahweh's awesome majesty in Psalms 97 and 99. Each begins with the statement Yahweh *mālak*, refers to Zion (97.8; 99.2), and focuses on Yahweh's holiness, especially Psalm 99 (97.12b; 99.3, 5, 9). Read in sequence, however, a progression can be seen in these four psalms. From general praise for Yahweh as creator who is coming (Psalm 96), we see him coming in clouds, fire etc. in Psalm 97 as those who worship idols are put to shame and those who hate evil rejoice. In Psalm 98 praise is summoned after Yahweh's victory as he prepares to judge the people which Psalm 99 declares him to have done. Moses, Aaron and Samuel stand as witnesses of those who have called on Yahweh's name and whom he has answered and avenged for the wrongs they have suffered (v. 8). The praise summoned in Ps. 96.10 echoes the summons of 93.1 thus joining this sequence to the earlier psalm in Book IV. We have also returned again to Zion in

Psalms 96–99 where Yahweh is enthroned (99.2) presuming again some future hope or a rebuilding of the temple.

The call to praise Yahweh widens in **Psalm 100** to the whole earth (v. 3; cf. Ps. 90.2). The reason given for this praise in v. 5 is partly because his steadfast love and faithfulness are eternal. That was declared at the start of Ps. 89.1-2 but questioned by the end of the psalm. Now it is fully asserted. We have moved beyond the dilemma of exile to a new level of praise and experience. Appropriately, Psalm 100 is designated a *mizmôr l^etôdâ*, i.e. 'a psalm for thanksgiving'. It is the climax of the psalms on Yahweh's kingship quoting Ps. 95.7 verbatim in v. 3 and alluding to 95.1-2 in v. 1, thus forming an *inclusio* around the sequence of Psalms 96–99. It also has a number of verbal connections with that group. The connection with Psalm 95 also serves to answer the open-endedness of that earlier psalm, where we were left at the end with only the example of the faithlessness of the wilderness generation of Israel. The summons of Psalm 100 calls not only a later generation of Israelites to praise but all the earth.

In the last section of Book IV we hear again the 'voice' of David in **Psalm 101** and 103. Psalm 101 is essentially a series of vows by the king to Yahweh as he sings of *ḥesed* (NRSV: 'loyalty') and justice, *mišpāṭ*. Whose loyalty and justice is not clear, but it is likely the ambiguity is intended since we have just heard about Yahweh's loyalty (cf. Pss. 99.4; 100.5) and are about to hear about David, who vows to study the way that is blameless (cf. Ps. 1.2). In a verse which anticipates the problems of his own dynasty David vows that those who practise deceit and utter lies will not be 'enthroned' (*yēšēb*; NRSV: 'remain') in his house (or 'dynasty') and will not be established. The psalm echoes the entrance liturgies in Psalms 15 and 24.3-6.

In **Psalm 102** we return to the genre of lament. The psalmist, unnamed but noted as one afflicted (*'ānî*), seeks an answer to their prayer in distress (v. 2; cf. Ps. 89.46). Since Yahweh answered the ancestors long ago (Ps. 99.6-9), the question is whether Yahweh will answer again? But the answer has already been set out in Book IV (cf. vv. 3, 11 with Ps. 90.3-6 and v. 10 with Ps. 90.7-9, 11). Now the psalmist has the assurance that Yahweh stands enthroned forever (v. 12). There can be confidence that Yahweh will have compassion on Zion, build it up again (v. 13) and the nations will flow to Zion (v. 22; cf. Isa. 2.2-4). This is the hope and prayer of Yahweh's servants (vv. 14, 17, 20). The hope (vv. 18-22) is clearly eschatological looking to a distant future as vv. 23-24 sees a return to the present plight. The reference to creation in v. 25 functions here not as the foundation for the eternal nature of Yahweh's steadfast love, but in contrast to it. Now even the heavens and earth can pass away, but Yahweh is the same without end. This is the security of Yahweh's servants (v. 28), who from v. 14 on, are addressed in the plural. An individual lament has turned into a prayer for Yahweh's people and v. 18, in language similar to Ps. 78.1-4, seeks to bear witness to later generations.

Psalm 103 is another psalm of David with Psalm 104 possibly a continuation. The Midrash Tehillim regards them as one with Psalm 104 starting as its predecessor concludes. David blesses Yahweh who forgives and redeems and who satisfies as long as we live (Ps. 103.2-5). Such vindication has been known since Moses (v. 7). While Yahweh can be angry he is slow to become so and his compassion and graciousness overwhelm his anger (vv. 8-10); so great is his steadfast love toward those who fear him (v. 11). Yahweh remembers the fragility of humankind (vv. 14-18; cf. 90.3) but this serves only to emphasize that his steadfast love extends to all generations of those who keep covenant and remember Yahweh's commandments (vv. 17-18), a reference to the Mosaic covenant. David ends with another blessing on Yahweh who rules all by all creatures (vv. 19-22).

Book IV begins to draw to a close with **Psalm 104**, a psalm of praise for Yahweh's creation of all life. David praises the works of Yahweh, a frequent theme in Book IV and now highlighted (vv. 13, 23, 24, 31; cf. Pss. 90.16; 92.4-5; 95.9; 96.3; 102.25; 103.22) drawing on earlier references (e.g. Pss. 78.7; 86.8). Yahweh satisfies all creatures. David prays that the glory of Yahweh will last forever (v. 31), that he will sing of Yahweh as long as he lives (v. 33; cf. Ps. 90.14-17), and that his meditation might be pleasing to Yahweh (v. 34).

While the voice of Moses stands firmly at the start of Book IV in Psalm 90, we also hear David's voice, at least in Psalms 101 and 103-104, and possibly in others, e.g. Ps. 92.10-11. In the midst of such a great disaster as the exile both Moses and the great king model piety and hope for their people.

Psalms 105–106

Book IV ends with two psalms that recite the early history of Israel. These psalms, although not necessarily related in their composition, are meant to be read together. Several things tie them together apart from historical recital. They each begin with a call 'to give thanks to Yahweh'. Ps. 105.1-3 and Ps. 106.47b form an *inclusio* around the psalms with the words 'to give thanks', 'holy name' and the Hebrew root *hll* (NRSV: 'glory' in 105.3; 'praise' in 106.47). Psalm 105 ends with a petition that Yahweh's people might 'keep his statutes and observe his laws' (v. 45) while Psalm 106 begins speaking of the blessed state of those 'who observe justice' and 'do righteousness' (v. 3). The same verb, *šāmar*, 'to keep, observe', appears in both verses.

While both psalms recite the earlier history of Israel, the forms of the recital are not the same (cf. also Psalms 78; 135; 136). Psalm 105 is a hymn calling for thanksgiving to Yahweh. Psalm 106, however, combines aspects of thanksgiving with confession and lament. It ends with a petition for Yahweh to save his people (v. 47a). Nevertheless, thanksgiving dominates the mood of this pair of psalms.

The core of each psalm consists of a series of episodes from Israel's early history, although the series are not identical. Each begins with an address to the people to give thanks (105.1-6; 106.1-3). Psalm 105 also includes an initial summary statement of the themes of the psalm stressing Yahweh's everlasting loyalty to the covenant he made with the ancestors and his promise of the land of Canaan as a gift (vv. 7-11). Psalm 106 also has brief prayers to Yahweh in vv. 4-7 and 47 surrounding the central section of historical recital. Smaller internal structures based on key words or word clusters can also be detected.

Psalms 105 and 106 both show signs of late exilic or post-exilic dating. There are allusions to Israel being scattered among the nations (Ps. 106.27, 47). There are also similarities to Pentateuchal traditions, although again differences are apparent. It is likely, however, that the two psalms did not come together until the final stages of formation of the Psalter. The evidence of 1 Chron. 16.8-36, where Pss. 105.1-15 and 106.47-48 are quoted, with Psalm 96 between, might suggest this happened in the first century after the exile but caution is required.

Psalm 105
The central themes of Psalm 105, and indeed of Psalms 105–106 together, are set out in vv. 7-11. They include the sovereignty of Yahweh over the earth, the everlasting nature of the covenant Yahweh made with Abraham, and the gift of the land of Canaan as Israel's 'portion for an inheritance.' Frequent repetition of

'land(s)' (10 times), of 'covenant' and its synonyms (e.g. 'word', 'promise'; 8 times) and of the names of the patriarchs (8 times), underline these themes. The psalmist stresses Yahweh's remembrance of his covenant in v. 8 (MT: *zākar*, 'he remembered'; NRSV: 'he is mindful') and v. 42 (MT: *zākar*). Yahweh's memory governs all that is recounted in the psalm, and by implication, everything involved in the ongoing relationship between Yahweh and his people. The use of 'forever', 'for a thousand generations' and 'everlasting' in these verses stresses the eternal nature of Yahweh's commitment. The relationship is further characterised by two words, 'servant' and 'chosen', used to describe Yahweh's people throughout Psalms 105–106. These terms are applied to the likes of Abraham and Moses of old (Pss. 105.6, 25-26, 42; 106.23) but also to later generations (Ps. 105.43) and those yet to come (Ps. 106.5). A vital part of this relationship is the gift of the land of Canaan, reference to which surrounds the recital of past events (Ps. 105.11, 44). The relationship between Yahweh and his people is not simply for mutual benefit. It has universal implications as vv. 1 and 7 imply.

Yahweh's injunction in v. 15, 'Do not touch my anointed ones; do my prophets no harm', is anachronistic if, as seems likely, the small number of sojourners (MT: *gārîm*; NRSV: 'strangers') wandering about (vv. 12-13) refers to the ancestors of Genesis as the reference to Joseph would imply. Prophets, like kings referred to here as 'anointed ones', did not arise until later in Israel's history. Even with the anachronism, there is a counter to the accusation of Yahweh's neglect made earlier in Psalm 89.

The passage on Joseph, vv. 16-22, is central to the historical recital. Joseph's experience of captivity, release and being set to rule over a foreign king's possessions, anticipates the experience of Israel recited in the psalm overall. Two things in this episode are important for understanding the whole psalm. As in the Joseph story in Genesis 37–50, the readers/hearers of the psalm are told that Yahweh is in charge of this piece of history. He sends Joseph to Egypt ahead of Israel to preserve and bless his people (Ps. 105.24; cf. Gen. 45.7; 50.20). Israel is to understand that behind the events recited in this psalm as well as in its application to later generations, there is the hand of Yahweh. Moreover, just as with Joseph, the time of hardship is one in which the word of Yahweh refines (MT: *ṣārap*; NRSV: 'tests') his people.

The wisdom to be gained from this recital is that Yahweh provides for his people even in the most difficult times. They will prosper with Yahweh even in captivity (v. 24) when their oppressors have the upper hand. In vv. 26-36 details of the way Yahweh provided in Egypt are given, namely in the mission of Moses and Aaron and the story of the plagues. This account differs in some detail from those in Exodus 7–12 and Ps. 78.44-51. For example, the plague of darkness comes first in Ps. 105.28 but second last in Exod. 10.21-29 and is missing entirely from Psalm 78. It is still debatable, however, whether Psalm 105 is using a different plague tradition to Exodus or they depend on oral variants of a general tradition which has not yet become fixed. The point made through the plague tradition in Psalm 105 is encapsulated in the pronouns and pronominal suffixes in the Hebrew. Fourteen times in vv. 27-36 the Egyptians are referred to by 'them', 'their' or 'they'. Without overt indication in vv. 37-42 the third person plural pronouns are now used to refer to Israel while Egypt is named fully (note the NRSV adds 'Israel' in v. 37 to clarify). It is clear who supplants whom.

The recital of past events ends in v. 44 with the gift of the lands of the nations and the wealth of the peoples. The emphasis in Psalm 105, however, is on the promise of land and not on descendants as is the case in Genesis. This suggests that for the intended readers/hearers of the psalm, land is the crucial issue as was certainly the case in the exile and after. The shift in naming from 'the land of Canaan' in v. 11 to the plural, less specific 'lands of the nations' in v. 44 suggests that the intended audience are those who need to understand the message of the psalm in a wider, more universal context. This recital of ancient events offers hope for them. Their faithful God will provide. But at the same time there is openness at the end of the psalm. The purpose of the gift of land is so that the people might keep Yahweh's statutes (v. 45). Obedience to the God who has remained faithful to his promises is part of the wisdom to be gained from the recital of past events. Faithful, divine memory calls for the corresponding quality in God's people (cf. Ps. 103.17-18).

Psalm 106

Psalm 106 opens as Psalm 105 ended with *hall^elûyâ* and a call to give thanks that Yahweh's 'steadfast love' lasts forever, a point which in the light of Psalm 105 can be asserted in answer to the question in Psalm 89. Psalm 106 then poses its own question, 'who can utter the mighty doings of Yahweh, or declare his praise?' (v. 2), followed by a blessing on the one who observes justice and does righteousness at all times (v. 3). This speaks about the one who accepts the invitation in Ps. 105.45 and who stands in the shoes of David as spelled out in Psalm 101. A further question is raised for the reader/hearer of the psalm. Who fills such shoes and who can utter Yahweh's mighty doings as has been done in Psalm 105? The first of two personal prayers to Yahweh in the psalm suggests the psalmist is one who shares Israel's present suffering and looks for the nation's redemption. Individual and national interests coincide.

As it develops we see that Psalm 106 is not simply a repeat of Psalm 105. The historical recital is similar but this time told from Israel's perspective. It begins starkly in v. 6 by stating literally 'we have sinned with our ancestors' (MT: ḥāṭāʾnû ʿim-ʾabôtēnû). The NRSV translation, 'Both we and our ancestors have sinned', is possible indicating especially the continuity of sin through the generations. Alternatively, the NJPS version has 'We have sinned like our forefathers' (similarly NJB) emphasizing the sin of the present generation. In either case the effect is that present generations, like their ancestors, do not remember Yahweh's steadfast love and his works as they were urged to do in Ps. 105.8. In a tradition not found in the Pentateuch, we are told that even in Egypt Israel forgot Yahweh (Ps. 106.7). While only the sins of the ancestors are mentioned, those sins, like the past acts of divine compassion in Psalm 105, are capable of repetition in the present generation.

In vv. 7-33 we have another recital of the events of deliverance from Egypt, wilderness wanderings and entry into the promised land. In spite of Yahweh saving them in the past (vv. 8-10), of his constant threats to destroy them (vv. 15b, 17-18, 23, 26-27, 29), and their deliverance only at the intercession of Moses and Phineas (vv. 23, 30), Israel constantly forget Yahweh's works and words. They sin seven times. Only on one of those occasions, the first after they left Egypt (vv. 7-12), did they believe Yahweh's words (lit. 'and they believed his words'; MT: wayyaʾamînû bidbārāyw) and praise him. Later they even despise the 'pleasant land' which is Yahweh's gift and 'did not believe his word' (MT: lōʾ-heʾĕmînû lidbārô; NRSV: 'having no faith in his promise'). The fickleness of Israel could not be more sharply drawn. Their punishment on occasion echoes what happened to Egypt (e.g. the plague in v. 29).

The recital of the exodus events in Psalm 106 is not presented in the geographical and temporal order found in the Pentateuchal account. It is presented in seven stanzas with episodes of cravings in the wilderness near the start and at the end (vv. 13-15 and 32-33 respectively). At the centre lies the episode of the golden calf with specific reference to Israel forgetting God and his works and worshipping an idol (vv. 21-22). Following this in vv. 24-27 is a reference to the spies (Numbers 13–14). Yahweh's determination to make Israel 'fall' in the wilderness parallels his oath to make their descendants 'fall' among the nations, a reference to exile (v. 27).

The recital in Psalm 106 goes beyond that in Psalm 105 including the period after Israel had entered the promised land. The events reflected in the Book of Judges are summarized in vv. 34-39 with the chief sin of the people being their serving the idols of Canaan. This matches the sin in the wilderness at the centre of the earlier recital, namely the worship of the calf at Horeb. The people do not change over time, even with the witness of past experience. Verses 40-46 then continue the story and, in spite of Yahweh saving them many times (v. 43), Israel remained rebellious. Nevertheless, for their sake Yahweh remembered the covenant, which in this context is clearly that mentioned in Ps. 105.8, 10, had compassion according to his abundant steadfast love and caused them to be pitied by their captors (vv. 44-46). This is Israel's hope in exile. It is what the psalmist asks from Yahweh for the people in v. 47. The move in vv. 34-39 to include events after the possession of the promised land opens up the significance of the recital of past events to new generations. We have already noted this effect through the use of the term 'chosen' in Pss. 105.43 and 106.5.

While Psalms 105 and 106 both recite the early history of Israel they stand in dialectical opposition to each other in terms of what that recital reveals. For one it primarily demonstrates Yahweh's faithfulness, for the other Israel's lack of faith. For one it is about possessing the promised land as a gift from Yahweh, for the other it is about losing that land. For one it is about Yahweh's unfailing memory of the covenant, for the other Israel's total forgetfulness. However, while the contrast is stark the similarities, the connections and the overall movement that takes place between the psalms cannot be overlooked. They both see Israel's history as one controlled by covenant. Together they stress the constancy of divine faithfulness and compassion. They stress that human sin arises when the divine word is ignored or despised. The two psalms are to be read together and not simply over against each another as if either divine grace or human sin can outweigh the other in significance. The two are present in Israel's relationship with God and contribute to the whole. The net effect is that the future of this relationship lies open for both Israel in terms of a commitment to obedience, and for Yahweh in terms of responding to the psalmist's petition to save. In the exilic or post-exilic context there is a basis for hope, but only where obedience to the divine word is taken seriously. The past may hold lessons for the present but it does not determine that present. A new start, as well as a new song (Psalms 96 and 98), is possible.

At the end of Book III of the Psalter Yahweh was accused of spurning his covenant with his servant David (Psalm 89). Earlier in the book (Psalms 74, 79) the destruction of the temple had been detailed. The old hopes associated with the Davidic monarchy needed to be modified in relation to national experience. Still, the association of those hopes with David was not totally to be dismissed. We also saw the beginning of collective interpretations of terms associated with the Davidic kings and the relation of the Davidic covenant to the Sinai one. Those moves are developed in Book IV. In Psalm 90 and elsewhere, no less at the end of the book in Psalms 105–106, we are taken back to times before that of David. In recounting the events of the exodus and early history of Israel the later community of faith re-engages with its roots and reclaims its identity precisely at a time when those things are challenged. In doing this emphasis is placed on the sovereignty of Yahweh over all nations and peoples, on Yahweh's faithfulness and on his *hesed*, 'steadfast love'. A new commitment to this is the key to both deliverance from present distress and the gift of future blessing. That does not mean present hardships can be easily dismissed. In the midst of a renewed celebration of and trust in the sovereignty of Yahweh and in the rediscovery of Yahweh as refuge and dwelling place, there is still a place for petition and lament as Psalms 94 and 102 show. There is also a necessary place for confession as Psalm 106 reveals. A faithful recognition of the contingencies of life is also necessary and has been repeated throughout the book (see Pss. 90.5; 102.4, 11; 103.15; cf. 89.47).

The position of David has receded somewhat with this new emphasis but it has not been entirely dismissed. He returned as psalmist in at least Psalms 101 and 103 where he sang of justice and loyalty and praised the steadfast love of Yahweh respectively.

He surely stands, in the words of Ps. 106.2, as one who can utter, and has done so, the mighty doings of Yahweh. The plea of the psalmist in 106.4 to be remembered when Yahweh shows his favour to his people, is consistent with the calls for Yahweh to remember in Ps. 89.50 (cf. 89.47). It was in that psalm that David was designated 'chosen' (v. 19) and 'servant' (vv. 20, 50), terms which are now widened to include the whole community of the faithful (cf. Pss. 90.13, 16; 102.14, 28; 105.25; 106.4).

Book V

Psalm 107

Book V opens with another community song of thanksgiving, one which begins in identical fashion to Psalm 106 at the end of Book IV (cf. 106.1; 107.1). But while Ps. 106.2 goes on to ask a question about who can utter such things, Ps. 107.2 continues the injunction calling for the 'redeemed of Yahweh' to do so. In addition to this, part of the refrain in Ps. 107.6, 13, 19, 28 shares a common theme and vocabulary with Ps. 106.43-44. Moreover, Ps. 108.1-4 is an expansion on the general theme of Ps. 106.1 and 107.1. Thus the sequence of psalms across the boundary between Book IV and V is bound closely together. Book V continues addressing an established theme.

Psalm 107 begins with the extended invitation to give thanks, including particularly those who are 'redeemed' (vv. 1-3). There is then a series of four stanzas each dealing with a particular group of people who have cried out to Yahweh: vv. 4-9 with those wandering in desert wastes; vv. 10-16 with those in prison; vv. 17-22 with those sick or 'foolish'; and vv. 23-32 with those who sail the seas in ships. Verses 33-42 contain instruction on how Yahweh can change aspects of creation for the blessing and deliverance of his people. The psalm ends with a call for the wise to consider Yahweh's steadfast love (v. 43). In its final form this thanksgiving also serves an instructional purpose.

Verses 1-3 call on 'the redeemed of Yahweh' to join in the thanksgiving song. This phrase occurs only here and in the early post-exilic passage Isa. 62.12, with the word 'redeemed' generally restricted to exilic and post-exilic passages. Verse 3 describes these people as ones gathered 'from the east and from the west, from the north and from the sea' (MT: *ûmiyyām*). The NRSV and other versions amend the last word to read 'and from the south', thus completing the four points of the compass. However, in terms of compass directions *yām* 'sea' indicates 'west', not 'south'. It is possible that east, west, north and 'sea' could indicate other than compass directions, although this does not rule out reading the psalm in the context of returned exiles.

The four stanzas, which describe groups that have cried to Yahweh and who, in the context of the psalm, are part of the redeemed of Yahweh, have the same structure. After a description of the group's distress (vv. 4-5; 10-12; 17-18; 23-27), an almost identical refrain occurs: 'Then they cried to Yahweh in their trouble, and he saved/delivered/brought them out from their distress' (vv. 6, 13, 19, 28). This is followed by a statement of deliverance appropriate to the group (vv. 7, 14, 20, 29-30). A final exhortation to thank Yahweh (vv. 8, 15, 21, 31) completes each stanza. In each of the first two stanzas (vv. 9 and 16) the final exhortation is appropriate to the act of deliverance, while in the last two stanzas (vv. 22 and 32) the exhortation continues with a call to sacrifice to Yahweh or to give praise.

The first stanza (vv. 4-9) speaks of people wandering in the wilderness, hungry and thirsty and without a city to dwell in. No reason is given for their situation but Yahweh responds to their cry. The stanza could apply to the exile but is also mindful of the exodus. The second stanza (vv. 10-16) speaks of those in darkness and deep darkness. The reference to irons, forced labour etc. suggests prison as the context although the exile also fits. In contrast to the first group, this group are where they are because they have rebelled against God's word (v. 11). The use of the word $ṣalmāwet$ 'deep darkness' (lit. 'shadow of death') recalls Ps. 23.4 and the trust of that psalm.

The third stanza (vv. 17-22) refers to some who are 'fools', $^{\prime e}wîlîm$, îbecause of their sinful ways (v. 17). The Hebrew adjective is used frequently in Proverbs and generally indicates someone of morally questionable behaviour (e.g. Prov. 1.7; 14.9; 15.5 etc.). The reference is commonly interpreted here as illness because of the lack of appetite, being close to death, and Yahweh healing them. The link between illness and foolish sinfulness and a thanksgiving offering (v. 22) was not impossible in ancient Israelite thought. The fourth stanza is the longest (vv. 23-32). It speaks of sailors at sea who witness the wonders of Yahweh, possibly the strange creatures of the seas. Fear of the power of storms is their problem and no indication is given of wrongdoing on their part. They too are saved when they cry out. A chiastic arrangement is thus achieved by having two situations involving deliverance from punishment related to sin or rebellion surrounded by two in which deliverance is from chaotic situations. In each case, however, all humanity is the intended recipient of Yahweh's deliverance (vv. 8, 15, 21, 31).

The emendation of 'sea' to 'south' in v. 3 gives the whole psalm a geographic/historic context. However, such a change is not necessary (cf. Isa. 49.12 with use of 'north' and 'sea' [NRSV: 'west']). The references in v. 3 relate to the four stanzas that follow. The directional references, which in some cases bear connections to geographic and historic circumstances—the desert wastes in the east, the darkness of the west where the sun sets, the dangers of sea travel—are also symbolic alluding to tradition and myth. The eastern desert wastes recall the exodus tradition as well as fit the situation of exile, as does the imagery of prison in the west. The 'north' carries a number of connotations. In Canaanite myth it is the place where Baal dwells. It is also the direction from which evil or disaster comes (Isa. 41.25; Jer. 1.13-15; Ezek. 23.24; 26.7 etc.) and when used as one direction from which exiles return to Israel signifies defeat of chaotic forces (e.g. Isa. 43.6; Jer. 3.12, 18; Zech. 2.6 etc.). The 'sea' also has both mythic (as a symbol of chaos) and exodus connections. It is most likely that the four directions in v. 3, developed later in the four stanzas, are used symbolically to speak of contexts from which people are redeemed. They carry mythic, traditional and geographic overtones to varying degrees. As such they allude to both exodus and exilic traditions.

The final section of the psalm, vv. 33-43, spells out Yahweh's sovereignty over the cosmos, thus underlining Yahweh's ability to answer the cry of those distressed. Yahweh's sovereignty is first described in destructive terms (vv. 33-34) in which Yahweh turns prosperity (rivers, pools, fruitfulness) into chaos because of people's sin. In vv. 35-38 Yahweh reverses that and turns desert places into springs, giving harvests and a home for the hungry and thereby reversing the first stanza above. Yahweh is the one who can both let chaos reign and overcome it. Similar expressions can be found in Isaiah (Isa. 35.5-7; 41.19; 43.19-20; 50.2; 51.3; cf. also Ps. 107.40 with Job 12.21-22). This is to the advantage of Yahweh's people. When they are low with oppression (vv. 39-41), Yahweh can reverse that also. Yahweh can restore the poor and needy.

The psalm closes with an injunction in v. 43 to let those who are wise consider 'these things' and Yahweh's steadfast love which stands behind these acts.

Psalm 107 plays a number of roles at the start of Book V. Book IV ended with the people waiting for deliverance from the (implied) context of exile. Now in Psalm 107 that deliverance, in many forms for many different people, comes about. People have literally been redeemed from many lands and many situations. The allusion to mythic themes in the four stanzas conveys that not only has a people been rescued historically but that forces beyond the earthly have been overcome. Yahweh's steadfast love and sovereignty have been exercized on all levels. The allusions to exodus themes sets that event up as a past example of Yahweh's steadfast love. But also the symbolic nature of the language in the four stanzas, the general statements regarding Yahweh's sovereignty in vv. 33-42 and the invitation in v. 43 mean that there is an openness to new acts of divine steadfast love. It is not only something to celebrate as past, but the focus of hope for the future. Psalm 107 and its close association with both Psalms 105–106, as well as the start of Psalm 108, bridges the gap between what is past and what is possible for the future. It stakes the hopes of Yahweh's people in Yahweh's steadfast love, that which was questioned so strongly in Psalm 89 but which stands the test.

Psalms 108–109

Psalm 108 introduces a short series of psalms ascribed to David (Psalms 108–110). Another series of 'Davidic' psalms will come near the end of Book V (Psalms 138–145). Psalm 108 combines two earlier psalms, Ps. 57.7-11 (= Ps. 108.1-5) and Ps. 60.5-12 (= Ps. 108.6-13), both of which are lament psalms. However, in the combination a new psalm with a new message is created. It still contains elements of petition and complaint (vv. 10-12) but it is now overwhelmingly a psalm of trust. It seeks to give thanks and praise to Yahweh among the nations because of Yahweh's steadfast love (vv. 1-4) and, therefore, continues the theme of Psalms 105 to 107. The psalmist has given heed to issues in earlier psalms (cf. Ps. 107.43) but their petition is no longer simply their own. It soon becomes one for the whole community (vv. 6b, 11-12). The reference to immediate neighbours, especially Edom, suggests that the troubles behind this psalm are those the exiles had with neighbouring peoples (especially Edom: Ps. 137.7-9; Isa. 34.2-17; 63.1-6; Obadiah). The designation of this psalm as Davidic, drawing on the words of two earlier Davidic psalms, sets the renowned king up as a model of prayer, whose very words can be used in new situations of distress. His trust in Yahweh alone (v. 12) is a model for those in later times. David becomes one who 'prays' for those who follow him in the faith. Even the list of nations in vv. 7-9 is reminiscent of the Davidic kingdom.

Psalm 109 is an individual lament with a set of extended curses in vv. 6-19. It is set as the voice of David who protests his innocence in the face of malicious words (vv. 2-3). In return for acts of compassion he has experienced hatred (vv. 4-5). Now he pleads that Yahweh not remain silent. He trusts in Yahweh's steadfast love (vv. 21, 26). The most intriguing part of the psalm, however, is the list of curses in vv. 6-19. In MT and LXX these could be read as a continuation of David's initial words. If so, then he is venting his anger in honest but harsh terms. In v. 20 he finally turns and hands the matter over to Yahweh (v. 21). Alternatively, we can read vv. 6-19 as a quotation of curses uttered by others against David. NRSV reads them this way adding 'They say' at the start of v. 6 (cf. NAB and NJB which set the verses in quotation marks). This interpretation is supported by the fact that v. 6 qualifies the 'accuser' or prosecutor (*śāṭān*) for David's trial with the parallel term *rāšāʿ*, 'wicked man'. Clearly a rigged trial is intended, hardly something David would claim. Moreover, the accusers are plural in vv. 2-5, 20, 27-29, but the one accused in v. 6-19 is singular, as in most laments. There is also contrast between David who trusts in Yahweh at the beginning and the end of the psalm, and vv. 6-19 where Yahweh is a pawn in the hands of the accusers. Having quoted the accusers, David then desires that the accusers' curses be upon their own heads (v. 20) and that Yahweh vindicate his poor and needy servant (v. 22). David exhibits great confidence even in a personally hopeless situation (v. 31) because Yahweh's steadfast love is his hope. Whereas the accusers sought to place a *rāšāʿ*, 'wicked man' at David's right hand (v. 6), in the end it is Yahweh who stands at the right hand of the needy (v. 31). This psalm, attributed to David, demonstrates again the trust required of those returning from exile as they seek to rebuild their lives again in the face of opposition that is both cruel and crafty.

Psalm 110

Psalm 110 is the last of the Davidic psalms at the start of Book V. It is a royal psalm which is both about the king and directly addressed to the king. It seems to have been composed by bringing together various oracles related to the king. These have been stitched together using a number of repeated words (e.g. Yahweh, 'enemies', 'right hand', 'on the day'). The oracles could have come from a coronation service or anniversary. Their function in the final form of the psalm is likely different. The content of the psalm could have lent itself to a liturgy related to battle preparations or some threat to the king. The date of the original composition is uncertain, from the time of king David himself through to the exile. In addition, the meaning of some verses in the MT is not clear. The Hebrew text is obscure in v. 3 while in vv. 5-7 the subject 'he' needs interpretation. The significance of the action described in v. 7 is also unclear.

The psalm breaks into two sections, vv. 1-3 and vv. 4-7, although the exact point of divide is debatable. Each section begins with a divine proclamation. Verses 1-3 begin with Yahweh (NRSV: 'LORD') calling on 'my lord' ($^a d\bar{o}n\hat{\imath}$) to take a position of honour at his 'right hand' (cf. 1 Kgs 2.19; Ps. 45.9) until the latter's enemies are overcome, i.e. made 'a footstool' for his feet. The imagery of a king sitting beside a god and of enemies being subdued under the foot of the victor is common in reliefs and documents across the ancient Near Eastern world and Egypt. In the context of Psalms 105–109 this imagery is sobering because the hoped for defeat of enemies, for which thanks was to be given to Yahweh, is not yet complete.

A question arises from Ps. 110.1. Who is addressed in the psalm, or who is 'my lord'? What follows in vv. 2-3, with reference to 'your mighty sceptre', to ruling others, and to people volunteering for battle, all suggests that 'my lord' is the Davidic king, referred to as such by a psalmist who is possibly a member of the court. However, we should not miss the point that the king is not the subject of any of the verbs in vv. 1-3. It is Yahweh who subdues the enemies and sends the sceptre from Zion. Not only is human help, even royal power, worthless in the struggle against enemies and foes (Ps. 108.12), but Yahweh stands at the right hand of the king as well as the needy (Ps. 109.31) to save them. This has the double effect of not only stressing the humanity of the king but of placing the king on equal footing with the needy in the community. As one among all, he also becomes a model for all. The intimacy between the king and Yahweh is promised to the whole.

The end of v. 3 is obscure. The difficulty is in relating the words 'womb', 'dawn' ($mish\bar{a}r$; NRSV: 'morning'), 'dew', and 'youth', and determining whether 'youth' is meant collectively for young men in the community or individually as a stage of the king's life. 'Your youth' could also be re-vocalised to read 'I begot you' (cf. NAB). In relation to this verse we note the use of sun, moon and rain imagery to describe the king's benefit to his people in Ps. 72.5-6 and that 'sun' was a common royal epithet in the ancient Near East. Depending on how we read the lines it would seem either to have something to do with youth volunteering for military service (so possibly the NRSV), or be connected to the 'holy splendour' (NRSV emends to 'holy mountains') and say something about the king's persona. On the other hand, we could read the lines as 'From your dawn, the dew of your youth, Yahweh has sworn …' seeing it as an introduction to Yahweh's proclamation in v. 4.

Verses 4-7 begin with the divine proclamation that the king is 'a priest according to the order of Melchizedek' (v. 4b, NRSV). The verse refers to the king/priest of Salem (Jerusalem) who blessed Abraham in Gen. 14.18-19. The connection with Jerusalem (i.e. Zion) might provide a link here. We also note that both David and Solomon acted as priests on occasion in their royal role (2 Sam. 6.17; 1 Kgs 3.3-4). However, an alternative translation is possible in which the name *malkî-ṣedeq* is translated literally. It reads 'You are a priest forever, according to my decree, O righteous king' (cf. NJPS), thus proclaiming the authority of the king's position.

Verses 5-7 provide a twist and some perplexities. The twist is that the sense of the 'right hand' reference changes. From the king being at Yahweh's right hand, Yahweh is now at the king's right hand (v. 5a), thus changing the image from one of honour to one of support and aligning the king with the needy in Ps. 109.31 (cf. Ps. 80.17). The perplexities relate to who is the 'he' of vv. 5b-7. In vv. 5b-6 it could be the king who does all these things because Yahweh is at his right hand. Alternatively, Yahweh could be the subject throughout. This would be consistent with the theme of vv. 1-2 where it is only Yahweh's power which can achieve such things. However, the subject of v. 7a, who drinks from the stream, must be the king. It is possibly a reference to some ritual of victory at a sacred stream or to the king's need to obtain drink wherever he can while pursuing his enemy. In v. 7b it is immaterial who lifts the king's head, Yahweh or the king himself; the imagery is of acceptance and honour (cf. Pss. 3.3; 24.7, 9; 27.6; 140.9).

In Psalms 108–109 we heard pleas to Yahweh to deliver from enemies and accusers. Those words were attributed to David through the superscriptions and the quotations from earlier Davidic psalms. In Psalm 110, another psalm associated with David, we hear the voice of a psalmist recalling the divine promises to the Davidic king. The king's victories over his enemies are the result of Yahweh standing at his 'right hand' even as Yahweh stands at the right hand of all the needy. For king and ordinary person alike, deliverance is not dependent on human power but on divine presence. For the post-exilic community, when the question of security is paramount, this is an important message.

The association of this and Psalms 108–109 with David is important but developments are taking place here in this regard. In Psalm 108, the earlier words of David from a time when he was in trouble are taken as the model for a plea for deliverance by the later community. In Psalm 110, we are reminded of David's own need of Yahweh's help in the face of adversity. The Targum on Psalms even offers an alternate translation for v. 1 which sees it as directly addressed to David. While the short oracles stitched together in Psalm 110 might have related once to the coronation or anniversary of the Davidic king, in the post-exilic context they must take on a new role. David functions as a model for the faith community, even in his royal capacity. But more than that is implied. As noted there is still an expectation of future adversaries and the need for further deliverance from Yahweh in Psalm 110. If David still provides a model for the prayerful community, he also provides a model for a future king. A messianic expectation is developing within the collection.

Psalms 111–117

In Ps. 107.43 those who are wise are urged to give thought to the events of both the recent and distant past and to Yahweh's steadfast love. Now in **Psalm 111**.10 we are reminded of that classic proverb: 'The fear of Yahweh is the beginning of wisdom; all those who practice it have a good understanding' (see Prov. 9.10; cf. 1.7; 15.33; Job 28.28). This follows a series of reasons (Ps. 111.2-9) why Yahweh ought to be praised and given thanks. There are echoes of the exodus in this list with reference to Yahweh's wonderful deeds ($nipl^{e\textsc{,}}\bar{o}t$) and his grace and mercy (Exod. 3.20; 33.19; 34.6, 10; cf. Pss. 105.2, 5; 106.7, 22), the provision of food and the gift and the heritage of the nations, i.e. their land. **Psalm 112** continues this public praise. Like Psalm 111, it begins with $hall^el\hat{u}\ y\bar{a}h$, 'praise Yahweh'. And like Psalm 111 it is an acrostic, with its twenty one lines beginning with successive letters of the Hebrew alphabet. However, unlike Psalm 111, Psalm 112 proceeds to spell out how ’ašrê-’îš 'blessed/happy is (the) man' who fears Yahweh and delights in his commandments. The echoes of Ps. 1.1-2 are strong and suggest the one here is associated with the individual signalled earlier, i.e. the king. The way Psalms 111 and 112 are set up shows that the blessed man reflects Yahweh whom he fears in his life and actions. While the community delights in the works of Yahweh (111.2) the blessed man delights in Yahweh's commandments (112.1). The clause 'his/their righteousness endures for ever' occurs in Ps. 111.3 in relation to Yahweh and in Ps. 112.3, 9 in relation to the man. Yahweh provides food (111.4) while the man distributes freely to the poor (112.5, 9). Yahweh is 'gracious and merciful' (111.4) as is the man (112.4) and the works of both are done in mišpāṭ, 'justice' (Pss. 111.7; 112.5). Yahweh remembers (yizkōr) his covenant forever (111.5) and the man who is righteous is remembered (zēker) forever (112.6). Finally, Yahweh's works/precepts are established (sᵉmûkîm) forever (111.8) and the heart of the man is established (sāmûk) and not afraid (112.8). A mirror image is thus created between the psalms, indicating that the wonderful deeds of Yahweh are reflected in the blessing and activity of the man, just as Yahweh's kingship was reflected in the Davidic king in Psalm 89.

Psalm 113 is a hymn beginning and ending with hallᵉlû yāh, and concluding the small collection Psalms 111–113 each of which begins hallᵉlû yāh. It also begins 'The Egyptian Hallel', Psalms 113–118 sung at major Jewish feats, especially pesaḥ, (Passover) and sukkōt (Tabernacles). Psalm 113 proclaims Yahweh's sovereignty (vv. 2-4) going on to ask who can compare with Yahweh. The reasons given for such praise include raising the poor and giving the barren woman a home and children recalling both the stories of the ancestors (Gen. 11.30; 25.21; 29.31), and the song of Hannah (1 Sam. 2.5, 8).

Psalm 114 returns to the exodus for its theme. Yahweh is not revealed as the god who does such marvels until v. 7 when the earth is called to tremble in his presence (NRSV replaces MT 'his' with 'God's' in v. 2 to clarify but the lack of clarity seems intended). This is the god who reverses expectations thus preserving Israel in the wilderness (v. 8; cf. Ps. 107.33-38).

Psalm 115 again praises Yahweh but for slightly different reasons. It proclaims the sovereignty of Yahweh in the face of the question posed by the nations 'Where is their God?' (v. 2).

This was the question posed twice in Ps. 42.3, 10 and in Ps. 79.10 (cf. Ps. 3.2). But the psalmist declares how Yahweh surpasses other gods who are mere manufactured idols (vv. 3-8) and urges Israel to trust in Yahweh (vv. 9-11) who will bless them (vv. 12-13). The exodus is not directly alluded to in this psalm but it reminds of the battle between Yahweh and the gods of Egypt at that time (see Exodus 5–12).

In **Psalm 116** we return again to hear the praise of an individual who has experienced Yahweh's deliverance. The psalm divides into two main parts, vv. 1-11 and 12-19. The first tells of the relationship between the psalmist and Yahweh. Verse 2 in isolation could suggest that thanksgiving is nothing more than obligation, but a complex relationship between Yahweh and psalmist is evident in vv. 1-11, where the latter loves Yahweh (v. 1), walks before Yahweh (v. 9) and keeps his faith even in the most difficult times, even in the face of death (v. 10; cf. vv. 3, 8, 15). In turn Yahweh is attentive (v. 2) gracious, merciful and just (v. 5), and protective (v. 6). The second part sees the psalmist pledge, in a repeated statement, to pay his vows 'in the presence of all (Yahweh's) people' (vv. 14, 18). What is an intimate relationship spills over into public praise. In the post-exilic context, the references to the temple and Jerusalem in v. 19 detail the bounty of Yahweh and the concrete reason for thanks. Yahweh has indeed been gracious and merciful, a developing theme in recent psalms (Pss. 103:8; 111:4; 112:4; 116:5; cf. 145:8).

Psalm 117 brings 'The Egyptian Hallel' almost to its completion. The general call to praise anticipates that which will be developed in Ps. 118.1-4, 29 and especially Psalm 136. It was already proclaimed at the end of Book IV (Ps. 106.1) and the start of Book V (Ps. 107.1). Two differences are evident, however, in Psalm 117. First, this is a call to all the nations (v. 1). All peoples are thereby drawn into the praise of Yahweh as already hinted at in Ps. 2.10-11. Secondly, the reason for the nations to praise Yahweh is that his steadfast love 'toward us' has been great and his faithfulness endures forever (v. 2). It is what Yahweh has done for his own people that gives reason for the nations to praise him. This presumes Yahweh's people have been delivered from the exile.

Psalm 118

Psalm 118 is a thanksgiving psalm (*tôdâ*) as the *inclusio* in vv. 1 and 19 clearly indicates. However, the form is complicated by some variations: there is a mixture of individual and communal elements in the psalm; the thanksgiving is combined with a further plea for deliverance, typical of laments; and an inordinate number of repeated phrases together with points of content lend the psalm to processional rites. The psalm has traditionally been seen as the last in 'The Egyptian Hallel' (Psalms 113–118). The original setting may have been some festival other than Passover or Tabernacles. The traditional association with the earlier psalms of the Hallel can be questioned, however, on the basis that this psalm has little to do with the exodus theme and is clearly a thanksgiving while the earlier psalms repeat the call *hallᵉlû yāh*, 'praise Yahweh'. This distinction is editorially important in the latter books of the Psalter.

The main body of the psalm falls into four sections: an invocation (vv. 2-4); a description of past deliverance (vv. 5-18); an entrance liturgy (vv. 19-24); and a final set of plea, blessings and direction of procession (vv. 25-28). Even these sections have been composed using shorter liturgical refrains and sayings, e.g. vv. 5-7, 8-9, 15-18 and 19-20. Just when the psalm was put together is not clear. Pre- and post-exilic dates could be suggested. In its present context in the Psalter, it is read as post-exilic.

The call to give thanks in the *inclusio* is a familiar one occurring elsewhere in the Old Testament (e.g. 1 Chron. 16.34; Jer. 33.11) and especially in the Psalter. Notably it spans the division between Books IV and V (Pss. 106.1 and 107.1). Psalm 136 develops the verse to its ultimate form.

Psalm 118 properly begins in vv. 2-4 with a threefold development of the initial call, addressed first to Israel, then the priestly house of Aaron, and finally to 'those who fear Yahweh'. Each group repeats the response from v. 1, 'His steadfast love endures forever.' The groups mentioned are the same as those listed in Ps. 115.9-10, 12–13, and could be associated specifically with the liturgical use of 'The Egyptian Hallel'. The one group which is not obvious is the third, 'those who fear Yahweh'. The 'fear of Yahweh' has a number of meanings. It can imply terror and fear in a negative sense (e.g. 2 Chron. 14.14; 17.10) or more positively a range of things from worship (e.g. Deut. 6.13; 10.20), to religious wisdom or knowledge (e.g. Ps. 111.10; Prov. 1.7), to trust or faith (Pss. 40.3; 115.11; 2 Chron. 19.9), and finally obedience to Yahweh's commands (e.g. Deut. 10.12; 13.4; 31.12; cf. Pss. 19.9; 112.1). Ps. 118.4 clearly refers to those in these latter categories.

Importantly we note that in Deut. 17.19 the king was to study the *torah* so that he may learn to 'fear Yahweh'.

Verses 5-18 give an example of the reasons for thanks. The psalmist recalls an occasion when he called to Yahweh who answered him. The nature of this deliverance is not clear. The MT reads in v. 5b *'ānānî bammerḥāb yāh* (lit.: 'he answered me—in a broad place—Yah'). NRSV has interpreted this to mean Yahweh literally sets the psalmist in a broad place while other translations (NAB, NIV, NJB, NJPS) understand 'in a broad place' metaphorically translating something like 'set me free'. The text does not specifically imply release from captivity although that is not inappropriate. It does imply release from distress whatever type.

The psalmist goes on to consider how it is better to have Yahweh on his side, to take refuge in Yahweh, than to trust in humans, even princes (vv. 6-9; cf. Ps. 146.3). He subdued surrounding nations in the name of Yahweh (vv. 10-13). The struggle was difficult as v. 13 implies. The NRSV reading 'I was pushed' follows the LXX, Syr., and Vulg. rather than the MT which reads *daḥōh dᵉḥîtanî*, 'you pushed me', implying Yahweh pressured the psalmist. However, this does not fit the sense of the verse for Yahweh becomes a helper in v. 13b and in v. 14 the psalmist's 'strength and song' (cf. Exod. 15.2a; Isa. 12.2; MT; NRSV: 'might').

The scene changes in vv. 19-20 to a procession through the 'gates of righteousness' which is the 'gate of Yahweh', as the psalmist gives thanks for deliverance by the right hand of Yahweh (cf. Pss. 20.6; 60.5; 98.1). Such customs are also evident in Mesopotamia. The gate through which the psalmist enters is the one through which all the righteous will enter (v. 20). Presumably we are thinking of the gates to the reconstructed temple.

With reference to all righteous entering through the gate, the psalm begins to move from an individual thanksgiving to a corporate prayer. What Yahweh has done is now marvellous in *our* eyes (v. 23) and *we* will rejoice in it. The psalmist invites others to join in thanksgiving, not just for his deliverance but in anticipation of further deliverance. This raises the question of who is this psalmist who celebrates his own deliverance in such a public way and also calls others to faith and celebration. We will return to this.

The proverb in v. 22 about the rejected stone becoming a cornerstone, one from which a building takes its alignment (cf. Isa. 28:16), is central in the interpretation of the psalm. Read in context the psalmist's experience is likened to the stone, at first rejected but then made central. The proverb occurs at the point where there is a change from singular to plural pronouns. It suggests that the psalmist's experience becomes an exemplar for the whole community. The community itself, i.e. Israel, is like the stone. Rejected, or oppressed and disregarded by the nations, Israel's experience becomes a key factor in Yahweh's plan. This is in accord with the emphasis in Psalm 117 where the nations were called to praise Yahweh because of Yahweh's steadfast love toward his own people. Israel's experience has significance beyond itself. The psalmist's entrance into the 'gate of Yahweh' symbolizes the entry of Israel returning from exile.

Just as we move from the individual to the corporate in the psalm we also move in vv. 25-28 from past celebration to a contemporary plea for deliverance. The prayer is made on behalf of the community so that it may prosper or have success. The same form of the verb (Hiphil of *ṣālaḥ*) is used as in Ps. 1.3 recalling the blessed man who is like the prosperous tree sustained by permanent waters. These are the only places this verb is used in the Psalter of those who trust Yahweh, thus drawing a deliberate connection between this victorious figure and the blessed one at the start of the Psalter. It stresses that prosperity in the community hinges on trust in Yahweh and *torah* obedience.

The community plea then changes to a liturgical celebration of Yahweh's response (vv. 26-28), although little detail is given of the exact nature of the liturgy. The community blesses 'the one who comes in the name of Yahweh' (v. 26), presumably the psalmist who seeks to enter the gates (v. 19). The entry of this individual has eschatological significance holding a key to the hope of the community. Clearly difficulties continue (v. 25), but this individual's experience has been symbolic for the community's own return from exile, and remains so in relation to future distress. The movement in the psalm from individual thanksgiving for past deliverance to community liturgy is indicative of the importance ongoing liturgical practice can hold for maintaining hope.

Psalm 118 offers no hint to the context in which it was composed. In the present Psalter it would appear to relate to the time after exile. But the timelessness of the psalm suggests it also has pertinence for times to come. However, the past is not forgotten. Aspects of the psalm suggest that things from its past influence the way it is now read. One such aspect relates to the identity of the psalmist. There are a number of points that suggest the psalmist is the king. These include: the threat by the nations (vv. 10-13) and the psalmist's subsequent victory over them (v. 15); the military language in vv. 10-11 and 15-16; the authority of the psalmist to call for the gates of the city/temple to be opened (v. 19); and the question of trust in princes implying allegiance and treaty (v. 9). In the psalm the king joins with the rest of the community in proclaiming the eternal nature of Yahweh's steadfast love. His proclamation in vv. 1 and 29 matches that called from Israel, the house of Aaron and all fearers of Yahweh (vv. 2-4). In the Deuteronomistic literature the king is clearly included among those who fear Yahweh. In the law of the king in Deut. 17.14-20 it is in the study of *torah* that the king learns to fear Yahweh (cf. Josh. 1.7-9). The king is also not to acquire many horses or wives for himself (vv. 16-17) lest he respectively enslave his own people or has his heart turned away. Both references pertain to the matter of forging political alliances for the sake of national security. Both Psalm 118 and Deuteronomy stress absolute trust in Yahweh. If the psalmist is the king then the psalm is consistent with this Deuteronomic outlook on kingship. The juxtaposition of Psalm 118 with the *torah* psalm, Psalm 119, is consistent with the association of royal themes to torah obedience.

Psalm 118, although it does not exhibit overt royal connections, has many images and ideas in common with other royal psalms, especially Psalms 18, 20, 21. We hear phrases and images familiar from Psalm 118 in, for example, Pss. 18.6, 17, 19, 29, 35; 20.1, 5, 6c, 7; and 21.7, 8, 9. These royal psalms also embrace the *torah* psalm, Psalm 19. The *torah*/king relationship is repeated.

In Psalm 118 we are returning to the figure of the blessed man who is also king in Psalms 1–2. That man was revealed as David in Psalm 3. But now both David and the Davidic monarchy lie in the past if in Book V we have moved beyond exile. In Psalm 118 the king as psalmist is also an example for his people. Memory of his victory and thanksgiving, and the faith behind those, is an example for later 'fearers of Yahweh' who experience distress and seek deliverance. Liturgical practice is the key to this memory. While David is no longer king the image of the faithful king lives on in hope of an end time. Such a hope is realized in one way in the New Testament's appropriation of the psalm to Jesus' death and resurrection (v. 22 cf. Mt. 21.42; Mk. 12.10-11; Lk. 20.17 etc.; v. 24 cf. Mt. 21.9; Mk. 11.9-10; Lk 13.35; 19.38).

Psalm 119

Psalm 119 dominates Book V of the Psalter by its sheer length. Its length also dominates the interpretation of the psalm. These 176 verses are homage to *torah* and its significance in the life of one who fears Yahweh. Every verse adds something to our appreciation of *torah*, the psalmist's devotion to it, and its importance in the psalmist's life. The length and the structure of the psalm make it more of an experience than a rational prayer or treatise on *torah*, although it is not without reason in its structure and themes.

The basic structure is simple. The psalm is an alphabetic acrostic consisting of twenty two stanzas, each with eighth lines, each of which begins with the letter of the Hebrew alphabet for that stanza. The stanzas work sequentially through the alphabet. The closest biblical parallel is the acrostic poem in Lamentations 3 where there are twenty two stanzas each with three lines. Within the overall structure of Psalm 119, a recitation on *torah* and its synonyms is developed. Eighth words are used to speak of *torah* with, for the most part, one used in each verse. They are *'imrâ, dābār, ḥuqqîm, miṣwōt, mišpāṭîm, ʿēdōt, piqqûdîm,* and *tôrâ* itself. In the NRSV they are translated: 'promise', 'word', 'statutes', 'commandments', 'decrees', 'precepts', and 'law' respectively. The words *derek* and *'ōraḥ* ('way') and *'emûnâ* ('faithfulness') are less frequent but could be added. While these words are synonyms for *torah*, they each add their own nuance to our understanding of *torah*. Such terms, as well as other aspects of and terms in the psalm (e.g. *lišmōr*, 'to observe, keep', and *bekol-lēb*, 'with all the heart'), bear similarities to the language of the Deuteronomistic History.

The structure of Psalm 119 bears on its interpretation. The alphabetic acrostic structure could indicate either that this psalm provides the A-Z of *torah* or that *torah* is complete and wholly adequate for the life of the faithful. The latter would seem more consistent with the lack of actual specific laws or prescriptions within the psalm. Moreover, completeness is also suggested by the inclusion of all parts of the psalmist's body in adherence to *torah*. For example, near the beginning we find: eyes—vv. 6, 15, 18, 37; mouth—vv. 13, 43; heart—vv. 2, 7, 10, 11, 34, 36; 'soul' (*napšî*, 'myself, body', lit. 'throat')—vv. 20, 25, 28. Each is repeated later in the psalm along with feet—vv. 59, 101, 105—and tongue—v. 172.

The psalm cannot be classified as a single form. We might think it belongs to the wisdom tradition with its frequent references to teaching and understanding (e.g. vv. 27, 29, 32, 34, 73 etc.) and, especially, the psalmist's prayer for Yahweh 'to teach me your statutes (vv. 12, 26, 33, 68, 124, 135, 171). In some of its themes it is closest to Psalms 1 and 19 which are also concerned with *torah*. However, there are strong elements of petition and plea within the psalm—more frequent in later verses (e.g. vv. 21-22, 50-51, 81-88, 121-128; 134; 137-176)—consistent with laments psalms. The date of the original composition and its setting are impossible to determine given the content of the psalm. The similarities with terminology and themes from Deuteronomy suggest an exilic to post-exilic date. It was also likely, given the form, that the psalm was penned as a unity.

While there is no clear thematic development through the psalm, some of the 22 stanzas do reveal thematic concerns, often associated with vocabulary or constructions related to the initial letter for the stanza. The *dalet* stanza (vv. 25-32) is a contemplation on the word *derek* ('way') which begins five of its verses. Seven of the eighth verses in the *hē* stanza (vv. 33-40) begin with Hiphil imperatives, thus giving the stanza a strong sense of command. In the *zayin* stanza (vv. 49-56) three verses spanning the stanza begin with a form of the verb *zākar*, 'to remember'. The *tet* stanza (vv. 65-72) constitutes a contemplation of 'good' with *ṭôb*, 'good', used six times in the stanza. The *yôd* stanza (vv. 73-80) begins with a series of supplications, while the *mêm* stanza (vv. 97-104) uses the preposition *min* in its comparative function to develop a series of 'better than' clauses. The most complex is the final stanza, *tāw* (vv. 169-176). Apart from the *tāw* at the start of each line, the masculine 2nd person suffix -^{e}kā ('your') occurs in each of fourteen half verses, mostly on the last word in the first half of a verse and on the second last word in the second half. Emphasis is thereby focused on Yahweh who is referred to by the 'you' or 'your' involved. Moreover, the second half verse starts with a 'k' sound in all but two lines (*kî*, 'for' in four cases, *k^e* 'like' in two) emphasising the sound of the suffixes.

The first two stanzas (*'ālep* and *bêt*, vv. 1-16) have an introductory function beginning with the general blessing upon those who 'walk in the *torah* of Yahweh' (v. 1). Verses 1 and 2 begin with 'ašrê (twice) recalling the blessed man of Psalm 1, although in Psalm 119 the blessing is extended to the whole community of the faithful. The divine command of precepts etc. is introduced along with the desire to observe them and thus not be shamed (v. 6). The psalmist's subsequent praise of Yahweh for such provision is noted. The second stanza then goes on to speak of the psalmist's response to the divine precepts (vv. 9-16).

Another connection to Psalm 1 and 2 is forged by the association of Psalm 119, with its focus on *torah* and blessing, with Psalm 118 which has royal features. This parallels the association set down at the beginning of the Psalter (cf. also Psalms 18–21 with the same association: Psalms 18, 20, 21 royal and Psalm 19 focussing on *torah*).

Learning and observing the precepts of Yahweh is the key to life. The psalmist trusts in Yahweh's word (v. 42) and loves and delights in Yahweh's commands (v. 47). Faithfulness and obedience even constitute the way to deal with distress (v. 30). The result of this *torah* obedience is not restriction but liberty in both activity and thought (vv. 32, 45). In this regard the psalmist classes himself among those who fear Yahweh (v. 38; cf. Ps. 118.2-4). But the psalmist is more than that, for he becomes both a teacher (v. 79) and an exemplar to others who fear Yahweh (v. 74). His experience has involved some hardship, or even now does (v. 126), but he sees that also as instructive (v. 71). Others plot against him (vv. 51, 53, 61, 69 etc.) and the arrogant get the upper hand (vv. 81-88). His opponents seem to be both near (v. 115) and far (v. 119). Yet his wisdom exceeds that of his predecessors, particularly because Yahweh has taught him (vv. 99-100). In his view Yahweh's steadfast love fills the earth (v. 64). Yahweh's promise, which is usually salvation of some kind, is continually before him and is intricately bound with Yahweh's word or commands (e.g. vv. 38, 41, 50, 82, 116, 148, 170, 172 etc.). Delight is his repeated response to *torah* (vv. 16, 24, 47, 70, 77, 92, 143). Verse 174 is an appropriate summation of the psalmist's message. In many ways this psalmist's experience parallels that of David in the Psalter to date. The final stanza is a fitting summation of the psalmist's praise and confidence in Yahweh.

The identity of this psalmist whose trust is an example to others is not made clear at any stage of the psalm. However, details within the psalm hint at the likelihood of a royal figure. The claim in v. 102 that Yahweh is the psalmist's teacher and that he understands more than the elders and teachers (vv. 97-100) suggests it is unlikely that this psalmist comes from a wisdom school. Such self assessment as this is not common in that context. Clearly, the psalmist is one of elevated rank. Other details point to a similar conclusion. The psalmist has dealings, for bad or good, with princes and kings (vv. 23, 46, 161). He speaks of himself as (Yahweh's) 'servant' (vv. 17, 23, 38 etc.) on occasion in relation to the mention of princes (esp. v. 23). He is of sufficient status for enemies to plot against and persecute him (vv. 23, 98, 161). He is familiar with the role of counsellors (v. 24). His comparison of Yahweh's *torah* with gold, silver and fine gold could also suggest someone of great wealth. It is reasonable to again see the psalmist as a king. Finally, the statement in v. 11, 'I treasure your word in my heart', echoes that of David in Ps. 40.9 where he says 'your *torah* is within my heart'. This was the goal of the Deuteronomistic law of the king (Deut. 17.14-20). Even expressions like we find in v. 116: 'Uphold me according to your promise, that I may live, and let me not be put to shame in my hope', could well be understood as referring to the Davidic covenant (cf. v. 76). With the additional similarities to earlier experiences in the Psalter where David was clearly indicated as psalmist, it could be envisaged that we have here the voice of one who speaks as David, an exemplar for all who fear Yahweh, and one who embodies the eschatological hope for a king of the stature and trust of his forebear. That is, 'David' speaks in a new way. The close association of this *torah* psalm with Psalm 118, echoing the associations noted earlier, reinforces the royal connection.

The nature of *torah* referred to in Psalm 119 is still a little unclear. David speaks in different ways about *torah* with *dābār* 'word' implying a body of teaching but words such as *ḥuqqîm* 'statutes', *'ēdōt* 'decrees', and *piqqûdîm* 'precepts' implying a body of discreet laws. In the body of the psalm, *torah* or its synonyms can be kept (v. 1 etc.), spoken (v. 13 etc.), studied (v. 18 etc.), and meditated on (v. 15 etc.). They strengthen one (v. 28 etc.), they are a way of faithfulness (v. 30 etc.), a word of salvation and hope (vv. 41, 43, 81-82 etc.) and invoke a public way of life (v. 74 etc.). David seeks to understand the way of the precepts, that is, seek the way that lies behind them (v. 27). At one time *torah* sounds like some form of natural law (v. 64) while at another learning the statutes can involve reflection on past experience (v. 71). At times one could perceive *torah* in Psalm 119 as something fixed and in relatively concrete form, such as the Pentateuch, although no specific laws are mentioned; at others, as some form of authoritative oral tradition or prophecy, or as revelation in a general form from nature or experience. What remains constant is the witness to Yahweh who always stands behind his word.

Psalms 120–134

Psalms 120–134 form an identifiable grouping within the Psalter, the 'songs of Ascents'. They are marked out by the common superscription *šîr hamma ʿălôt* 'a song of ascents'. Just what that indicates is debatable. It could be related to the use of the verb *ʿālâ*, 'to go up', in regard to the exiles returning to Jerusalem in Ezra 2.1; 7.9. It could indicate the collection is related to pilgrimage in general. Alternatively, the Mishnah implies a liturgical function seeing one psalm sung on each of the fifteen steps between the women's court and the court of Israel in the temple complex (*Mid.* 2.5; *Sukk.* 5.4). The collection has traditionally been used in the festival of *Sukkot* (Tabernacles) recalling the wilderness wanderings. Several genres are present in the collection including lament, hymns of praise, psalms of trust and a royal psalm. The unity of the collection lies in their common usage as well as in repeated themes and a linear progression through the collection.

The collection falls into three groups: Psalms 120–124; 125–129; and 130–134. There is constant stress on reliance upon Yahweh and on Zion as the place of blessing. The collection bears marks of a complex editorial history but took its final form in the post-exilic period. A number of phrases repeated throughout the collection helps bind the collection. These include: 'I lift up my eyes' (Pss. 121.1; 123.1); 'who made heaven and earth' (Pss. 121.2; 124.8; 134.3); 'let Israel now say' (Pss. 124.1; 129.1); 'from this time on and forevermore' (Pss. 121.8; 125.2; 131.3); 'peace be upon Israel' (Pss. 125.5; 128.6); 'Yahweh bless you from Zion' (Pss. 128.5; 134.3); and 'O Israel, hope in Yahweh' (Pss. 130.7; 131.3).

The collection begins in **Psalm 120** with a plea for deliverance from distress picking up the lament at the end of Psalm 119. The psalmist lives in a foreign place. In Ps. 118.5 it was the king who made this plea but in Ps. 120.1 it is the psalmist's own expression and in the present tense. The psalmist speaks in v. 5 as an alien in Meshech (NW of Jerusalem in Asia Minor) and in Kedar (E of Jerusalem in the desert). He thus speaks as an exile on behalf of all exiles. It is little wonder that his plea in v. 1 is similar to the refrain of the people in Ps. 107.6, 13, 19, 28. **Psalm 121** follows as a psalm of pilgrimage. The greater context of the Songs of Ascents suggests that the psalmist is arriving at his destination. The image of the hills could be negative (i.e. a place of danger) or positive (the place of Yahweh's dwelling and source of help) in which case v. 2 could be either a statement or a question. Yahweh is Israel's protector with a form of the verb 'to keep' used six times in the psalm.

Psalm 122 is designated as a psalm of David. The psalmist expresses joy at having been invited to come to Jerusalem. That is where the thrones of David's dynasty have been set up. The Davidic dynasty has become a point of hope. The psalm ends with a prayer for peace (cf. 121.6-7). In **Psalm 123**, having had enough of the contempt he has received from others, the psalmist pleads with Yahweh for mercy. He lifts his eyes again (cf. 121.1) but now to the one enthroned in the heavens. This image suggests that the start of Psalm 121 ought to be read positively.

The last psalm in this section, **Psalm 124**, also has a superscription attributing it to David. It is a psalm of thanksgiving for Yahweh's presence with his people and deliverance of them. It is only through Yahweh that they have been delivered. The first five psalms in these Songs of Ascents give a combined picture of the pilgrim, thankful for deliverance from distress in foreign places, journeying back to Jerusalem.

Psalms 125–129 all relate to a time when Israel have settled in the land and face new difficulties. **Psalm 125**, a psalm of trust, compares Yahweh's care for his people to the hills that surround Zion. Yahweh will not let wickedness come upon them. It ends with a prayer for justice for those who are good and for peace upon Israel (cf. 120.6-7; 122.6-9). **Psalm 126** considers the time 'when Yahweh restored the fortunes of Zion' (v. 1; so NRSV) although the MT could be translated more directly in terms of the return of the exiles to Zion (cf. NIV, NJB). The psalmist longs for further restoration and looks to a time of great blessing and fertility (cf. Ps. 107.33-42).

At the centre of this section we find **Psalm 127** which is attributed to King Solomon. The reference to 'building the house' (v. 1) suggests this but it also implies that the 'house' is the temple. Without Yahweh's aid, this task especially is in vain (v. 1). But this is a dictum that applies to all of life (v. 2). It goes on to speak of the blessings of Yahweh in terms of children declaring the man who has lots of sons 'happy' (v. 5; 'ašrê, cf. Ps. 1.1). The large number of children is also relevant to Solomon in a number of ways but it could refer to the Davidic dynasty which ran through him, i.e. lots of sons in terms of descendants on the throne.

Psalm 128 begins as Psalm 127 finished with another 'ašrê phrase, this time relating to those who fear Yahweh. It also speaks in terms of the blessing of family, and even in this way the king functions as a model of the one who receives blessing. The psalm ends with desire for further blessings of long life, the prosperity of Jerusalem and peace for Israel (vv. 5-6). The section ends with **Psalm 129**, a prayer for the downfall of Israel's enemies. This too depends on Yahweh who is righteous. The refrain turns an individual psalm into a communal one (cf. Psalm 124).

The final section of the Songs of Ascents speaks of hope for the future with further reflection on the Davidic covenant toward the end of the collection. **Psalm 130** is a lament in unknown circumstances. The psalmist is aware that his only hope is in Yahweh's word (v. 5 recalling the mood of Psalm 119) and he waits diligently for Yahweh. He calls Israel in turn to hope in Yahweh who has steadfast love and the power to redeem (vv. 7-8). **Psalm 131** picks up the mood of a quiet confidence in Yahweh, finishing again on a call to Israel to hope in Yahweh.

At the centre of this section stands the longest of the Songs of Ascents, **Psalm 132**. It begins asking Yahweh to 'remember' in David's favour all his hardships (v. 1), particularly David's desire to 'find a place for Yahweh' (v. 5). It recounts some of the history of the ark coming to Jerusalem, with Jaar and Ephrathah (v. 6) probably references to Kiriath-Jearim (1 Sam. 7.1-2). The prayer at the end of the first half of the psalm seeks Yahweh's continued attention to David and his covenant (v. 10). The second half begins parallel to the first with Yahweh's oath (v. 11; cf. David's in v. 2). This reiterates Yahweh's promise that a descendant of David will sit on the throne. Yahweh has chosen Zion as his resting place forever and will bless it and its people (vv. 13-18). He promises that a horn will sprout for David (vv. 17-18). There is thus an eschatological reshaping of the promise to David. This psalm looks back to the historic David and anticipates a new descendant for David.

The collection ends with two psalms of blessing, **Psalm 133** speaking of the goodness of unity among kindred which is part of a blessing of life forever, and **Psalm 134** which speaks of people in turn blessing Yahweh even as Yahweh blesses them. This is an eschatological hope following from Psalm 132.

Psalms 135–145

The next section of Book V opens with two psalms recounting Israel's early history in praise of Yahweh. **Psalm 135** calls all who worship Yahweh to praise his name (vv. 1-4). Verses 1-2 echo Ps. 134.1 in this call, thus linking the psalm to the Songs of Ascents, but extending the invitation to a wider congregation. Psalm 135 is also linked to 'The Egyptian Hallel' through the phrase *hall^{e}lû-yāh* 'Praise Yahweh' (vv. 1a, 21c) which is frequent in Psalms 111–117, and a number of phrases from Psalm 115. From the rebuilt temple (v. 2) the psalmist calls all to praise Yahweh as sovereign on the basis of creation (vv. 5-7) and the exodus and wilderness wanderings to the entry into the land (vv. 8-12). In contrast to the idols, which are the work of human hands (vv. 15-18), Yahweh's name endures forever (vv. 13-14). All groups in the temple are finally called to bless Yahweh who resides in Jerusalem (vv. 19-21a; cf. Ps. 118.2-4). The psalm conveys a sense of confidence in Jerusalem and its temple.

The companion psalm, **Psalm 136**, is a great responsorial hymn of praise celebrating Yahweh's everlasting steadfast love. This response is frequent in the Psalter but its use as an *inclusio* in Ps. 118.1, 29 ties Psalm 136 back to earlier psalms. After affirming the sovereignty of Yahweh in vv. 1-3 (cf. the modified *inclusio* in v. 26), Psalm 136 catalogues aspects of creation (vv. 4-9), the exodus and wilderness wanderings to the entry into the promised land (vv. 10-22) in parallel to the sequence in Ps. 135.5-12. This historic recall in both psalms anticipates the return to the land after exile.

However, the pain of the experience of exile in Babylon is not forgotten as **Psalm 137** shows. It remembers the distress of that experience (vv. 4-6) and seeks vindication against the Edomites who cooperated with the Babylonians (v. 7-9; cf. Obadiah). Central to the psalm is the question: 'How can we sing Yahweh's song in a foreign land' (v. 4; *'admat nēkār*). *nēkār* occurs elsewhere in the Psalter only in Pss. 18.45-46 and 144.7, 11 to which we will return (cf. Ps. 81.10 'foreign god'). As well as voicing the bitter experience of exile Psalm 137 anticipates the question of continued foreign domination after return from exile.

There follows a series of psalms, Psalms 138–145, ascribed to David. The first such psalm, **Psalm 138**, is a thanksgiving psalm to Yahweh for his steadfast love and faithfulness. Psalm 138 with Psalm 145 form a frame around this Davidic collection through common motifs: namely the 'name' of Yahweh (Pss. 138.2; 145.1-2, 21); 'glory' (Ps. 138.5; 145.11); and 'great' (Pss. 138.5; 145.3, 6). In Psalm 138 Yahweh has answered the psalmist's call in Psalm 137, and the psalmist looks to a time when all kings will acknowledge Yahweh, for he 'regards the lowly' (vv. 4-6). Even now the psalmist trusts in Yahweh's deliverance in difficult times. By way of exploring the 'work of (Yahweh's) hands' (v. 8) and showing how Yahweh regards the lowly, the psalmist turns to **Psalm 139**, a personal account of a faithful relationship with Yahweh. It is not possible for the psalmist to escape Yahweh who is all present and all knowing. Given the vulnerability of human life (cf. Pss. 39.4-6; 62.9; 144.4) such a presence could be oppressive but in this psalm it leads only to wonder and praise (v. 14). The psalm ends with a desire for the death of the wicked and a claim that the psalmist hates that which Yahweh hates (vv. 21-22), a statement principally of loyalty rather than emotion. But in the end, just as the psalmist is aware that Yahweh has searched him out in the past (vv. 1-6), he asks Yahweh to search him out again so that he will not be like the wicked but be led 'in the way everlasting' (v. 24).

A series of lament psalms (Psalms 140–143), with their own internal connecting motifs, follows. It begins in **Psalm 140** with the psalmist seeking deliverance from the enemies whom he hated at the end of Psalm 139. He relies on Yahweh's justice and care for the needy to ensure the upright will live in his presence (v. 12-13). **Psalm 141** follows with a prayer for preservation from evildoers. As in Psalm 139, the psalmist knows his ways are not upright in themselves and thus needs Yahweh to be a refuge and guard him (šāmar 'to keep'; cf. Psalm 121). **Psalm 142** is a traditional lament. It is, however, the only psalm attributed to David outside Books I-II which is given a context in David's life—'when he was in the cave'. This connection seems to be stirred by vv. 6b-7a and could refer to either the episode of the cave of Adullam (1 Sam. 22.1-2) or that at En-gedi (1 Sam. 24.1-15) although neither fits exactly with the psalm (cf. also Psalm 57 superscription). The final psalm in this sequence of laments is **Psalm 143**. Remembrance of the days of old (v. 5; cf. Psalms

135–136) gives the psalmist reason for his prayer (v. 6). In almost every verse, especially from vv. 5-11, there are echoes of, allusions to or even quotes of phrases from earlier psalms, particularly ones in Books I-II (e.g. v. 5: Ps. 77.5, 12; v. 6: Pss. 88.9; 42.2; 63.1 etc.). The words of the psalmist literally echo those of David from earlier in the Psalter.

Psalm 144 is the last royal psalm in the Psalter (see v. 10). It too is attributed to David. Like its predecessor it draws heavily on earlier psalm material: with v. 3 cf. Ps. 8.4; with v. 4 cf. Ps. 39.11. Several phrases in Psalm 144 have also been borrowed from Psalm 18: with v. 1 cf. Ps. 18.2, 46; with v. 2 cf. 18.2; with v. 5 cf. 18.9; and with vv. 7, 11 cf. 18.44-45. The connection to Psalm 18 is important and focuses on the phrase $b^e n\hat{e}$-$n\bar{e}k\bar{a}r$ 'foreigners, aliens'. In Psalm 18 David had just said how Yahweh had helped him defeat his enemies (vv. 18.31-42) and described how foreigners came cringing to him as a result of his victory (vv. 43-45). In Ps. 144.7, 11 the psalmist prays again for rescue from foreign hands. The use of the same phrase founds the request in Psalm 144 on David's past experience. Moreover, the use of $n\bar{e}k\bar{a}r$ in only these places and Psalm 137 (note also 'foreign god' in Ps. 81.10) ties these psalms together. In Psalm 144 the psalmist prays for relief from continuing oppression like that described in Psalm 137. He proclaims Yahweh's saving action and seeks deliverance on a national scale. Yahweh rescued his servant David, so the psalmist says he can 'rescue me' (vv. 10-11). The psalmist then invokes a blessing on the people in eschatological terms and seeks no further exile (vv. 12-14). Such a people are happy ($'a\check{s}r\hat{e}$; cf. Ps. 1.1). The psalm turns from an individual prayer to one on behalf of the community from v. 12 and the psalmist bases his own hope for rescue on that of David, his predecessor and example (v. 10).

The final psalm in the section is **Psalm 145**, an acrostic hymn of praise, which provides a fine summation and climax for Book V. Verse 4, in speaking of one generation declaring Yahweh's mighty acts to another, epitomizes the Psalter itself. It passes on the prayers and faith of one who trusts in the steadfast love of Yahweh, from David to succeeding generations. The psalmist, in the voice of David, vows to meditate on the works of Yahweh and celebrate and proclaim Yahweh's unsearchable greatness, abundant goodness and righteousness (vv. 1-9). Verse 8 quotes the divine qualities from Exod. 34.6-7. The rest of the psalm sees the praise of Yahweh's goodness, compassion and steadfast love etc.

spreading out from David (vv. 1-9) to 'all' Yahweh's works (v. 10) and to 'all' flesh (v. 21). The particle *kôl*, 'all', occurs seventeen times in the psalm, pointing to the comprehensive nature of the praise and the ones who give it. The end of the psalm, vv. 13b-20, speaks further of Yahweh's qualities—faithfulness, upholding those who fall, raising up those bowed down, supplying needs, acting justly and kindly, being near, fulfilling all desires, hearing cries, keeping those who love him (*šāmar*; NRSV: 'watch over'), and destroying the wicked; all things that happen in the Psalter. At the centre of this acrostic psalm we have the verses beginning with the letters *kap* ('k'), *lāmed* ('l'), and *mêm* ('m'). Reversed these three letters make up the word *melek* 'king'. In each of these three verses the word *malkût* 'kingdom' appears. All Yahweh's works speak of the glory, power, splendour and the everlasting nature of his kingdom. It is that which governs all in the Psalter and that to which all flesh vows praise (v. 21). In this sense Psalm 145 looks forward to the praise that follows in Psalms 146–150. But it also looks back as v. 20 closely resembles Ps. 1.6 providing an *inclusio* to Psalm 1 and thus concluding the Psalter in one sense.

Psalms 146–150

There is no doxology at the end of Book V of the Psalter as in the case of each of the preceding books (Pss. 41.13; 72.18-19; 89.52; and 106.48). Instead, Psalms 146–150, a collection of post-exilic hymns, function as a great doxology which concludes both Book V and the Psalter as a whole. These five hymns, each with its call and reason for praise, form another collection of Hallel psalms. Each psalm begins and ends with *hallᵉlû-yāh*, 'Praise Yahweh' (cf. Psalms 113–118).

This cacophony of praise takes its leave from Ps. 145.21. It begins in Psalm 146 with the psalmist opening his mouth with praise (cf. 145.21a) and concludes with 'everything that breathes' praising Yahweh (Ps. 150.6; cf. 145.21b). Thus Psalm 145 is a point around which the end of the Psalter pivots. It is a summation of all that goes before and it opens the way for what follows. Each of the following psalms adds to the voices which praise Yahweh—first the psalmist, then Jerusalem, then all in heaven and earth, then the faithful in Zion and Israel, and finally 'everything that breathes'. Various dimensions of praise are evident in this movement—personal, community, political, and liturgical. The use of the phrase *zōqēp* (*lᵉkol-hak*)*kᵉpûrîm* 'one who lifts up (all) those who are bowed down' in Pss. 145.14 and 146.8, and nowhere else in the Psalter further binds Psalm 145 to the following.

Psalms 146–150 are themselves linked together through a number of catchwords and motifs. For example, the address to Zion in Ps. 146.10 is picked up again in Ps. 147.12, with a further reference to Zion in 149.2 and the location of Psalm 150 in the sanctuary (v. 1). The references to dancing and making melody in Ps. 149.3 are picked up in Psalm 150. Kings are mentioned in Pss. 148.11 and 149.8. The praise or glory of the faithful is a motif that spans the whole collection (Pss. 145.10; 148.14; and 149.1, 5, 9).

Early in this final collection of hymns, there is a focus on the various qualities of Yahweh. This extends the catalogue of descriptive phrases in Psalm 145. Ps. 146.6-7b list aspects of Yahweh's creative works followed by qualities of truth and justice and finally 'bread for the hungry'. Verses 7b-9 speak of Yahweh's dealing with those bowed down finishing with care for the orphan and widow. In contrast, the way of the wicked will only bring destruction (cf. Ps. 1.6). Ps. 147.3-6 speak of Yahweh rebuilding Jerusalem and gathering its outcasts. A mixture of Yahweh's attributes and actions follows including healing, creating the heavens, understanding, supporting the poor, and defeating the wicked. The catalogue continues in vv. 8-9 with images of Yahweh as sustainer having called the people to give thanks (v. 7). The theme of Yahweh's word is strong in this last section with reference to the command of Yahweh (v. 15) in relation to creation (cf. vv. 18-19). Finally, Yahweh is trustworthy (Pss. 147.4-5, 15–18; and 148.5-6) and faithful to his exiled people (Pss. 147.2-3; 148.14; 149.4).

Praise is the fitting response for such a god. At the centre of this final collection lies Psalm 148 in which we hear in antiphonal form first praise from the heavens (vv. 1-6), with a series of *hallûhû* clauses calling all heavenly entities (the heights, divine messengers, heavenly hosts, sun and moon, stars, the highest heaven and the waters above the heavens) to praise Yahweh. The reason for praise is that Yahweh created them (vv. 5-6). In vv. 7-13b there is the call for praise from the earth. All creatures and peoples are called to praise Yahweh, including creatures of cosmic significance (sea monsters, fire, hail, mountains etc.), ones of national importance (kings and princes) and all people (young and old, men and women). Praise spills out beyond the faithful. Heaven and earth give thanks for Yahweh has raised a horn for his people (vv. 13-14). Those in Israel and in Zion are to rejoice and praise Yahweh for he delights in his people and gives them salvation (Ps. 149.2-4). This praise culminates in Psalm 150 with 'all flesh' called to praise. Thus praise has spread out from the individual to the heavenly and earthly hosts to 'all flesh' as we have moved through Psalms 146–150. The faithful, and all creation, are called to unbounded praise, praise with words, movement and music.

Yahweh's name is praised in these psalms. In Psalm 148 the heavens and the earth are called to praise Yahweh's name which alone is exalted (vv. 5 and 13). The focus on Yahweh's 'name' tied Psalms 145 and 146 together. 'All flesh' will bless Yahweh's name (Ps. 145.21b) and in Psalm 146 we hear the name 'Yahweh' no less than eleven times. This focus on the divine name as an object of praise continues through Pss. 148.5, 13; and 149.3.

Yahweh's kingship is again reiterated throughout Psalms 146–150. It is stated in Ps. 145.1 and taken up again in Ps. 146.10. By comparison the power, steadfastness and plans of human leaders are deceptive. They cannot last (Ps. 146.3-4). The point is underlined in Ps. 147.10 with the use of holy war language. Yahweh's strength does not lie in horses, which were used in late Old Testament times with war chariots, or with infantry. The motif is strengthened in Psalm 148 through the use of creation language. The one exalted over creation, especially over those things which symbolize chaos (the sea monsters and the deeps, Ps. 148.7), is sovereign. In the end, the kings and princes of the earth will confirm what is patently clear from creation itself; Yahweh is king (cf. Ps. 149.2). Ultimately this king will be victorious over the nations who continue to oppress Israel (Ps. 149.6-9).

Psalm 149 needs particular comment. This psalm focuses on 'the faithful' (MT: $h^a sîdîm$) who praise Yahweh. One might expect the subject to be all creation or 'all flesh' following Psalm 148 and anticipating Psalm 150. However, Psalm 149 takes us back to Yahweh's own people. Moreover, they are not a people who have acted in their own strength or power. Verse 3 describes them as the $^{c}a nāwîm$ (NRSV: 'the humble'; elsewhere 'the poor'). The same term has been used in the past to refer to those who are dependent upon Yahweh's compassion (Pss. 9.19; 10.17; 22.27; 25.9; 34.3; 69.33; 147.6). Yahweh's people play a special role in the establishment and proclamation of Yahweh's kingship. His people are not lost in the flood of kings, princes, young and old who join in Yahweh's praise (Ps. 148.11-12). Just as Zion is a cornerstone in that burgeoning praise (Psalm 147), so are Yahweh's faithful. Psalm 149 goes on, however, to speak of the faithful praising Yahweh 'in their throats' but having 'a two-edged sword in their hands' to execute 'vengeance' on the nations (vv. 7-9a). This vengeance, however, is not their own but *mišpāṭ kātûb* (NRSV: 'the judgment decreed'). The presumption in the context is that it is Yahweh's judgment which is executed. A parallel can be drawn with Psalm 2 where Yahweh derides those who reject his reign saying he has set his king in Zion (Ps. 2.6). Yahweh's king is his weapon against his opponents. In Psalm 149 the faithful replace the king in his role. The functions of the king have been democratized; David has become exemplar. The faithful not only emulate him in terms of piety but they begin to fulfil the role the king once had. Moreover, while there is the chance for the nations to 'be wise' as Ps. 2.10 says, there will still be those who oppose Yahweh's ways and his faithful people, which is what Psalm 149 anticipates (cf. Ps. 148.11-12). The picture is an eschatological one with a vision of things yet to be; things that will only be achieved through struggle. Psalm 150 could also be read that way. The psalmist's call for all to praise Yahweh 'for his mighty deeds', *gᵉbûrōtāyw*, among other things reminds us of the great works of salvation from the past (cf. *gᵉbûrōt* in Ps. 71.16). Even the unbounded praise of Psalm 150 does not neglect the struggles and the deliverance from them in the past. And by its open-endedness it suggests that praise may yet be a response to arise from further deliverance.

The connection between the end of the Psalter and its beginning goes beyond a parallel between the function of the people and that of the king. Ps. 146.3-4 speak of not trusting in princes or their plans. Both perish together when breath departs. So too the nations in Psalm 2 who conspire and plot (v. 1) and take counsel together (v. 2). Yahweh laughs at their vain pursuits (vv. 1, 4). Moreover, Ps. 146.9 expresses Yahweh's care for strangers, widows and orphans and anticipates the demise of the way of the wicked in language very close to Ps. 1.6. A very similar sentiment is expressed in Ps. 145.20. The end of the Psalter echoes in small but clear ways its beginnings. The journey from one place to another is assured. Its course may not be smooth as the presence of lament psalms even near the end makes clear (see Psalms 140–143). Nevertheless, the final word in this journey will always be *hallᵉlû-yāh* and the title of the Psalter in Hebrew always *tᵉhillîm*, 'praises'.

Bibliography

Allen, L.C., *Psalms 100–150* (Waco, TX: Word, 1983).
— *Psalms* (Biblical Word Themes; Waco, TX: Word, 1987).
Anderson, B.W., with S. Bishop, *Out of the Depths* (3rd edn, rev. and expanded; Louisville: Westminster John Knox Press, 2000).
Bellinger, W.H., *Psalms: Reading and Studying the Book of Praises* (Peabody, MA: Hendrickson, 1990).
Brown, W.L., *Seeing the Psalms: A Theology of Metaphor* (Louisville: Westminster John Knox, 2002).
Broyles, C.C., *Psalms* (Peabody, MN: Hendrickson, 1999).
—*The Conflict of Faith and Experience in the Psalms* (JSOTSup 52; Sheffield: JSOT, 1989).
Brueggemann, W., *The Message of the Psalms* (Minneapolis: Augsburg, 1984).
—*Israel's Praise: Doxology against Idolatry and Ideology* (Philadelphia: Fortress, 1988).
—*Finally Comes the Poet* (Minneapolis: Fortress, 1989).
—*Abiding Astonishment: Psalms, Modernity, and the Making of History* (Louisville: Westminster/John Knox, 1991).
—*The Psalms and the Life of Faith* (ed. P.D. Miller; Minneapolis: Fortress, 1995).
Bullock, C.H., *Encountering the Book of Psalms: A Literary and Theological Introduction* (Grand Rapids: Baker Book House, 2001).
Clifford, R.J., *Psalms 1–72* (Nashville: Abingdon, 2002).
—*Psalms 73–150* (Nashville: Abingdon, 2004).
Craigie, P.C., *Psalms 1–50* (2nd edn with Supplement by M. Tate; Nashville: Thomas Nelson, 2004).
Craven, T., *The Book of Psalms* (Message of Biblical Spirituality 6; Collegeville, MN: Liturgical Press, 1992).
Crenshaw, J.L., *The Psalms: An Introduction* (Grand Rapids: Eerdmans, 2001).
Croft, S.J., *The Identity of the Individual in the Psalms* (JSOTSup 44; Sheffield: JSOT, 1987).
Davidson, R., *The Vitality of Worship: A Commentary on the Book of Psalms* (Grand Rapids: Eerdmans, 1998).
Day, J., *Psalms* (Sheffield: JSOT, 1989).
deClaisse-Walford, N.L., *Introduction to the Psalms: A Song from Ancient Israel* (St. Louis: Chalice, 2004).
Eaton, J.H., *Kingship and the Psalms* (2nd edn; Sheffield: JSOT, 1986).
—*The Psalms: A Historical and Spiritual Commentary with an Introduction and New Translation* (London: T & T Clark, 2003).
Flint, P.W., *The Dead Sea Psalms Scrolls and the Book of Psalms* (Leiden: Brill, 1997).

Bibliography 195

Flint, P.W., and P.D. Miller (eds.), *The Book of Psalms: Composition and Reception* (Leiden: Brill, 2005).
Futato, M.D., *Interpreting the Psalms: An Exegetical Handbook* (Grand Rapids: Kregel, 2007).
Gerstenberger, E.S., *Psalms Part 1, with an Introduction to Cultic Poetry* (Grand Rapids: Eerdmans, 1988).
—*Psalms Part 2, Lamentations* (Grand Rapids: Eerdmans, 2001).
Goldingay, J., *Psalms. Volume 1: Psalms 1–41* (Grand Rapids: Baker Academic, 2006).
Grant, J.A., *The King as Exemplar: The Function of Deuteronomy's Kingship Law in the Shaping of the Book of Psalms* (Atlanta: SBL, 2004).
Gunkel, H., *The Psalms: A Form-Critical Introduction* (Philadelphia: Fortress, 1967).
—*An Introduction to the Psalms* (Macon, GA: Mercer University, 1998).
Holladay, W.L., *The Psalms Through Three Thousand Years: Prayerbook of a Cloud of Witnesses* (Minneapolis: Fortress, 1993).
Hossfeld, F.-L., and E. Zenger, *Psalms 2* (Minneapolis: Fortress, 2005).
Human, D.J., and C.J.A. Vos (eds.), *Psalms and Liturgy* (London: T & T Clark International, 2004).
Hunter, A.G., *Psalms* (London: Routledge, 1999).
Johnston, P.S., and D.G. Firth (eds.), *Interpreting the Psalms: Issues and Approaches* (Leicester: Apollos, 2005).
Keel, O., *The Symbolism of the Biblical World: Ancient Near Eastern Iconography and the Book of Psalms* (New York: Seabury, 1978).
Kraus, H.J., *Theology of the Psalms* (Minneapolis: Augsburg, 1986).
—*Psalms 1–59: A Commentary* (Minneapolis: Augsburg, 1988).
—*Psalms 60–150: A Commentary* (Minneapolis: Augsburg, 1989).
Levine, H.J., *Sing unto God a New Song: A Contemporary Reading of the Psalms* (Bloomington: Indiana University, 1995).
Limburg, J., *Psalms* (Loiusville: Westminster/John Knox, 2000).
Lohfink, N., and E. Zenger, *The God of Israel and the Nations: Studies in Isaiah and the Psalms* (Collegeville: Liturgical Press, 2000).
Magonet, J., *A Rabbi Reads the Psalms* (London: SCM, 1994).
Marttila, M., *Collective Reinterpretation in the Psalms* (Tübingen: Mohr Siebeck, 2006).
Mays, J.L., *Psalms* (Louisville: John Knox, 1994).
—*The Lord Reigns: A Theological Handbook to the Psalms* (Louisville: Westminster John Knox, 1994).
—*Preaching and Teaching the Psalms* (ed. P.D. Miller and G.M. Tucker; Louisville: Westminster John Knox, 2006).
McCann, J.C., *A Theological Introduction to the Book of Psalms: The Psalms as Torah* (Nashville: Abingdon, 1993).
—(ed.), *The Shape and Shaping of the Psalter* (JSOTSup 159; Sheffield: JSOT, 1993).
—'Psalms' in *The New Interpreter's Bible* (Nashville: Abingdon, 1996), Vol. IV, pp. 639–1280.
Miller, P.D., *Interpreting the Psalms* (Philadelphia: Fortress, 1986).
—*The Way of the Lord: Essays in Old Testament Theology* (Tübingen: Mohr Siebeck, 2004).

Mowinckel, S., *The Psalms in Israel's Worship* (2 vols; Nashville: Abingdon, 1962).
Parrish, V.S., *A Story of the Psalms: Conversation, Canon, and Congregation* (Collegeville: Liturgical Press, 2003).
Sarna, N., *Songs of the Heart: An Introduction to the Book of Psalms* (New York: Schocken, 1993).
Schaefer, K., *Psalms* (Collegeville: Liturgical Press, 2001).
Seybold, K., *Introducing the Psalms* (Edinburgh: T & T Clark, 1990).
Smith, M.S., *Psalms: The Divine Journey* (New York: Paulist, 1987).
Tate, M.E., *Psalms 51–100* (Waco, TX: Word, 1990).
Terrien, S.L., *The Psalms: Strophic Structure and Theological Commentary* (Grand Rapids: Eerdmans, 2003).
Westermann, C., *The Praise of God in the Psalms* (Richmond: John Knox, 1965).
—*Praise and Lament in the Psalms* (Atlanta: John Knox, 1981).
—*The Psalms: Structure, Content and Message* (Minneapolis: Augsburg, 1980).
Whybray, N., *Reading the Psalms as a Book* (Sheffield: SAP, 1996).
Wilson, G.H., *The Editing of the Hebrew Psalter* (Chico, CA: Scholars, 1985).
Zenger, E., *A God of Vengeance? Understanding the Psalms of Divine Wrath* (trans. L.M. Maloney; Louisville: Westminster/John Knox, 1996).

Index

Abraham, 41, 78, 121, 159, 172
animal terms, 56, 101
anointed, 16-18, 20, 46, 71, 75, 79, 94, 97, 99, 141, 146, 147, 153, 160
ark of the covenant, 22, 24, 28, 36, 64, 66, 96, 139, 186
Asaph Psalms, 6, 92, 99, 123, 142
Assyrians, 17, 94, 118
authorship of Psalms, 2, 9

Baal, 43, 47, 64-66, 72, 130, 168
blessing, 10, 12, 14-16, 18-20, 23, 25-27, 40, 51, 60, 64, 66, 69, 70, 72, 75, 76, 81, 85-87, 91, 117, 119, 121, 122, 144, 147, 158, 159, 161, 164, 166, 172, 174, 176, 178, 179, 181, 182, 184-186, 189

Canaanites, 29, 43, 71, 74, 168
Christ, 24, 57
Christian, 24, 54, 57
Chronicles, Books of, 2, 6, 7, 90, 92, 99
community, 4, 24, 30, 38, 54, 55, 58, 59, 65, 67, 68, 71-73, 77-81, 84, 93, 99, 101-103, 108, 109, 116, 122, 125, 127, 133, 138, 139, 147, 150-153, 156, 164-166, 169, 171, 173, 174, 178, 179, 182, 189, 190
covenant, 8, 62, 66, 68, 69, 71, 75, 84, 99, 100-102, 121, 131, 134, 137, 139, 144, 146, 148, 150, 154, 158, 159, 163, 164, 174, 183, 186
creation, 22, 31-33, 47-49, 51, 52, 63, 64, 66, 72-75, 77, 82, 94, 95, 97, 100, 107, 116, 130, 133, 144, 145, 151, 153-156, 158, 166, 187, 191, 192
cult, 3, 4, 6, 35, 53, 63, 129

David, 2, 7, 8, 10
David as model, 3, 9, 10, 14, 19, 25, 27, 39, 46, 52, 68, 71, 87, 90, 109, 116, 158, 169, 171, 173, 186
Davidic dynasty, 5, 6, 127, 132, 133, 138, 144, 148, 164, 179, 185, 186
Dead Sea Scrolls, 2, 5, 9, 72, 80
death, 24, 26, 36, 42, 54, 56, 60, 61, 77, 81, 88, 98, 100, 107, 124, 126, 142, 144, 153, 167, 175, 180, 188

doxology, 3, 4, 85, 90, 121, 147, 150, 190

Egyptian influence, 37, 59, 74, 115, 118, 120, 126, 135, 136, 150, 160-162, 171, 174-176, 187
enemies, 17, 21-24, 26, 27, 30, 32, 35, 37, 38, 40-43, 45, 51, 53, 55, 56, 58-60, 62, 63, 67, 70, 71, 78, 79, 86-90, 93, 107, 110, 112, 115-117, 120, 121, 128-130, 132, 135, 136, 140, 142, 143, 145, 146, 151, 171-173, 183, 186, 188, 189
Ephraim, 134-137
eschatology, 6, 7, 9, 10, 15, 20, 39, 40, 57, 63, 77, 96, 97, 109, 142, 157, 178, 183, 186, 187, 189, 193
exile, 5-8, 10, 60, 70, 72, 73, 80, 93, 98, 106, 108, 112, 117, 123, 128, 129, 134, 142, 143, 146, 151, 152, 154, 157-159, 161, 163, 164, 166-171, 173, 175, 176, 178, 179, 181, 184, 187, 189, 190
exodus, 73, 74, 100, 136, 161, 175
Exodus, 60, 69, 74, 82, 116, 117, 120, 128,

Index

130, 133, 162, 164, 167-169, 173-176, 187

faith, 8, 10, 19-22, 24, 33, 36, 39, 46, 50, 52, 55, 60, 66, 67, 69, 72, 77, 80, 81, 87, 90, 95, 97, 99-103, 105, 108-110, 113, 116, 122, 127, 129, 132, 144, 145, 147, 148, 151, 154, 157, 161-165, 170, 173, 175-177, 179, 180, 182, 188-192
fear of Yahweh, 13, 18, 22, 38, 50, 61, 62, 69, 71, 73-76, 78, 79, 81, 85, 95, 97, 98, 102, 109, 113, 116, 119, 133, 142, 158, 167, 173, 176, 179, 182, 183, 186
Feast of Tabernacles, 116, 174, 176, 184
fools, 38, 98, 166, 167
forgiveness, 67-70, 72, 103, 105-109, 141

Hallel, 174-176, 187, 190
history of Israel, 9, 10, 158, 159, 163, 164
hymns, 30, 53, 54, 63, 71, 129, 143, 144, 159, 174, 187, 189

inclusio, 19, 29, 30, 33, 34, 37, 42, 44, 46, 49, 60, 71, 87, 94, 104, 106, 107, 111, 112, 124, 135, 138, 147, 150, 153, 157, 159, 175, 176, 187, 190
Israel, 8, 9, 10, 14, 32, 41, 55, 58-60, 70, 74, 75, 80, 90, 93, 96, 101, 110, 124, 127, 128, 130-132,
134-137, 139, 140, 142, 143, 145, 147, 148, 157-164, 168, 174-176, 178, 179, 184-187, 190, 192

Jerusalem, 5, 20, 22, 24, 43, 63, 64, 92, 94, 95, 98, 108, 109, 117, 125, 127, 138, 139, 140, 143, 144, 172, 175, 184-187, 190, 191
Jewish interpretation, 5, 7, 8, 20, 28, 54, 59, 63, 82, 87, 174
justice, 14, 27-29, 34, 38, 49, 61, 69, 73, 86, 89, 94, 117-119, 140, 141, 144, 155, 157, 159, 162, 164, 174, 185, 188, 191

King Saul, 26, 41, 42, 53, 78, 79, 83, 85, 110-113, 134
kingship, 2-10, 13, 15-22, 25, 27, 29, 31-41, 43-46, 51-56, 58-60, 63-65, 67, 71, 72, 76-78, 83, 84, 86, 92-94, 97-99, 104, 113, 115-123, 126-128, 130, 132-134, 141-143, 145-148, 154-158, 160, 169-174, 177, 179, 182, 184-186, 189, 190, 192, 193
Korah Psalms, 6, 92, 98, 99, 123, 140-143

lament psalms, 4, 8, 10, 21, 23, 26, 30, 32, 34-40, 53-58, 66, 67, 70, 71, 78, 79, 81, 84, 85, 87, 89, 90, 92, 93, 99, 100, 103, 109-112, 117, 118, 120, 128, 130, 133,
138-140, 142, 143, 145-147, 150-154, 157, 159, 164, 169, 170, 176, 181, 184, 186, 188, 193
Levites, 2, 92, 99, 123
liturgy, 3, 7, 8, 24, 39, 54, 58, 63, 65, 66, 90, 91, 118, 134, 157, 171, 176, 178, 179, 184, 190

memory, 34, 35, 58, 68, 93, 135-137, 139, 160, 161, 163, 179
Mesopotamian influence, 19, 49, 56, 67, 74, 95, 101, 126, 130, 144, 146, 150, 152, 171, 177
messiah, 5, 8-10, 20, 122, 149, 173
Midrash Tehillim, 59, 60, 72, 104, 158
Moses, 5, 7, 14, 41, 59, 69, 150, 156, 158, 160-162
Most High, 3, 29, 34, 95, 136, 140, 154
Mt Sinai, 43, 69, 100, 101, 148, 150, 163, 164

nations, 16, 18, 19, 34-38, 45, 54, 58, 74, 75, 93, 96-98, 102, 116, 117, 120, 121, 138, 140-142, 157, 159, 161, 163, 164, 169, 173-175, 177-179, 192, 193

penitential psalms, 103
pilgrimage, 140, 184, 185
poor, 34-39, 44, 84-87, 90, 91, 110, 118-120, 125, 131, 168, 170, 174, 191, 192
post-exilic period, 6, 8, 73, 80, 106, 148, 159,

Index   199

164, 166, 173, 175, 176, 181, 184, 190
praise, 4, 6, 10, 29, 30, 32, 34-36, 38-40, 42, 44-47, 49, 53-55, 57, 58, 63, 65, 70-74, 76-79, 81, 83, 84, 90, 94, 97, 107, 109-111, 113-118, 127, 129-133, 139, 142-145, 151, 156-159, 161, 162, 167, 169, 173-176, 178, 182, 184, 187-193
Psalm superscriptions, 2, 3, 6, 7, 9, 20, 21, 25, 26, 29, 33, 34, 38, 41, 42, 46, 47, 51, 54, 59, 63, 72, 78, 92, 93, 104, 105, 110-113, 118, 136, 139, 147, 150, 154, 173, 184, 185, 188

redeemer, 52, 120, 135
refuge, 19, 21, 25-27, 29, 32, 39, 44, 46, 70, 79, 93-97, 110, 112, 116, 124, 126, 127, 148, 151, 154, 164, 177, 188
repentance, 28, 29, 105, 107, 135, 150, 152
righteousness, 14, 15, 27-29, 34-37, 39, 41, 43, 50, 61, 62, 64, 70, 72, 73, 76-78, 80, 83, 100, 110, 111, 118, 119, 123-125, 127, 132, 141, 144, 155, 159, 162, 172, 174, 177, 186, 189
rock, 40, 42, 44, 45, 52, 126, 135, 140

sacrifice, 52, 53, 62, 67, 82, 83, 99, 100,
101-103, 106-110, 116, 117, 127, 131, 167
servant, 19, 24, 41, 51, 52, 78, 82, 110, 136, 138, 141, 143, 144, 146, 147, 153, 160, 164, 165, 170, 183, 189
shepherd, 59-61, 63, 71, 75, 98, 136, 139
sin, 8, 30, 68-71, 80, 88, 99, 103-109, 112, 116, 132, 134-136, 138, 139, 142, 146, 148, 151-154, 162, 163, 167, 168
Solomon, 8, 43, 55, 72, 92, 118, 121-123, 128, 131, 138, 148, 172, 185
sovereignty, 6, 22, 28, 29, 30, 33, 38, 43, 55, 58, 64, 68, 81, 139, 143-146, 152, 155, 159, 164, 168, 169, 174, 187, 192
steadfast love, 73, 76, 79, 83, 93, 104, 112, 114, 141, 142, 144, 145, 147, 153, 155-158, 161-164, 166, 168-170, 173, 175, 176, 178, 179, 182, 186-189

temple, 2-4, 7, 8, 13, 22, 24, 29, 39, 42, 49, 52, 53, 62, 63, 65, 67, 72, 91, 95, 96, 117, 123, 125, 127-132, 138-140, 142, 143, 148, 151, 154, 155, 157, 164, 175, 177, 179, 184, 185, 187
Ten Commandments, 99, 102
thanksgiving, 29, 34, 35, 38, 39, 40, 42, 43,
53, 57, 58, 62, 72, 73, 77, 78, 81-85, 87, 89, 99, 101, 103, 107-111, 115-117, 132, 143, 155, 156, 157, 159, 161, 166, 167, 169, 171, 173, 175-179, 185, 188, 191, 192
theophany, 43, 45, 47, 99, 100, 117, 125, 129, 135
torah, 5, 7, 9, 10, 12, 13, 15, 18, 20, 21, 46-52, 71, 82, 85-87, 127, 134, 137, 177-183

Ugarit, 47, 64, 65, 95, 130, 152

vengeance, 155, 193

wicked, 12-16, 21, 23, 25, 26, 29, 34-40, 70, 75, 78-80, 99, 100, 102, 103, 110, 124-127, 132, 140, 155, 170, 188, 190, 191, 193
wilderness, 28, 36, 41, 59, 60, 113, 130, 134-137, 156, 157, 162, 163, 167, 174, 184, 187
wisdom, 3-5, 10, 16, 19, 48, 51, 52, 87, 98, 105, 107, 111, 113, 123, 128, 150-153, 160, 161, 173, 176, 181-183

Zion, 17-19, 25, 35, 36, 40, 92, 94-96, 98, 100, 101, 108, 116, 117, 127, 129, 132, 134, 136-140, 142, 154, 156, 157, 171, 172, 184-186, 190-193

www.ingramcontent.com/pod-product-compliance
Lightning Source LLC
Chambersburg PA
CBHW072127160426
43197CB00012B/2017